MW01233523

E-LEARNING: 21ST CENTURY ISSUES AND CHALLENGES

E-LEARNING: 21ST CENTURY ISSUES AND CHALLENGES

AUDREY R. LIPSHITZ AND STEVEN P. PARSONS
EDITORS

Nova Science Publishers, Inc.
New York

Copyright © 2008 by Nova Science Publishers, Inc.

All rights reserved. No part of this book may be reproduced, stored in a retrieval system or transmitted in any form or by any means: electronic, electrostatic, magnetic, tape, mechanical photocopying, recording or otherwise without the written permission of the Publisher.

For permission to use material from this book please contact us:
Telephone 631-231-7269; Fax 631-231-8175
Web Site: http://www.novapublishers.com

NOTICE TO THE READER

The Publisher has taken reasonable care in the preparation of this book, but makes no expressed or implied warranty of any kind and assumes no responsibility for any errors or omissions. No liability is assumed for incidental or consequential damages in connection with or arising out of information contained in this book. The Publisher shall not be liable for any special, consequential, or exemplary damages resulting, in whole or in part, from the readers' use of, or reliance upon, this material. Any parts of this book based on government reports are so indicated and copyright is claimed for those parts to the extent applicable to compilations of such works.

Independent verification should be sought for any data, advice or recommendations contained in this book. In addition, no responsibility is assumed by the publisher for any injury and/or damage to persons or property arising from any methods, products, instructions, ideas or otherwise contained in this publication.

This publication is designed to provide accurate and authoritative information with regard to the subject matter covered herein. It is sold with the clear understanding that the Publisher is not engaged in rendering legal or any other professional services. If legal or any other expert assistance is required, the services of a competent person should be sought. FROM A DECLARATION OF PARTICIPANTS JOINTLY ADOPTED BY A COMMITTEE OF THE AMERICAN BAR ASSOCIATION AND A COMMITTEE OF PUBLISHERS.

LIBRARY OF CONGRESS CATALOGING-IN-PUBLICATION DATA

E-learning : 21st century issues and challenges/Audrey R. Lipshitz and Steven P. Parsons(editors)
    P. cm.
ISBN 978-1-60456-156-2(hardcover)
    1. Distance education—Computer –assisted instruction.I. Lipshitz,Audrey R. II. Parsons,Steven P.
    LC5803.C65E15 2007
    378.1'758—dc22

                    2007045192

Published by Nova Science Publishers, Inc. ✢ New York

CONTENTS

PREFACE

Electronic learning, or e-Learning, is a general term used to refer to computer-enhanced learning. It is used interchangeably in so many contexts that it is critical to be clear what one means when one speaks of 'e-Learning'. In many respects, it is commonly associated with the field of advanced learning technology (ALT), which deals with both the technologies and associated methodologies in learning using networked and/or multimedia technologies. By 2003, more than 1.9 million students were participating in on-line learning at institutions of higher education in the United States alone. Many higher education, for-profit institutions now offer on-line classes. By contrast, only about half of private, non-profit schools offer them. The Sloan report, based on a poll of academic leaders, says that students generally appear to be at least as satisfied with their on-line classes as they are with traditional ones. Private institutions may become more involved with on-line presentations as the cost of instituting such a system decreases. Properly trained staff must also be hired to work with students on-line. These staff members must be able to not only understand the content area, but also be highly trained in the use of the computer and Internet. On-line education is increasing dramatically around the world. This book presents the latest research in the field.

Chapter 1 - With the development of Internet technology, e-Learning has gradually become an important focus in the field of education (Brook, 2000; Brown and Johnson-Shull, 2000; Cerny and Heines, 2001; Kovacs and Rowell, 2001; Sun, Bender, and CECIL Fore III, 2003). The characteristics of the Internet environment also bring great changes to teaching and learning behaviors in the e-Learning environment. These changes in turn gradually influence the educational paradigm (Flake, 2001). Therefore, in recent years, the educational researches related to e-Learning has received increasing attention.

In comparison with the traditional learning environment, the e-Learning environment has its own distinguishing characteristics. According to Bodzin and Cates (2003) and Hoffman, Wu, and Krajcik (2003), e-Learning is an effective and alternative kind of learning. It can provide more bountiful resources to improve student learning than the traditional classroom. Besides, Flake (2001) also points out that learners in an e-Learning environment are independent; they should be responsible for their own learning. Concluding from related literature, Wang (2007) argues that the main benefit of e-Learning lies in its breakthrough of the limits in time and space, and this is what traditional teaching fails to do. This breakthrough equips learners with the opportunities to learn independently, but also leads to the lack of teacher supervision which traditional teaching can provide (Wang, 2007). Therefore, in an e-Learning environment, if learners cannot be their own teachers, their learning effectiveness can be low (Sujo de Montes and Gonzales, 2000). The literature review above proves the importance of developing the strategies which can facilitate students to learn actively. Regarding the problem that "e-Learning environment can provide learners with the opportunities to learn independently but lacks the teacher supervision which traditional teaching provides," Wang proposes effective solving strategies. He believes that the assessment-centered learning environment suggested by Bransford, Brown, and Cocking (2000) can be applied to designing an effective e-Learning environment. Bransford et al. argue that in the assessment-centered learning environment, a successful teacher will keep on evaluating students and offer proper feedbacks during the teaching process. This helps learners cultivate the ability of self-assessment, with which they can evaluate their own learning and improve the learning effectiveness by themselves.

In a traditional learning environment, it is difficult to successfully construct the assessment-centered learning environment as Bransfod et al. have suggested because the teachers often have to deal with many learners at the same time and face the pressure resulting from catching up with the scheduled teaching progress. They seldom can effectively administer tests for all students and provide them with proper feedback (Buchanan, 2000; Wang, 2007). However, with the help of information technology (IT), the assessment-centered learning environment can be easily realized in an e-Learning environment because there learners can directly interact with the Web-based assessment system. When they encounter difficulties in the process of assessment, the Web-based assessment system will be able to help teachers provide learners with immediate feedbacks. The workload of teachers can therefore be lessened. Moreover, if the database of the Web-based assessment system is equipped with well-prepared information, the programs wifeedbacks. When students gain assistance (more effective feedbacks) in learning, their learning effectiveness in the e-Learning environment can in turn be improved.

The Web-based formative assessment system introduced in this research is developed on the basis of the WATA system (Web-based Assessment and Test Analysis system) (Wang, Wang, Wang, Huang, and Chen, 2004), which contains FAM-WATA (Formative Assessment Module of the WATA system) (Wang, 2007) and GAM-WATA (Game Assessment Module of the WATA system) (Wang, Wang and Wang, 2007). FAM-WATA mainly includes six effective strategies: "repeat the test," "correct answers are not given," "query scores," "ask questions," "monitor answering history," and "all pass and then reward." As to GAM-WATA, besides the six strategies of FAM-WATA, it includes the "Ask-Hint Strategy," which consists of two designs – the "Prune Strategy" and the "Call-in Strategy." The "Ask-Hint strategy" endows Web-based formative assessment with the characteristics of Web-based quiz-game. Learners cannot only obtain on-line hints with the "Ask-Hint Strategy" but also gain more feedback in the process of taking Web-based formative assessment. The Web-based quiz-game-like formative assessment is expected to motivate learners to actively do self-assessment. GAM-WATA and FAM-WATA share the same development objectives. It is hoped that the two systems can both be practically used in the e-Learning environment to promote the meaningful interaction between teachers and learners, and even improve the dilemma commonly seen in the traditional learning environment, that is, teachers do not have enough time to effectively administer formative assessment and provide meaningful feedbacks.

Besides introducing the designs of FAM-WATA and GAM-WATA, this research further investigates how the two systems help improve the e-Learning effectiveness. This research is composed of two studies. In Study 1, it examines the "repeat the test" strategy in FAM-WATA, trying to clarify how the number of repeated tests is related to the e-Learning effectiveness. Study 2 aims at the "Ask-hint Strategy" of GAM-WATA, exploring how the design of the "Prune Strategy" and the "Call-in Strategy" helps improve e-Learning effectiveness.

Chapter 2 - This chapter describes how aspects of intercultural communicative competence can be fostered and assessed in on-line collaborative projects. In order to do so, the authors present the findings of an on-line exchange carried out by the Department of Applied Languages at Nebrija University in Madrid and Dublin City University during the academic year 2006-2007. Students collaborated electronically by e-mail and in wikis, using their native language (L1) and their L2 to interact with a partner and exchange personal, linguistic and socio-cultural information. Data was gathered from a triangulation of instruments, such as e-mail and wiki content, language learning diaries, critical incidents, essays, compositions and self-evaluation questionnaires. On the basis of Byram's (1997) model of Intercultural Communicative Competence (ICC) and the guidelines for assessment of intercultural experience (Byram 2000), the authors attempted to assess qualitatively whether the different components of ICC can be developed in e-Learning environments. Their findings seem to suggest that the instruments mentioned can help us to describe some evidence of development with regard to a) interest in knowing other people's way of life and introducing one's own culture to others, b) ability to change perspective, c) knowledge about one's own and others' culture for intercultural communication, and d) knowledge about the intercultural communication process. Further research needs to be carried out on how best to encourage students to exhibit 'a readiness to suspend disbelief and judgment with respect to others' meanings, beliefs and behaviours' and a 'willingness to suspend belief in one's own meanings and behaviours, and to analyse them from the viewpoint of the others with whom one is engaging' (Byram 1997: 34).

Chapter 3 - The main focus on e-Learning portals has so far been on technical issues and conformity to SCORM, which initially was developed for people in military training. Other user groups with totally different needs and abilities have so far not received much focus by platform developers, apparently caused by limited knowledge about, for example, disabled or elderly people's life conditions and their need for Internet and related technologies. Quality assurance and how to design platform learning activities to assure long-lasting knowledge achievements by the students taking part in distance learning are additional areas in need of more development and research.

At the same time, a need for e-learning platforms accessible to everybody in society is growing. As elderly (65+) and disabled people now account for around 25 % of the population in Europe and the USA, there is a substantial unexplored market for education providers as well as e-Learning platform producers. Research has started in the field of "Web for All" and the interest for elderly people's Internet habits are intensively discussed among researchers.

One conclusion in this paper is that "e-Learning for All" is possible to obtain. Experiments on how to make examinations on the Internet with high reliability have been done and found difficult but possible to develop. However, it is another issue to prevent students from cheating on tests over the Internet which calls for new technical solutions.

Chapter 4 - The World Wide Web is currently changing dramatically. The buzzword Web 2.0 describes how we deal with the Internet. "The user is the content" is one of the famous descriptions. Users create their own (learning) content by blogging, podcasting or producing mashups. Of course the innovations summed up with the word Web 2.0 influence the traditional e-learning world.

In this paper, the authors focus on how learning will change in the future. The combination of traditional research work combined with emerging technologies leads to an assumption of the learning behaviour of tomorrow. Will today's teaching soon be a matter of the past? What will a lecture look like by integrating emerging technologies? The authors conclude that information anytime and anywhere influences the world of digital natives arbitrarily and causes the death of e-Learning in the present sense. Using computer and mobile technologies for learning purposes will be as normal as writing a letter with pencil.

Chapter 5 - This study compares two mathematical e-Learning instructions supported by different forms of feedback: E-Learning with metacognitive feedback (EL+MF), and e-Learning with result feedback (EL+RF). Metacognitive feedback was based on the IMPROVE self-questioning strategy (e.g., Kramarski and Mevarech, 2003), and result feedback included correctness of the solution.

The participants were 62 ninth-graders who practiced mathematical problem-solving through interactive tasks accessible on the Web. Results showed that EL+MF students significantly outperformed the EL+RF students in procedural and transfer problem-solving, and used more conceptual arguments when providing mathematical explanations. Furthermore, at the end of the study the EL+MF students exhibited more self-efficacy in learning mathematics in a computer-based environment.

Chapter 6 - "Free and open learning for all everywhere at all times" is a noble aspiration written in global strategies and heard so many times from the highest political levels. It should lead towards a "better world", but the research and experiences shows that there are several obstacles in the way. The relationship of "lifelong learning" and its technology foundation "e-Learning" is explored in the chapter. Directions of e-Learning technology development for efficient lifelong learning are identified and some guidelines for major research tracks are suggested.

Personalization is a key technology success factor for wide implementation of e-Learning. Personalization can make the ICT based e-Learning platform friendly and even intimate which is a critical aspect to overcome the so called "technology barier". The personalized e-learning system will be able to respond to the individual learning styles, explicit and implicit preferences, role and the existing level of knowledge. Personalization will be achieved without or with as little user intervention as possible with tracking their usage data and history. "Cognitive-based personalization" is based on monitoring learner behavior in a real time, and predicting what the user would like to do next - finally leading to the "whole-person personalization" which seeks to understand the deep-seated psychological sources.

The quality of an e-Learning educational offering depends not only on products, such as learning material or services, but also on the interaction of the learner with contents, tasks, tutors and other learners. E-Learning quality is a broad concept which has yet to develop unified guidelines. Several issues for this development are described and questions to be anwered are identified.

Open educational resources (OER) in e-Learning are the future source of information for lifelong learners. Open source and open standards are defined as the basis of the "Open educational resource movement" that is beginning to form on a global level at the dawn of the

21st century. Several good practices, ideas and existing initiatives are presented and the vision of the future of open educational resources is introduced.

Chapter 7 - A question that has gained widespread interest is 'how can learning tasks be structured to encourage creative thinking in the classroom through technology?' Contemporary applications of learning theories towards educational technology design are influenced by constructivist and constructionist learning approaches. This chapter draws upon theories of learning and creativity to provide a design method to encourage creative thinking in the classroom. It is suggested here that learning theories may provide insights towards understanding the creative process. Extending upon this, a generative framework for creative learning is presented which exists as a design support tool in planning lesson materials for the classroom and the design of educational software. An example of how this framework can be applied in the design of educational technology is provided through the instantiation of the framework in a collaborative music composition task.

Chapter 8 - This study investigated whether collaborative PBL in conjunction with blended learning would improve preservice teachers' critical-thinking skills and their personal teaching efficacy. Employing the before-and-after design, the researcher conducted an 18-week experimental instruction program with 34 preservice teachers enrolled in an undergraduate class of "Critical-thinking Instruction." The program incorporated collaborative PBL with blended learning, where face-to-face instruction was combined with e-Learning. It was found that: (a) all participants held positive views about the instructional design of this study, claiming that it provided them with opportunities to put theory into practice, increased their motivation to participate, encouraged authentic thinking, and provoked multiple-perspective thinking; (b) the experimental instruction considerably improved both the preservice teachers' critical-thinking skills and their personal teaching efficacy; and (c) the precise mechanisms that facilitated such positive effects were evidently the problem-based learning, guided practice, discussions and sharing, observational learning, and the self-reflection activity.

Chapter 9 - Despite the numerous initiatives undertaken towards in-service teacher training, there are just a few cases where their actual effect on classroom teaching has been analyzed. We probably need to get to the root of the cause since serious evaluations into learning acquired by teachers attending any educational/training course have very rarely been carried out. As shown in this chapter, learning evaluation is a necessary requisite for a reliable follow-up analysis in education. It is indeed a fairly onerous evaluation process generally dealt with by a special monitoring team, which is rarely allocated specific resources within an educational programme. The question arising in this chapter is therefore to understand whether a follow-up analysis can be carried out all the same with the aid of survey tools capable of 'replacing' the task of a special monitoring team. Therefore a methodological approach tailored to the design, development and evaluation of a questionnaire to support the follow-up analysis is illustrated. Although this approach has been developed for a specific educational programme, useful elements will emerge from discussion showing its generalizability even to contexts other than what it was originally designed for.

Chapter 10 - BEPI – from Basic Epidemiology – is an e-Learning course in epidemiology for medical students and for public health training. The course is supported by the Swiss Virtual Campus and by the medical faculties of the Swiss universities. The leadership as well as the coordination are situated at the Institute for Social- and Preventive Medicine in Basel.

This e-Learning course offers realistic scenarios through which the student learns the epidemiological methods and becomes familiar with the important medical and public health data sources in Switzerland.

The course is targeted for medical students at different levels in different universities as well as for people in public health training. In order to comply with different requirements of the learning environment, the authors created an independent tool suitable for people without e-Learning experience.

Epidemiology offers ideal examples with illustrating material for learning the methods and testing the knowledge that is crucial to profit from the possibilities of E-Learning. Getting involved in these realistic scenarios requires motivation and time, but then a deeper understanding of the content can be achieved.

However, the authors have to become familiar with e-Learning and know the different didactic scenarios to take advantage of the possibilities e-Learning offers.

E-Learning can be seen as another learning- and teaching-aid, as an alternative to a textbook or to a lecture offering many didactical advantages: it adapts to individual pace, the question-answer-options (multiple choice, complete a text, calculations, put in order, form pairs) can be tailored to the subject, exercises can be prepared for different levels of understanding, elaborative feedback facilitates the learning process and references and links to authentic data sources create a methodological and up-to-date background for practical and understandable exercises.

Although e-Learning will never replace lectures with a more personal contact or books providing the theoretical background in a compact form, it can be seen as a supplement.

Chapter 11 - The aim of the present chapter is to answer the question: Has neuropsychology anything to say about e-Learning? The authors' review is organized as follows: The first section deals with some key issues of multimedia and computer-supported instructions which set them apart from a 'classical' teaching approach. In the second section, they briefly examine some of the methods that are used to infer brain-cognition relations (e.g., reaction time, EEG and different imaging techniques, like MRI, fMRI and PET). Reviewed are also some animal and lesions studies. Next, they describe what these methods have revealed about the brain with a special focus on findings that have direct relevance to the field of educational psychology and e-Learning. Findings related to attention and memory are discussed, as well as individual differences related to ability (giftedness and creativity) and gender are reviewed. Finally, the authors discuss neuropsychological studies of e-Learning, and suggest new avenues of research.

Chapter 12 - This chapter is about the 'connectedness' of different ways of presenting health information. Information for individual patients can be tailored via 'user-models' which may include the patient's own medical record. There is evidence that tailoring information in this way can make it more relevant and useable for patients and their families. For example, in rigorous randomised trials, the authors have shown that tailored information is more likely to be shown by cancer patients to their confidants. There may be impact on psychological well-being, but this has been more difficult to show.

Traditional e-Learning for students has well known advantages such as convenience of time and being able to work at the student's own pace and review material in different ways. However, the reduced 'connection' with the lecturer and other students may mean that students are less motivated to engage with the material. The authors have been developing simple ways of delivering live webcasting with a simultaneous chat room. User reaction from students has been favourable but there are many practical aspects to improve, although there is evidence that computers can be used successfully for psychological therapy and patient education approaches to this could be improved by inclusion of live webcasting. For example, computerised cognitive behavioural therapy has proved successful for anxiety and depression but there is also some evidence that this approach is less successful if there is no human contact. A combination of live webcasting to provide human contact and motivation together with tailored information education may be the best way forward.

However, there are many unanswered questions about the use of these technologies, particularly amongst new user groups. For example, how does the use of asynchronous methods such as email differ from synchronous methods such as chat rooms. Chat rooms may provide more 'connection' but perhaps users need time to think. We will be exploring such issues with groups of older people.

In: E-Learning: 21st Century Issues and Challenges
Editor: Audrey R. Lipshitz and Steven P. Parsons
ISBN : 978-1-60456-156-2
©2008 Nova Science Publishers, Inc.

Chapter 1

WEB-BASED FORMATIVE ASSESSMENT: ISSUES AND TRENDS

Tzu-Hua Wang*

Department of Education, National Hsinchu University of Education, Taiwan

ABSTRACT

In an e-Learning environment, the unique features of Web technology have driven great changes in teaching and learning. The main advantage of e-Learning lies in its breakthrough of the limits of time and space. However, there is also a lower level of teacher supervision, and students are required to learn more actively and be responsible for their learning effectiveness. This research introduces two effective Web-based formative assessment modules in the Web-based Assessment and Test Analysis system (WATA system), named Formative Assessment Module (FAM-WATA) and Game Assessment Module (GAM-WATA). There are six effective Web-based formative assessment strategies in FAM-WATA. As to GAM-WATA, it includes a unique strategy, "Ask-Hint Strategy." Both FAM-WATA and GAM-WATA aim to help teachers construct an assessment-centered learning environment and to enable students to obtain more feedback when taking a Web-based formative assessment. GAM-WATA further turns a Web-based formative assessment into an online quiz game. It is expected that this design can encourage students to perform self-assessment spontaneously. In addition to introducing FAM-WATA and GAM-WATA, this research also integrates these two systems into an e-Learning environment and explores the effectiveness of their strategy designs.

Keywords: e-Learning, FAM-WATA, GAM-WATA, WATA system, Web-based formative assessment.

* Department of Education, National Hsinchu University of Education, No.521, Nanda Rd., Hsinchu City 300, Taiwan, Email: tzuhuawang@gmail.com

1. INTRODUCTION

With the development of Internet technology, e-Learning has gradually become an important focus in the field of education (Brook, 2000; Brown and Johnson-Shull, 2000; Cerny and Heines, 2001; Kovacs and Rowell, 2001; Sun, Bender, and Fore, 2003). The characteristics of Internet environment also bring great changes to teaching and learning behaviors in an e-Learning environment. These changes in turn influence the educational paradigm (Flake, 2001). Therefore, in recent years, the educational researches related to e-Learning have received increasing attention.

In comparison with the traditional learning environment, the e-Learning environment has its own distinguishing characteristics. According to Bodzin and Cates (2003) and Hoffman, Wu, and Krajcik (2003), e-Learning is an effective and alternative kind of learning. It can provide more bountiful resources to improve student learning than the traditional classroom. Flake (2001) also points out that students in an e-Learning environment are independent; they should be responsible for their own learning. Concluding from the related literature, Wang (2007) argues that the main benefit of e-Learning lies in its breakthrough of the limits in time and space, and this is what traditional teaching fails to do. This breakthrough on the one hand equips students with the opportunities to learn independently, but on the other hand leads to the lack of teacher supervision which traditional teaching can provide (Wang, 2007). In an e-Learning environment, if students fail to be their own teachers, their learning effectiveness can be low (Sujo de Montes and Gonzales, 2000). Developing the strategies which can facilitate students to learn actively in an e-Learning environment is therefore quite important. Regarding the problem that e-Learning environment can provide students with the opportunities to learn independently but lacks the teacher supervision which traditional teaching provides, Wang proposes effective solving strategies. He believes that the concepts about assessment-centered learning environment suggested by Bransford, Brown, and Cocking (2000) can be applied to design an effective e-Learning environment.

Bransford et al. argue that in the assessment-centered learning environment, a successful teacher will keep on evaluating students and offer proper feedback during the teaching process. This helps students cultivate the ability of self-assessment, with which they can evaluate their own learning and improve the learning effectiveness by themselves. In a traditional learning environment, teachers often have to deal with many students at the same time and face the pressure resulting from catching up with the scheduled teaching progress. Teachers seldom can effectively administer tests for all students and provide them with proper feedback (Buchanan, 2000; Wang, 2007). Therefore, it is difficult to successfully construct the assessment-centered learning environment as Bransford et al. have suggested. However, with the help of information technology (IT), the assessment-centered learning environment can be easily realized in an e-Learning environment because there students can directly interact with the Web-based assessment system. When students encounter difficulties in the process of assessment, the Web-based assessment system will be able to help teachers provide them with immediate feedback. The workload of teachers can therefore be lessened. Moreover, if the database of the Web-based assessment system is equipped with well-prepared information, the feedback the system offers will be even more effective. With the feedback as the assistance during the learning process, student learning effectiveness in an e-Learning environment can in turn be improved.

The Web-based formative assessment system introduced in this research is developed on the basis of the WATA system (Web-based Assessment and Test Analysis system) (Wang, Wang, Wang, Huang, and Chen, 2004; Wang, Wang, and Huang, 2008). WATA system is currently composed of two formative assessment modules: FAM-WATA (Formative Assessment Module of the WATA system) (Wang, 2007) and GAM-WATA (Game Assessment Module of the WATA system) (Wang, 2008). FAM-WATA mainly includes six effective strategies: "repeat the test," "correct answers are not given," "query scores," "ask questions," "monitor answering history" and "all pass and then reward." As to GAM-WATA, it includes a unique strategy, "Ask-Hint Strategy," which consists of two designs: the "Prune Strategy" and the "Call-in Strategy." The "Ask-Hint Strategy" endows Web-based formative assessment with the characteristics of Web-based quiz games. Students can not only obtain online hints with this strategy, but also gain more feedback in the process of taking Web-based quiz-game-like formative assessment. The Web-based quiz-game-like formative assessment is expected to motivate students to actively do self-assessment. GAM-WATA and FAM-WATA share the same development objectives. It is hoped that when practically used in an e-Learning environment, these two systems can not only promote the meaningful interaction between teachers and students, but also further solve the dilemma commonly seen in the traditional learning environment, that is, teachers do not have enough time to effectively administer formative assessment and provide meaningful feedback.

Besides introducing the designs of FAM-WATA and GAM-WATA, this research also investigates how the two systems help improve e-Learning effectiveness. This research is composed of two studies. Study 1 examines the "repeat the test" strategy in FAM-WATA, trying to clarify how this strategy is related to e-Learning effectiveness. Study 2 aims to investigate the "Ask-Hint Strategy" of GAM-WATA and explore how the design of the "Prune Strategy" and the "Call-in Strategy" helps improve e-Learning effectiveness.

2. LITERATURE REVIEW

2.1. Formative assessment and learning effectiveness

Formative assessment and summative assessment are two important types of assessment commonly seen in teaching activities. Scriven (1967) uses "formative" and "summative" to describe the various roles of evaluation in curriculum development and instruction (Ebel and Frisbie, 1991, p.24). Ebel and Frisbie point out that the main purpose of formative assessment is to monitor student learning process and to ensure that their learning proceeds in the planned way. As to summative assessment, it is often administered at the last stage of teaching. It mainly aims to evaluate whether planned learning outcomes are successfully achieved and to make sure students can proceed with the next stage of learning.

Besides Ebel and Frisbie (1991), Bell and Cowie (2001) also discuss the concepts of formative and summative assessment. Bell and Cowie believe that in early times, the concept of formative assessment was used to distinguish the continuous summative assessment done by teachers inside the classroom from the summative assessment (such as standardized assessment) administered by some testers outside the classroom. According to Bell and Cowie, early formative assessment was called "continuous summative assessment" (p.537). It could provide teachers with some information related to student learning in midst of the semester, but Bell and Cowie think that the information was quite rough and Brown (1996) even called this kind of assessment "weak formative assessment" (Bell and Cowie, 2001, p.537). This "continuous summative assessment" was often questioned in many ways. The exemplary questions often directed are as the following:

> "...how many separate assessments have to be recorded for the aggregated mark or grade to be reliable and valid; how best to store the multiple assessment documentation; how to aggregate the marks or grades; the problems with reducing many assessment results into one grade; and whether all the achievement objectives in the science curriculum have to be assessed and how often." (Bell and Cowie, 2001, p.537)

When formative assessment was put into practice in the early times, its summative assessment nature used to make itself be criticized from the angle of summative assessment. Its way of scoring, its frequency, the content it covered, its reliability and validity were all questioned. However, in recent years, the definition of formative assessment has undergone changes. Generally speaking, it is no longer regarded as "continuous summative assessment" but as a kind of assessment which occurs within the interaction between teachers and students. It is administered during, rather than after, the process of teaching and learning and provides students and teachers with feedback (Bell and Cowie, 2001); the feedback contributes to the main assistance in student learning (Bell and Cowie, 2001; Perrenoud, 1998; Sadler, 1989). According to the above we know that the definition of formative assessment has lately gotten rid of the characteristics of summative assessment. The focus is no longer placed on its scoring, frequency and content covered, but on the interactive feedback between teachers and students. Formative assessment is now integrated with teaching, learning and courses. The main purpose of formative assessment is to realize and enhance students' "formative learning (Orsmond, Merry, and Callaghan, 2004)" through the feedback. However, the feedback is no longer limited to scores.

Student learning effectiveness is quite closely related to formative assessment (Bell and Cowie, 2001; Black and Wiliam, 1998; Gipps, 1994). Bell and Cowie (2001) believe that the main function of formative assessment is to improve student learning. Both teachers and students can understand students' learning condition through formative assessment and provide feedback based on it. After reviewing the related literature, Black and Wiliam (1998) claim that formative assessment can indeed be used to improve learning effectiveness to a considerable extent. Gipps (1994) also argues that formative assessment is the process of appraising, judging or evaluating students' work or performance and using this to shape and improve students' competence. The literature review stated above show that formative assessment not only plays an important role in teaching activities but also exerts considerable influence on student learning effectiveness.

2.2. Web-based formative assessment and learning effectiveness

Besides in a traditional learning environment, formative assessment also plays an important role in an e-Learning environment. Many researchers indicate that student learning effectiveness can improve if Web-based formative assessment is included in an e-Learning environment. In recent years, with the development of Internet technology, many commercial and academic Web-based assessment systems have been developed. Some researchers begin to investigate the role of Web-based assessment system in an e-Learning environment, and their studies end up with positive results.

Broadly speaking, the inclusion of Web-based formative assessment in an e-Learning environment can improve student learning effectiveness (Brewer, 2004; Buchanan, 2000; Gardner, Sheridan, and White, 2002; Henly, 2003; Justham and Timmons, 2005; Khan, Davies, and Gupta, 2001; Peat and Franklin, 2002; Velan, Kumar, Dziegielewski, and Wakefield, 2002; Wang, 2007; Wang, 2008). Brewer makes use of "BioBytes" to construct an environment for Web-based formative assessment and puts it into practice in a college course, "Introductory Biology." It is found that the environment can help improve students' general understanding of biology principles and concepts. As to Buchanan, he makes use of "PsyCAL" to construct another environment for Web-based formative assessment and applies it in a college course, "Psychology." The results indicate that Web-based formative assessment can help improve students' learning interests and effectiveness. In addition, Gardener et al. integrate a Web-based formative assessment tool, "Self-Assessment," into an e-Learning environment. This tool allows college students to enter the environment any time to practice with the tests prepared by teachers. The results show that the design of "Self-Assessment" is helpful regarding learning effectiveness, and that students like to assist their own learning online with this function. In an e-Learning course, "Introductory Biochemistry and Molecular Biology," Henly makes use of "WebCT (http://www.webct.com)" to administer Web-based formative assessment for dentistry students. As a result, 80 % of the participating students find the Web-based formative assessment quite helpful to their learning. Justham and Timmons make use of "WebCT" to construct a Web-based formative assessment and apply it to the teaching of "Statistics" for post-registration nursing students. It is found that after students do learning in the environment, their knowledge and understanding about statistics are both improved. In an e-Learning course on "Gynaecology and Obstetrics," Khan et al. adopt "Questionmark Perception (http://www.questionmark.com)" to administer Web-based formative assessment for undergraduate medical students. The results reveal that Web-based formative assessment enables students to monitor their educational progress and directs their learning. Velan et al. also resort to "Questionmark Perception" to administer Web-based formative assessment for undergraduate medical students in an e-Learning course on "Pathology." It is found that Web-based formative assessment can effectively promote student learning effectiveness. With "Adobe Macromedia Authorware (http://www.adobe.com)," Peat and Franklin develop "SAM (Self-Assessment Module)" and integrate it into an e-Learning environment they developed for the teaching of "Biology." This module allows students to take formative assessment online in the process of learning. The results show that Web-based formative assessment can promote student learning.

Taking the design by Buchanan (2000) and other researchers' comments on formative assessment as reference, Wang (2007) develops a Web-based formative assessment module on the basis of the Web-based Assessment and Test Analysis system (WATA, Wang et al., 2004; Wang et al., 2008). This module is called Formative Assessment Module of the WATA system (FAM-WATA). FAM-WATA has been integrated into the e-Learning environment of junior high school "Nature and Life Technology" course in Taiwan. The results indicate not only that FAM-WATA is effective in promoting student e-Learning effectiveness but that students hold positive attitudes towards FAM-WATA. Wang also points out that if the formative assessment in an e-Learning environment can be administered in the form of Web-based test and more feedback strategies, such as the strategies in FAM-WATA, can be included in, it will be more effective than the formative assessment administered in the form of paper-and-pencil test (see Section 2.3 and Section 2.4.2 below for more discussion about FAM-WATA). Besides, Wang (2008) further develops a Web-based quiz-game-like formative assessment module – Game Assessment Module of the WATA system (GAM-WATA). This module proves to motivate students to actively participate in Web-based formative assessment and improve their learning effectiveness in an e-Learning environment. Wang indicates that GAM-WATA can help teachers construct the "challenge mechanism" and "game mechanism" in an e-Learning environment by administering Web-based quiz games. GAM-WATA has been integrated into the e-Learning environment of elementary school "Nature and Life Technology" course in Taiwan. The results reveal that GAM-WATA makes students have better learning effectiveness and more actively participate in Web-based formative assessment to do self-assessment than normal Web-based test (only turns the paper-and-pencil formative assessment tests into Web-based tests). In addition, formative assessment administered in the form of GAM-WATA also better improve student learning effectiveness than that administered in the form of paper-and-pencil test (see Section 2.3 and Section 2.4.3 below for more discussion about GAM-WATA).

From the literature review above, we know that formative assessment is effective in both the traditional and the e-Learning environment. However, related empirical studies and the construction of theoretical basis are obviously inadequate. Some researchers believe that further investigation into formative assessment is necessary (Bell and Cowie, 2001; Bransford et al., 2000; Black and Wiliam, 1998). Bell and Cowie note that the process of how formative assessment is administered should be explored; Bransford et al. claim that future studies of formative assessment should focus on the development of new strategies. Black and Wiliam believe that there is a need to explore the interrelationships between learning and formative assessment. They also claim that there is a call for further research and theorizing on formative assessment. Taking these researchers' comments into consideration, this research tries to figure out what kind of strategy design in a Web-based formative assessment can help students promote their e-Learning effectiveness the most.

2.3. Design of Web-based formative assessment

Regarding the design of Web-based formative assessment, the literature on formative assessment in traditional learning environment raises some suggestions deserving to be taken into consideration. Bransford et al. (2000, p.140-141) believe that teachers should make use of formative assessment to provide students with opportunities to gain feedback and revise their thinking. Based on the viewpoints of Bransford et al., Wang (2007) suggests that in a Web-based formative assessment, the strategy design of "repeat the test" and "timely feedback" (Brown and Knight, 1994; Wiliam and Black, 1996) are quite important. Buchanan (2000) also believes that the strategy design of Web-based formative assessment should contain "repeat the test" and "timely feedback." In addition, to enable better effectiveness of Web-based formative assessment, these two strategies should function along with the "correct answers are not given" strategy. Buchanan and Wang both argue that if the "repeated the test" strategy and the "correct answers are not given" strategy can be used together and test takers can be provided with answer references as "timely feedback," they will focus more on learning the teaching materials and gradually master the content of the course. In other words, if the Web-based formative assessment students take includes "repeat the test," "timely feedback" and "correct answers are not given" strategies, they will be able to make use of the feedback to "correct" the faults of thinking in the learning process. This is the same as what they can gain from taking formative assessment in the traditional learning environment.

Referring to the design suggestions raised in the related literature, Wang (2007) develops a Web-based formative assessment system, FAM-WATA. This system contains six strategies: "repeat the test," "correct answers are not given," "query scores," "ask questions," "monitor answering history" and "all pass and then reward." Besides, there is an innovative mechanism in FAM-WATA. When taking Web-based formative assessment, if students can answer an item correctly three times consecutively in total (two times consecutively in repeated tests), the item will never appear again in future tests. Thus, the number of items will gradually decrease with each iteration of the test. In other words, if they can answer more items correctly three times consecutively in total (two times consecutively in repeated tests), there will be fewer items included in future tests. When all items are answered correctly three times consecutively, the system will tag the successful student with a "pass the test" mark and play an Adobe Macromedia Flash animation as the reward. After passing the test, the student will be allowed to query his/her own answering history. However, if students answer an item wrongly before they can answer it correctly three times consecutively, the answer count will be reset to zero and begin again because the system judges that the students answer the item correctly simply by guessing (Wang, 2007). In order not to make the students feel bored when repeating the test, both the options and the items are arranged in random order. Wang integrates FAM-WATA into the e-Learning environment of junior high school "Nature and Life Technology" course in Taiwan, and probes into its effectiveness. It is found that students in FAM-WATA group hold positive attitudes towards the six FAM-WATA strategies, believing that theses strategies can facilitate them to do e-Learning. It is also found that the e-Learning effectiveness of the students in FAM-WATA group is significantly better than that of the students in N-WATA group (formative assessment is administered in the form of normal Web-based test and does not include the six strategies of FAM-WATA) and in PPT group (formative assessment is administered in the form of paper-and-pencil test). Wang also investigates the relationship between students' cognitive styles and the effectiveness of FAM-WATA. It is found that FAM-WATA is more effective to field-independent students. Moreover, FAM-WATA assesses student performance in FAM-WATA based on the "Accumulated Score (AS)" equation (see Section 2.4.2.4). It is also found that Student performance in FAM-WATA bears correlation with the e-Learning effectiveness. Wang finds that the e-Learning effectiveness of those students belonging to the upper-AS group and middle-AS group is significantly better than that of those belonging to the lower-AS group. He believes that the AS provides effective information for students to monitor their own learning and for teachers to understand students' learning condition. The strategy designs of FAM-WATA and AS can be taken into consideration when researchers develop other Web-based formative assessment systems in the future.

Besides FAM-WATA, Wang (2008) also develops the Web-based quiz-game-like formative assessment system, GAM-WATA. GAM-WATA can help teachers to construct the "challenge mechanism" and "game mechanism" in an e-Learning environment by administering Web-based quiz games. Vogel, Greenwood-Ericksen, Cannon-Bower, and Bowers (2006) argue that the four main components of a game are "play," "interactivity," "appropriate challenge" and "rewards and scores." Referring to their idea and other suggestions about formative assessment design raised in related literature, Wang devises seven strategies in GAM-WATA: "repeat the test," "correct answers are not given," "query scores," "ask questions," "monitor answering history," "all pass and then reward" and "Ask-Hint Strategy." These strategies work together to turn a Web-based formative assessment into an online quiz game. Among these strategies, "Ask-Hint Strategy" is a unique design. "Ask-Hint Strategy" is composed of the "Prune Strategy" and the "Call-in Strategy" (see Section 2.4.3 below for more discussion). When students take Web-based formative assessment and encounter problems, "Ask-Hint Strategy" allows them to gain online hints. The design of "Ask-Hint Strategy" mainly aims to allow students of different competency levels to have "appropriate challenge" in the Web-based quiz game. "Ask-Hint Strategy" can reduce the difficulty of an item for the less-competent students in two ways. It either reduces the number of options (Prune Strategy) or provides the info about how their peers answer each item (Call-in Strategy). Wang integrates GAM-WATA into the e-Learning environment of elementary school "Nature and Life Technology" course in Taiwan, and finds that GAM-WATA can make students more actively participate in Web-based formative assessment to do self-assessment than normal Web-based test (merely turns the paper-and-pencil formative assessment tests administered in traditional classroom into Web-based tests but does not make the tests quiz-game-like). It is also found that students taking formative assessment in the form of GAM-WATA have better learning effectiveness than those taking formative assessment in the form of normal Web-based test and paper-and-pencil test.

2.4. WATA system

The WATA system can provide each user with personalized interface (Figure 1). It now contains three modules: SAM-WATA (Summative Assessment Module of the WATA system), FAM-WATA (Formative Assessment Module of the WATA system), and GAM-WATA (Game Assessment Module of the WATA system). These modules are introduced as the following:

2.4.1. SAM-WATA

The design of SAM-WATA is mainly derived from the idea of summative assessment. This system integrates Triple-A Model (Assembling, Administering, Appraising) (Wang et al., 2004) and helps teachers administer Web-based summative assessment. The development of Triple-A Model is based on the idea of "basic steps in classroom testing (Gronlund & Linn, 1990, p.109-141, 228)" and the interviews with 17 in-service teachers and assessment experts. The basic steps range from "determining the purpose of testing," "constructing the Two-Way Chart (also known as the table of specifications)," "selecting appropriate items according to the Two-Way Chart," "preparing relevant items," "assembling the test," "administering the test" to "appraising the test." Triple-A Model is composed of three parts:

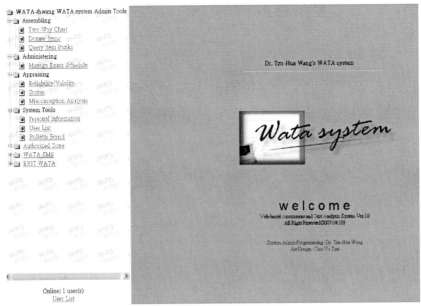

Figure 1. Personalized interface of the WATA system

Assembling Engine: teachers can construct the item bank by themselves and
assemble a test paper on the basis of Two-Way Chart.

Administering Engine: teachers can simultaneously manage and administer multiple
examinations securely and effectively.

Appraising Engine: teachers can analyze the information collected during the process
of assessment and then obtain educational statistical information to appraise their
teaching, student learning and item construction.

The "Assembling Engine" and "Administering Engine" are equipped with the functions
of common online databases systems. They can be used to construct a multimedia item bank
which supports items of various media types, such as text, figure, video, Adobe Macromedia
Flash and etc. (Figure 2), and to manage multiple examination schedules. As to "Assembling
Engine", its main function is to ensure the validity of examinations. It asks teachers to create
a Two-Way Chart before they assemble a test paper (Figure 3). Teachers have to take the
Two-Way Chart as criteria to search for proper items in the item bank and then generate a test
paper.

Lastly, the "Appraising Engine" can be used to do "Test Analysis," "Item Analysis"
(Figure 4) and "Misconception Analysis" (Figure 5). It concludes every kind of statistic data
after analyzing the information recorded down during the process of tests and presents
analysis results in Web pages. All of the results are divided into the following categories:
"student misconception analysis according to Two-Way Chart," "variance, standard deviation
and mean of all scores," "T-score, z-score and Z-score of each student," "average difficulty of
the test," "KR20 reliability," "discriminating power (DP)," "item difficulty (ID)," "distracter
analyses of each item," "analyses of all, upper group and lower group students' answers on
each item" and so on. With these comprehensive analyses, teachers can not only monitor
student learning and their own instruction but also understand whether their tests and items
are properly constructed.

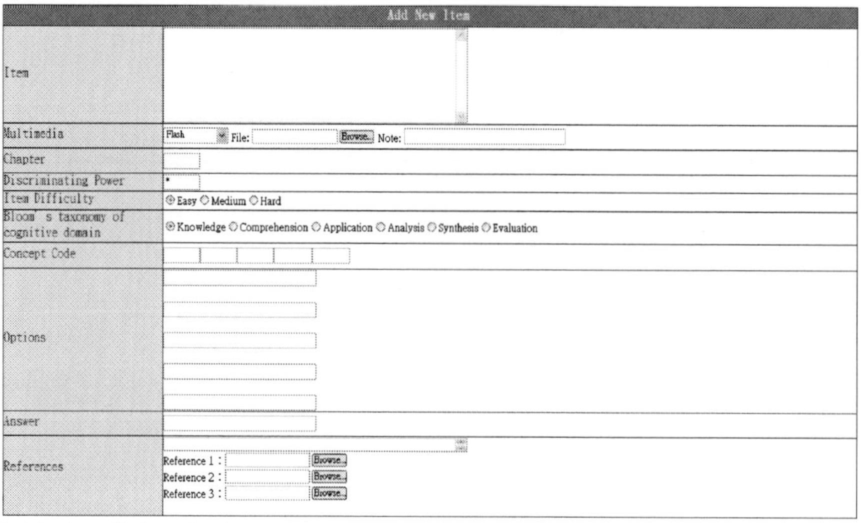

Figure 2. Multimedia item bank

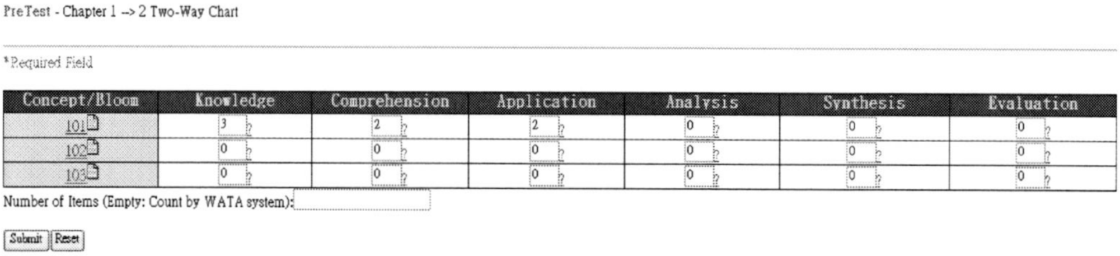

Concept/Bloom	Knowledge	Comprehension	Application	Analysis	Synthesis	Evaluation
101	3	2	2	0	0	0
102	0	0	0	0	0	0
103	0	0	0	0	0	0

Figure 3. Assemble a test paper based on Two-Way Chart

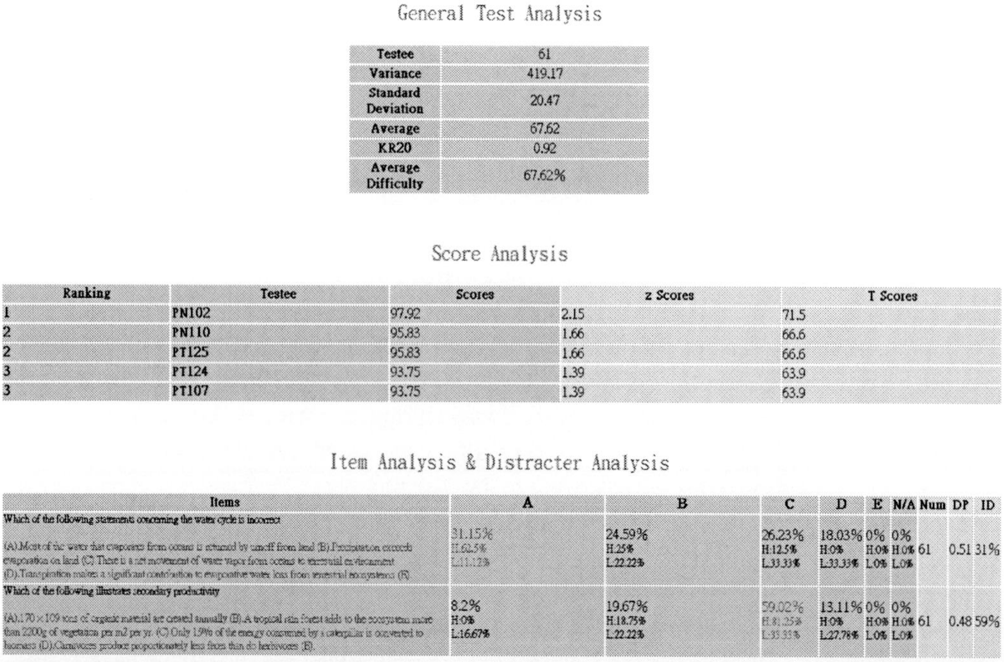

General Test Analysis

Testee	61
Variance	419.17
Standard Deviation	20.47
Average	67.62
KR20	0.92
Average Difficulty	67.62%

Score Analysis

Ranking	Testee	Scores	z Scores	T Scores
1	PN102	97.92	2.15	71.5
2	PN110	95.83	1.66	66.6
2	PT125	95.83	1.66	66.6
3	PT124	93.75	1.39	63.9
3	PT107	93.75	1.39	63.9

Item Analysis & Distracter Analysis

Items	A	B	C	D	E	N/A	Num	DP	ID
Which of the following statements concerning the water cycle is incorrect (A).Most of the water that evaporates from oceans is returned by runoff from land (B).Precipitation exceeds evaporation on land (C) There is a net movement of water vapor from oceans to terrestrial environment (D).Transpiration makes a significant contribution to evaporative water loss from terrestrial ecosystems (E).	31.15% H:62.5% L:11.11%	24.59% H:25% L:22.22%	26.23% H:12.5% L:33.33%	18.03% H:0% L:33.33%	0% H:0% L:0%	0% H:0% L:0%	61	0.51	31%
Which of the following illustrates secondary productivity (A).170×109 tons of organic material are created annually (B).A tropical rain forest adds to the ecosystem more than 2200g of vegetation per m2 per yr. (C) Only 19% of the energy consumed by a caterpillar is converted to biomass (D).Carnivores produce proportionately less feces than do herbivores (E).	8.2% H:0% L:16.67%	19.67% H:18.75% L:22.22%	59.02% H:81.25% L:33.33%	13.11% H:0% L:27.78%	0% H:0% L:0%	0% H:0% L:0%	61	0.48	59%

Figure 4. Test Analysis and Item Analysis

Testee/Concept	STS	science	material	earth	life	health	eco	elec	gene
a01	0%	22.73%	7.14%	6.67%	8.33%	5.26%	40%	45.45%	30%
a02	6.25%	40.91%	14.29%	6.67%	12.5%	10.53%	80%	36.36%	20%
a03	0%	40.91%	42.86%	13.33%	16.67%	5.26%	80%	54.55%	30%
a04	12.5%	31.82%	14.29%	20%	8.33%	15.79%	60%	54.55%	40%
a05	0%	22.73%	28.57%	33.33%	4.17%	10.53%	80%	36.36%	50%
a06	0%	27.27%	14.29%	6.67%	8.33%	5.26%	20%	45.45%	0%
a07	12.5%	27.27%	7.14%	20%	12.5%	10.53%	80%	27.27%	40%
a08	0%	40.91%	14.29%	13.33%	20.83%	15.79%	80%	18.18%	40%
a09	6.25%	22.73%	7.14%	6.67%	8.33%	10.53%	40%	36.36%	40%
a10	0%	40.91%	21.43%	20%	12.5%	15.79%	40%	27.27%	30%
a11	12.5%	40.91%	14.29%	6.67%	12.5%	10.53%	60%	36.36%	30%
a12	6.25%	22.73%	14.29%	13.33%	16.67%	5.26%	40%	63.64%	10%
a13	0%	31.82%	14.29%	26.67%	16.67%	31.58%	40%	36.36%	40%
a14	0%	27.27%	14.29%	6.67%	8.33%	5.26%	20%	45.45%	0%
a15	18.75%	31.82%	14.29%	13.33%	8.33%	5.26%	40%	45.45%	40%
a16	6.25%	40.91%	7.14%	6.67%	12.5%	15.79%	60%	36.36%	30%
a17	0%	36.36%	0%	6.67%	12.5%	5.26%	60%	18.18%	20%
a18	0%	36.36%	7.14%	13.33%	16.67%	10.53%	40%	27.27%	20%
a19	6.25%	36.36%	7.14%	13.33%	4.17%	5.26%	40%	36.36%	10%
a20	0%	27.27%	14.29%	20%	8.33%	15.79%	60%	54.55%	30%
a21	0%	40.91%	14.29%	13.33%	16.67%	21.05%	80%	18.18%	20%
a22	6.25%	36.36%	14.29%	6.67%	16.67%	10.53%	80%	36.36%	20%

Figure 5. Misconception Analysis

2.4.2. *FAM-WATA*

FAM-WATA is a Web-based formative assessment system (see Section 2.3 for more discussion about FAM-WATA). It targets at enabling teachers to construct an "assessment-centered learning environment (Bransford et al., 2000, p.139)" in an e-Learning environment. The design of the strategies included in FAM-WATA is mainly based on the viewpoints proposed by Bransford et al. (2000, p.140-141) and Buchanan (2000). Bransford et al. state that the addition of opportunities for formative assessment increases students' learning and transfer, and they learn to value opportunities to revise (Barron et al., 1998; Black and Wiliam, 1998; Vye et al., 1998). According to Buchanan, if the "correct answers are not given" strategy is used along with the "repeat the test" strategy, and students can gain answering references as "timely feedback" when answering incorrectly, they will concentrate more on learning the teaching materials and gradually become familiar with the course contents.

The screen students see when taking the formative assessment in FAM-WATA is shown in Figure 6. FAM-WATA includes six main strategies: "repeat the test," "correct answers are not given," "query scores," "ask questions," "monitor answering history" and "all pass and then reward." These six strategies are introduced below.

2.4.2.1. "Repeat the test," "correct answers are not given" and "ask questions" strategies

According to the related literature, combining the "repeat the test," "correct answers are not given" and "timely feedback" strategies in a Web-based formative assessment can effectively promote e-Learning effectiveness (Buchanan, 2000; Wang, 2007). To further engage students in self-assessment, Wang revises the "repeat the test," "correct answers are not given" and "timely feedback" strategies with some innovative designs. These designs aim to arouse students' interests and desire to compete, and motivate them to do self-assessment actively. The operation of these strategies is introduced below.

"Repeat the test" strategy is integrated with "correct answers are not given" strategy. When students log in to do self-assessment, FAM-WATA would randomly choose several items (the number of items is set by the teacher) from the assigned item bank. These items and their respective options would appear in random order. This design aims to decrease the possibility that the effectiveness of assessment is impaired by the fact that students feel bored about the repeated items when they repeat the test. When taking assessments, students have to do their best to figure out the correct answers. If they can answer an item correctly for three times consecutively in total (two times consecutively in repeated tests), the item will never appear again in future tests. Contrarily, if students answer an item wrongly before they can answer it correctly three times consecutively, the answer count will be reset to zero and begin again (because the system assumes that they answer correctly by guessing) (Wang, 2007). In other words, the more items students can answer correctly for three consecutive times, the fewer items there will be in future tests. The process will keep on going until no item remains in the assigned item bank, and the system will tag the successful student with a "pass the test" mark. With this design, it is expected that students can be motivated to spontaneously participate and challenge, and be encouraged to be more focused and careful when answering.

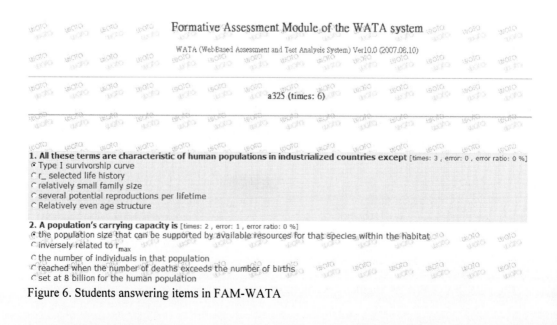

Figure 6. Students answering items in FAM-WATA

In addition, "timely feedback" is also integrated with "correct answers are not given" strategy. After students submit their test papers, they will know their scores and whether they answer each item correctly. For the item answered wrongly, FAM-WATA will immediately present reference materials (timely feedback) to help students figure out correct answers. As to the "ask questions" strategy, students can have asynchronous interaction with teachers by asking questions online and getting feedback.

2.4.2.2. "Query scores" strategy

As shown in Figure 7, after students take the tests, there will be an interface in FAM-WATA through which they can query the scores of their peers and easily view whether they have passed the test. Knowing the scores of other students can enhance their learning motivation. This design mainly aims to enable the positive interaction between students. Those who pass the test will be marked with star signs, identifying their role as others' models. This design can make those who have passed the test feel proud of their achievement and in turn enhance their learning motivation.

Student ID	Scores	Test Time	Used Time
★ a10524 (Times: 1)	80	2007-06-08 09:02:54	0.29
a10514 (Times: 1)	60	2007-06-08 09:03:33	0.44
a10517 (Times: 1)	60	2007-06-08 09:03:40	0.32
a10505 (Times: 1)	100	2007-06-08 09:04:08	1.54
a10502 (Times: 1)	60	2007-06-08 09:04:22	0.64
a10529 (Times: 1)	60	2007-06-08 09:04:24	0.19
a10513 (Times: 1)	80	2007-06-08 09:04:27	0.69
★ a10524 (Times: 2)	100	2007-06-08 09:03:23	0.35
a10517 (Times: 2)	60	2007-06-08 09:03:58	0.17
a10514 (Times: 2)	60	2007-06-08 09:04:15	0.39
a10506 (Times: 2)	80	2007-06-08 09:05:00	0.22
a10513 (Times: 2)	80	2007-06-08 09:05:12	0.29

Figure 7. "Query score" strategy in FAM-WATA

2.4.2.3. "All pass and then reward" strategy

As shown in Figure 8, after students pass the tests, FAM-WATA will play an Adobe Macromedia Flash animation as the reward. It is expected that the visual effect can stimulate students' learning motivation and enhance students' sense of achievement after passing the tests.

Figure 8. "All pass and then reward" strategy in FAM-WATA

2.4.2.4. "Monitor answering history" strategy

As shown in Figure 9, after students pass the tests, FAM-WATA will provide an interface through which they can query their own answering history. They can not only know the rate at which the whole class answers an item correctly and chooses a particular option of a particular item but also properly monitor their own learning condition. Moreover, they will get an Accumulated Score (AS) generated from the system. The calculation of AS is shown below:

$$\textbf{Item Score (IS)} = \begin{cases} \textbf{Failed Item: IS} = 0 \\ \text{(Item NOT correctly answered } N \text{ time(s) consecutively)} \\ \\ \textbf{Passed Item: IS} = (N/Times)*(100/Total) \\ \text{(Item correctly answered } N \text{ time(s) consecutively)} \end{cases}$$

$$\textbf{AS (Accumulated Score)} = \sum_{n=1}^{n=Total} ISn$$

Times: Total number of times each item is answered

Total: Total number of items in the FAM-WATA assessment

N: Number of times students are required to correctly answer an item consecutively during the repeated tests before they can be taken as passing the item

With the AS, students can know their performance in FAM-WATA. Wang (2007) conclude that the AS provides an effective feedback mechanism for students to monitor their formative learning and for teachers to understand the learning condition of their students.

Item (63.03 %)	Which of the following statements concerning the water cycle is correct?
Options	⊙ (22.69 %) There is a net movement of water vapor from terrestrial environment to oceans ⊙ (7.57 %) Evaporation exceeds precipitation on land ⊙ (5.33 %) Most of the water that evaporates from oceans is returned by urnoff from land ⊙ (63.03 %) Transpiration makes a significant contribution to evaporative water loss from terrestrial ecosystems ⊙ (1.13 %) <<No answer>>
Concept Code	ch2_0103 ch2_0105
Answer	Transpiration makes a significant contribution to evaporative water loss from terrestrial ecosystems
Hint	Reference 1: Click Here!! Reference 2: Click Here!! Internet Resources:http://www.chinatimes.org.tw/river/
c214 Correct Ratio: 75 %	Times 1: There is a net movement of water vapor from terrestrial environment to oceans Times 2: Transpiration makes a significant contribution to evaporative water loss from terrestrial ecosystems YES!! Times 3: Transpiration makes a significant contribution to evaporative water loss from terrestrial ecosystems YES!! Times 4: Transpiration makes a significant contribution to evaporative water loss from terrestrial ecosystems YES!! IS (Item Score):6.82

Figure 9. "Monitor answering history" strategy

2.4.3. GAM-WATA

GAM-WATA is a system for Web-based quiz-game-like formative assessment (see Section 2.3 for more discussion about GAM-WATA). Its main purpose is to offer "game mechanism" and "challenge mechanism" in an e-Learning environment, and to motivate students to actively participate in Web-based formative assessment (Wang, 2008). GAM-WATA includes a unique design - "Ask-Hint Strategy." Students can get online hints using this strategy when feeling uncertain about the correct answers. In addition, teachers can set how many times the "Ask-Hint Strategy" can be used by students during a test based on test difficulty. The operation of "Ask-Hint Strategy" is introduced below.

2.4.3.1. "Prune Strategy"

As shown in Figure 10, instead of directly providing correct answers, the "Prune Strategy" turns the 4-option item into a 2-option or 3-option one to make it easier. Only if the times students use the "Ask-Hint Strategy" do not exceed the preset limit, they can press the scissors icons located before the items to gain assistance when they are not sure of the correct answers. The screen which appears when students use the strategy is shown in Figure 10. The number of the cartoon icons in the lower left of the screen represents the remaining times the student can use the "Ask-Hint Strategy." Since the "Prune Strategy" is one kind of "Ask-Hint Strategy," whenever they use the "Prune Strategy," one cartoon icon will be removed. As to the cartoon icon on the left upper corner of the screen, it indicates how many percent of items students have answered correctly three times consecutively.

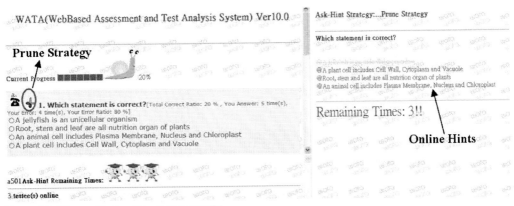

Figure 10. "Prune Strategy" in GAM-WATA

2.4.3.2. "Call-in Strategy"

As shown in Figure 11, the "Call-in Strategy" does not provide the correct answers, either. Instead, it provides the rate at which an option is chosen by other students. Taking the information as reference, students using the strategy can decide which option to choose. Only if the times students use the "Ask-Hint Strategy" do not exceed the preset limit, they can press the telephone icons located before the items to gain assistance when they are not sure of the correct answers. The screen which appears when students use the strategy is shown in Figure 11. Other descriptions of Figure 11 are the same as those of Figure 10 stated above.

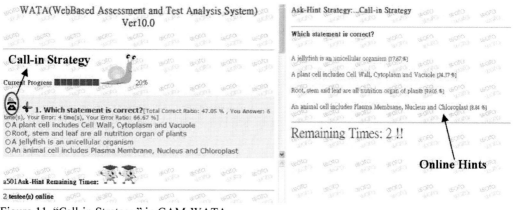

Figure 11. "Call-in Strategy" in GAM-WATA

3. STUDY ON THE EFFECTIVENESS OF STRATEGIES IN FAM-WATA AND GAM-WATA

This research is composed of two studies. Study 1 explores the "repeat the test" strategy in FAM-WATA, while Study 2 focuses on the "Ask-Hint Strategy" in GAM-WATA. Study 1 expects to clarify when the "repeat the test" strategy is used along with the "correct answers are not given" strategy, how many times students should correctly answer an item consecutively during the repeated tests before they can be taken as passing the item can lead to the best effectiveness of FAM-WATA. As to Study 2, in addition to comparing paper-and-pencil formative assessment with GAM-WATA formative assessment regarding their effectiveness in an e-Learning environment, it also probes into the effectiveness of the two designs of "Ask-Hint Strategy" - the "Prune Strategy" and the "Call-in Strategy." There are five ways to combine these two designs, termed "P2," "P3," "P2C," "P3C" and "C." With "P2," students can turn a 4-option item into a 2-option item by using the "Prune Strategy." As to "P2C," it adopts the design of "P2" but further includes the "Call-in Strategy." The design of "P3" allows students to turn a 4-option item into a 3-option item with the "Prune Strategy." "P3C" combines the design of "P3" and the "Call-in Strategy." As to "C," it only includes the "Call-in Strategy."

3.1. Study 1

Study 1 adopts quasi-experimental design to investigate the "repeat the test" strategy in FAM-WATA. It tries to understand when the "repeat the test" strategy is used along with the "correct answers are not given" strategy, how many consecutive times students should answer an item correctly during the repeated tests before they can be taken as passing the item can lead to the best effectiveness of FAM-WATA.

3.1.1. Participants

Six elementary school science teachers experienced in Web-based instruction, along with 225 forth graders from their classes, were invited to participate in this study. The teachers came from four different schools in central Taiwan and the 225 forth graders were from eight different classes. They were divided into four groups, with two classes as a group. These groups were named by the number of times for which students should correctly answer an item consecutively during the repeated tests before they can be taken as passing the item. There were "0-time" group, "1-time" group, "2-time" group and "3-time" group (see Table 1). All of the students had taken computer classes before. They were equipped with basic computer skills and able to use the e-Learning system.

Table 1 Participant distribution by RT group and Gender

RT group / Gender	0-time	1-time	2-time	3-time	Sum
Female	33	29	26	25	113
Male	27	29	29	27	112
Sum	60	58	55	52	225

RT group: repeat times group

3.1.2. Instruments

3.1.2.1. FAM-WATA and e-Learning environment

For the introduction of FAM-WATA, please refer to Section 2.4.2. The contents of the e-Learning materials used in this study were closely related to the local culture of Taiwan. The Gray-faced Buzzard, a migratory bird often seen in Taiwan, was taken as the topic. The e-Learning materials covered its growth, migratory route and flying movements. The presentation screen (as shown in Figure 12) was divided into two parts, the part for learning guide and the part for learning contents. In the learning guide part, the structure of e-Learning materials was presented in branches. It included the topics of e-Learning materials and FAM-WATA. Most of the contents of the e-Learning materials were summarized in the form of illustrations and tables, and no lengthy description was used. Some Adobe Macromedia Flash animations were also used to facilitate student learning.

3.1.2.2. Summative assessment and formative assessment

In this study, the learning contents were divided into three sections, and there was one formative assessment for each section. This study constructed the items of the three formative

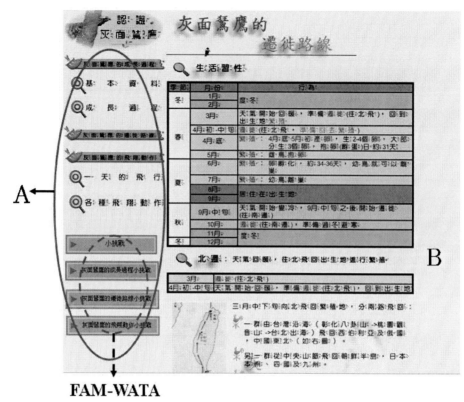

FAM-WATA

Figure 12. e-Learning environment. (A) The part for learning guide; (B) The part for learning contents.

assessments according to the learning contents of each section. They respectively focused on three topics: the growth of Gray-faced Buzzards, their migratory route, and their flying movements. Items in the three formative assessments did not appear again in the summative assessment. All of the items in the summative assessment were designed to evaluate students' understanding of the e-Learning materials. The Two-Way Chart was also taken as reference to ensure that the items comprehensively covered the concepts students should learn. The difficulty of the summative assessment was 0.583 and Cronbach's α was 0.882. Prior to the e-Learning, the pre-test of summative assessment was administered to understand students' entry behavior of learning; after the e-Learning, the post-test of summative assessment was administered to assess student e-Learning outcome.

3.1.3. Study design and procedures

This study took two weeks in total. Eight classes of students were divided into four groups, with each group containing two classes. The four groups were termed as "0-time" group, "1-time" group, "2-time" group and "3-time" group. Four groups of students used the same e-Learning materials and took the same Web-based formative assessment. The only difference among these groups was the consecutive times for which they should answer an item correctly during the repeated tests before the item never appeared again in future tests (that is, "pass the item"). For example, in "2-time" group, students should correctly answer an item for three times consecutively in total (two times consecutively in repeated tests) so that they could be taken as "passing the item." As to the students in "3-time" group, they had to pass an item by correctly answering an item four times consecutively in total (three times consecutively in repeated tests).

Before the 2-week e-Learning course, all students took the pre-test of summative assessment and were allowed time to get familiar with the e-Learning environment. They understood how to navigate the e-Learning materials and how to use FAM-WATA. The objectives of this study and the way of teaching were also explained to the participating teachers. This was to prevent that their ignorance or misunderstanding might have negative effects on students' learning outcome. Then the four groups of students began the 2-week e-Learning course, during which they could freely do learning and took FAM-WATA formative assessment. After the 2-week e-Learning course, all students had to take the post-test of summative assessment.

3.1.4. Data collection and analysis

The data collected in this study, the pre-test scores of summative assessment (PRE) and post-test scores of summative assessment (POST), were all quantitative. The PRE was taken to represent the entry behavior of learning, while the difference between the PRE and the POST was taken to represent the learning effectiveness. SPSS Ver.12.0 was used to conduct ANCOVA on these data. The PRE was taken as the covariate, the POST was taken as the dependent variable, and the repeat times (RT) was taken as the fixed factor. The LSD method was also used to compare the effectiveness of these four different RT groups.

3.1.5. Results

In this study, ANCOVA was used to understand how the students in the "0-time" group, "1-time" group, "2-time" group and "3-time" group differ in their e-Learning effectiveness. During ANCOVA, the relationship between the POST and RT was tested with the PRE as the covariate, the POST as the dependent variable and the RT as the fixed factor. Before ANCOVA, the homogeneity of variance assumption was tested. The Levene's test for equality of variances was not significant ($F_{3,221}$=2.249, p > 0.05). In addition, the assumption of homogeneity of regression coefficients was also tested ($F_{3,217}$=1.347, p > 0.05). These results indicated that both homogeneity assumptions were not violated.

Table 2 shows that the PRE has a significant impact on the POST ($F_{1,220}$ = 47.085, p < 0.01), and the RT is also found to have a significant impact on the POST ($F_{3,220}$ = 12.240, p < 0.01). Furthermore, the LSD method was used to compare the effectiveness of the four different RT groups (Table 2). Table 2 shows that "0-time" and "1-time" group appear to be the least effective; "2-time" and "3-time" group appear to perform better in the e-Learning environment. Additionally, students in the "2-time" group perform significantly better than those in the other three groups, and students in the "3-time" group perform significantly better than those in the "0-time" and the "1-time" group. In summary, the RT appears to have a significant impact on student e-Learning effectiveness. Requiring students to answer an item correctly three times consecutively in total (two times consecutively in repeated tests) appear to be the most effective in an e-Learning environment.

Table 2 ANCOVA and Post Hoc test (n=225)

Variable	Level	Mean (Std. Error)[a]	F	Post Hoc
PRE	0-time		47.085**	
	1-time			
	2-time			
	3-time			
RT	0-time	45.299 (1.663)	12.240**	2-time > 3-time**
	1-time	45.354 (1.691)		2-time > 1-time**
	2-time	57.992 (1.736)		2-time > 0-time**
	3-time	50.666 (1.788)		3-time > 1-time*
				3-time > 0-time*

** $p< 0.01$; * $p< 0.05$

[a] Covariates appearing in the model are evaluated at the following values: PRE = 33.829

PRE: pre-test scores of summative assessment

RT group: repeat times group

0-time: students should answer an item one time correctly (do not repeat the test).

1-time: students should answer an item correctly two times consecutively during the repeated tests in total (one time in the repeated test).

2-time: students should answer an item correctly three times consecutively during the repeated tests in total (two times consecutively in repeated tests).

3-time: students should answer an item correctly four times consecutively during the repeated tests in total (three times consecutively in repeated tests).

3.2. Study 2

Study 2 adopts quasi-experimental design to compare paper-and-pencil formative assessment with GAM-WATA formative assessment regarding their effectiveness in an e-Learning environment. This study also examines the effectiveness of the "Prune Strategy" and the "Call-in Strategy."

3.2.1. Participants

Six junior high school science teachers experienced in Web-based instruction, along with the seventh graders from 18 classes they teach, were invited to participate in this study. The teachers came from five different counties in central Taiwan. The 18 classes totaling 566 (281 female and 285 male) valid participants were randomly divided into six different groups. In the random division, the whole class was regarded as a unit, which means students from the same class would not be divided into different groups. Each group was assigned one of the six different types of formative assessment and labeled "P2" group, "P3" group, "P2C" group, "P3C" group, "C" group and "PPT" group (see Table 3). All of the students took the same e-Learning course, but each group took one of the six different types of formative assessment. The 566 students all had taken computer classes in the elementary school. They were equipped with basic computer skills and able to use the e-Learning system.

Table 3 Participant distribution by TFA and Gender

TFA \ Gender	P3	P2	P3C	P2C	C	PPT	Sum
Female	34	52	62	55	56	22	281
Male	51	37	58	53	45	41	285
Sum	85	89	120	108	101	63	566

TFA: types of formative assessment. P3: Prune Strategy- turn the original 4-option item into a 3-option item by eliminating one incorrect option. P2: Prune Strategy- turn the original 4-option item into a 2-option item by eliminating two incorrect options. P3C: P3 and Call-in Strategy. P2C: P2 and Call-in Strategy. C: Call-in Strategy. PPT: Paper-and-Pencil Test.

3.2.2. Instruments

3.2.2.1. GAM-WATA and e-Learning environment

For the introduction of GAM-WATA, please refer to Section 2.4.3. As to the e-Learning materials in this study, they covered the topic, "Atmosphere and Water," in the junior high school "Nature and Life Technology" course in Taiwan. Figure 13 shows the e-Learning environment composed of PowerPoint-generated e-Learning materials, concept maps, reference materials, Adobe Macromedia Flash animations and so on.

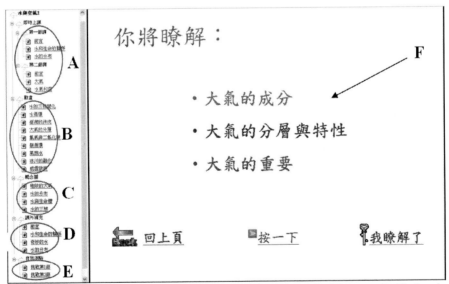

Figure 13. e-Learning environment. (A) Learning materials; (B) Adobe Macromedia Flash animations; (C) Concept maps; (D) Reference materials; (E) GAM-WATA; (F) The part for learning contents.

3.2.2.2. Summative assessment and formative assessment

The items in the formative assessment were constructed according to the e-Learning contents. Students taking the six different types of formative assessment practiced the same items. The items in the summative assessment were also constructed according to the e-Learning contents but were different from those used in the formative assessment. It aimed to assess student learning outcome in an e-Learning environment. In this study, the pre-test scores of the summative assessment represented the entry behavior of learning, and the post-test scores represented the learning outcome. The average difficulty of the summative assessment was 0.633 and the Cronbach's α was 0.814.

3.2.3. Study design and procedures

This study took two weeks in total. All participating students were divided into six groups and each group took one of the different types of formative assessment (Table 3). The six different types of formative assessment include paper-and-pencil test and five different types of Web-based quiz-game-like formative assessment (GAM-WATA). The five different types of Web-based quiz-game-like formative assessment were constructed on the basis of the two designs in the "Ask-Hint Strategy" - the "Prune Strategy" and the "Call-in Strategy" (see Section 2.4.3 for detailed descriptions). When students are divided into groups, each class is taken as a unit, which means students in the same class would not belong to different groups. Before the 2-week e-Learning course, all students took the pre-test of the summative assessment and familiarized themselves with the e-Learning environment. During the 2-week e-Learning course, students in "P2" group, "P3" group, "P2C" group, "P3C" group and "C" group learned on the Web and took part in the Web-based quiz-game-like formative assessment at any time. Students in "PPT" group also did learning on the Web at any time, but the formative assessment (paper-and-pencil test) was administered after each class. For "PPT" group, correct answers were given but not actively explained by the teachers. Besides, test papers were returned to students for review. When students had any queries about the correct answers, they were supposed to actively ask the teachers or try to find the answers on the Web pages by themselves. The six groups of students did learning in the same e-Learning environment and practiced the same items in six different types of formative assessment. After the 2-week instruction, all of the students had to take the post-test of the summative assessment.

3.2.4. Data collection and analysis

In this study, two sets of quantitative data were collected, including the pre-test scores of summative assessment (PRE) and post-test scores of summative assessment (POST). After the data was gathered, the scores were analyzed with SPSS Ver.12.0. The PRE was taken to represent the entry behavior of learning, while the difference between the PRE and the POST was taken to represent the learning effectiveness. This study used ANCOVA, taking the PRE as the covariate and the POST as the dependent variable, to test the relationship between the POST and the "types of the formative assessment (TFA)." There were six different types of formative assessment ("P2," "P3," "P2C," "P3C," "C" and "PPT"). The LSD method was also used to compare the effectiveness of these six different types of formative assessment.

3.2.5. Results

In this study, ANCOVA was used to examine the effectiveness of the six different types of formative assessment. During ANCOVA, the relationship between the POST and TFA was tested with the PRE as the covariate, the POST as the dependent variable and the TFA as the fixed factor. Before ANCOVA, the homogeneity of variance assumption was tested. The Levene's test for equality of variances was not significant ($F_{5,560}= 1.322$, $p> 0.05$). In addition, the assumption of homogeneity of regression coefficients was also tested ($F_{5,554}=2.078$, $p > 0.05$). These results indicated that both homogeneity assumptions were not violated.

Table 4 shows that the PRE has a significant impact on the POST ($F_{1,559}$= 460.050, p < 0.01), and the TFA is also found to have a significant impact on the POST ($F_{5,559}$ = 8.535, p < 0.01). The LSD method was used to further compare the effectiveness of the six different types of formative assessment (Table 4). As shown in Table 4, students in the "PPT" group appear to be the least effective in their learning. However, students in the "P2C" group and "P3C" group appear to learn more effectively in the e-Learning environment. According to Table 4, there is no significant difference in the learning effectiveness between the "P3C" and "P2C" group. Students in both the "P3C" group and the "P2C" group appear to perform significantly better than those in the "P3" group, "P2" group, "C" group and "PPT" group. Table 4 also shows that students in the "P3" group, "P2" group and "C" group appear to perform significantly better than those in the "PPT" group. In summary, the types of formative assessment appear to affect e-Learning effectiveness, and students appear to have better effectiveness in an e-Learning environment equipped with GAM-WATA, especially when the Web-based formative assessment is administered in the form of "P3C" and "P2C."

Table 4 ANCOVA and Post Hoc test (n=566)

Variable	Level	Mean (Std. Error)[a]	F	Post Hoc
PRE	P3		460.050**	
	P2			
	P3C			
	P2C			
	C			
	PPT			
TFA	P3	54.443(1.238)	8.535**	P3C > P3**
	P2	53.039(1.207)		P3C > P2**
	P3C	58.754(1.034)		P3C > C**
	P2C	58.264(1.090)		P3C > PPT**
	C	54.566(1.133)		P2C > P3*
	PPT	48.941(1.435)		P2C > P2**
				P2C > C*
				P2C > PPT**
				P3 > PPT**
				P2 > PPT*
				C > PPT**

** p< 0.01; * p< 0.05

[a] Covariates appearing in the model are evaluated at the following values: PRE = 39.790

PRE: pre-test scores of summative assessment

TFA: types of formative assessment. It includes "P2" (Prune Strategy- turn the original 4-option item into a 2-option item), "P3" (Prune Strategy- turn the original 4-option item into a 3-option item), "P3C" (P3 and Call-in Strategy), and the other is "P2C" (P2 and Call-in Strategy), "C" (Call-in Strategy) and "PPT" (Paper-and-Pencil Test).

4. CONCLUDING REMARKS

In an e-Learning environment, students are required to learn more actively, be their own teachers and be responsible for their learning effectiveness (Sujo de Montes and Gonzales, 2000; Wang, 2007). Therefore, stimulating student motivation and making them learn more actively have become important issues in the field of e-Learning. Wang believes that the idea of assessment-centered learning environment proposed by Bransford et al. (2000) is an ideal basis on which an effective e-Learning environment can be established. The main characteristic of assessment-centered learning environment is that during the teaching process, teachers would constantly administer formative assessment for students and provide them with proper feedback. It is expected that students can cultivate the ability of self-assessment and improve their learning effectiveness any time with this ability. This research introduces two Web-based formative assessment modules of the WATA system - FAM-WATA and GAM-WATA. They can be used to help teachers construct an assessment-centered e-Learning environment. In addition to assisting teachers to administer Web-based formative assessment in an e-Learning environment, the two modules also enhance the interaction between teachers and students and offer timely feedback to students. Thanks to the interaction and feedback, student learning effectiveness can be facilitated with their ability of self-assessment.

After surveying the literature related to formative assessment, Wang (2007) develops FAM-WATA on the basis of the WATA system. This Web-based formative assessment system includes six effective strategies – "repeat the test," "correct answers are not given," "query scores," "ask questions," "monitor answering history" and "all pass and then reward." According to Wang, students hold positive attitudes towards the six strategies in FAM-WATA. In comparison with the formative assessment administered in the form of paper-and-pencil test and normal Web-based test in an e-Learning environment, formative assessment administered in the form of FAM-WATA is more effective. Analyzed from the angle of students' cognitive styles, FAM-WATA is proved to be the most effective in facilitating the learning of field independent students. On the other hand, Wang also proposes using the Accumulated Score (AS) equation to assess student performance in FAM-WATA formative assessment. He claims that the AS provides an effective feedback mechanism for students to monitor their formative learning and for teachers to understand the learning condition of their students. Continuing the efforts of the previous researches, this research further investigates the "repeat the test" strategy in FAM-WATA. It aims to explore how many times students should correctly answer an item consecutively during the repeated tests before they can be taken as passing the item can lead to the best effectiveness of FAM-WATA. The results indicate that in terms of improving the effectiveness of FAM-WATA, the design of "2-time" group (correctly answer an item three times consecutively in total, or two times consecutively in repeated tests) is the best, while that of "3-time" group (correctly answer an item four times consecutively in total, or three times consecutively in repeated tests) is the second best. As to the design of "1-time" group (correctly answer an item two times consecutively in total, or one time in the repeated test) and "0-time" group (correctly answer an item one time, or do not repeat the test), they are not significantly different. Based on the findings, it is suggested that FAM-WATA should adopt the design of "2-time" group. This design can ensure the best effectiveness of FAM-WATA in facilitating student learning in an e-Learning environment.

The findings also suggest that when researchers try to develop Web-based formative assessment systems in the future, they should consider incorporating the "repeat the test" strategy into the systems along with the "correct answers are not given" and "timely feedback" strategies, and the times for which students should correctly answer an item consecutively before they can be taken as passing the item should be three.

As to GAM-WATA, it includes a unique strategy-"Ask-Hint Strategy." This strategy is composed of two designs: the "Prune Strategy" and the "Call-in Strategy." GAM-WATA aims to create a Web-based quiz-game-like formative assessment in an e-Learning environment. It is expected that the quiz-game-like characteristics can make the formative assessment more interesting. When students take Web-based quiz-game-like formative assessment in an e-Learning environment, they can feel like playing quiz games. In this way, students will be motivated to actively participate in the Web-based formative assessment and their learning interest and effectiveness can also be promoted (Wang, 2008). Concerning how effectively GAM-WATA facilitates e-Learning when used to administer formative assessment, it proves better than paper-and-pencil test. Moreover, the design of combining the "Prune Strategy" with the "Call-in Strategy" ("P3C" and "P2C") can lead to better effectiveness than the designs of using only "Prune Strategy" or only "Call-in Strategy." These findings suggest that more feedback strategies should be provided in a Web-based formative assessment system. Student e-Learning effectiveness will be improved if students can gain more timely feedback when encountering difficulties during the process of taking Web-based formative assessment.

In the future, continuous researches will be conducted on the mechanism of how FAM-WATA and GAM-WATA facilitate student learning in an e-Learning environment. The theoretical basis of this mechanism will also be constructed. There will also be further researches conducted to explore how students' individual differences, such as learning style, cognitive style, prior knowledge, self-efficacy, motivation and etc., influence their learning effectiveness in the e-Learning environment which includes FAM-WATA formative assessment and GAM-WATA formative assessment. The topic about why the design of "2-time" group makes FAM-WATA the most effective and why the designs of "P2C" group and "P3C" group make GAM-WATA the most effective will also be explored. Factors influencing students' interaction with the "Ask-Hint Strategy" are another important topic deserving further investigation.

At the end, based on the review of related literature and findings of this research, some topics that researchers should keep on exploring in the future are herein proposed:

1. The administration of (Web-based) formative assessment (Bell and Cowie, 2001)
2. The interaction between students and (Web-based) formative assessment and the construction of the theoretical basis of (Web-based) formative assessment (Black and Wiliam, 1998)
3. Explore the potential of new technologies that provide the opportunity to incorporate (Web-based) formative assessment into teaching in an efficient and user-friendly fashion (Bransford et al., 2000, p.258)
4. The informativeness of the feedback provided in (Web-based) formative assessment (Narciss, 1999)

5. The effective feedback strategies in (Web-based) formative assessment; the theoretical basis of these strategies and the reasons for their effectiveness (Wang, 2007).

It is expected that with the continuous and deeper investigation of the five issues, the mechanism of how Web-based formative assessment influences student learning in an e-Learning environment can be clarified, and the proper theoretical basis can in turn be constructed. The future design of Web-based formative assessment system can then rely on the basis and come closer to perfection. The improved system will effectively assist teachers to provide students with proper and useful feedback in an e-Learning environment. Thanks to Web-based formative assessment and the feedback it offers, students can do formative learning and cultivate the ability of self-assessment. Once students take the initiative in learning, their e-Learning effectiveness will surely be improved.

NOTES

It is herein stated that all the trademarks and product names referred to in this chapter are the property of their respective owners.

ACKNOWLEDGEMENTS

The author deeply appreciates the National Science Council in Taiwan for the financial support and encouragement under Grant No. 95-2511-S-134-002-MY3. The author also thanks Dr. Shih-Chieh Huang, Dr. Kuo-Hua Wang and Dr. Wei-Lung Wang, professors of National Changhua University of Education in Taiwan, for their assistance in this research. Lastly, the author would like to thank "Giant Riches (http://www.ttv.com.tw /drama/2003/GiantRiches)," a TV program produced by Taiwan Television Enterprise (TTV), and "Who Wants to be a Millionaire (http://millionaire.itv.com/millionaire/home.php)," a U.K. TV program produced by Independent Television (ITV). These two programs give rise to the original concept of designing "Ask-Hint Strategy."

REFERENCES

Barron, B. J. S., Schwartz, D. L., Vye, N. J., Moore, A., Petrosino, A., Zech, L., Bransford, J., and The Cognition and Technology Group at Vanderbilt (1998). Doing with understanding: Lessons from research on problem- and project-based learning. *Journal of the Learning Sciences*, 7, 271-311.
Bell, B. and Cowie, B. (2001). The characteristics of formative assessment in science education. *Science Education*, 85, 536–553.
Black, P. and Wiliam, D. (1998). Assessment and classroom learning. *Assessment in Education*, 5(1), 7-74.

Bransford, J. D., Brown, A., and Cocking, R. (2000). *How people learn: Mind, brain, experience and school* (expanded ed.). Washington, DC, USA: National Academy Press.

Brewer, C. A. (2004). Near real-time assessment of student learning and understanding in Biology courses. *BioScience*, 54, 1034-1039.

Brook, B. (2000). Going to college on the Web. *Hispanic*, 13(9), 64-66.

Brown, S. (1996). *Summary comment. Symposium on validity in educational assessment.* Educational Assessment Research Unit, University of Otago, Dunedin, New Zealand.

Brown, S. and Knight, P. (1994). *Assessing learners in higher education*. London, UK: Kogan Page.

Brown, G. and Johnson-Shull, L. (2000). Teaching online: Now we're talking. *The Technology Source*, May/Jun.

Bodzin, A. M. and Cates, W. M. (2003). Enhancing preservice teachers' understanding of Web-based scientific inquiry. *Journal of Science Teacher Education*, 14, 237-257.

Buchanan, T. (2000). The efficacy of a World-Wide Web mediated formative assessment. *Journal of Computer Assisted Learning*, 16, 193-200.

Cerny, M. G. and Heines, J. M. (2001). Evaluating distance education across twelvetime zones. *Technological Horizons in Educational Journal*, 28 (7), 18-25.

Ebel, R. L. and Frisbie, D. A. (1991). *Essentials of educational measurement* (5th ed). Englewood Cliffs, NJ, USA: Prentice Hall.

Flake, J. L. (2001). Teacher education and the World Wide Web. *Journal of Technology and Teacher Education*, 9(1), 43-61.

Gardner, L., Sheridan, D., and White, D. (2002). A Web-based learning and assessment system to support flexible education. *Journal of Computer Assisted Learning*, 18, 125–136.

Gipps, C. (1994). *Beyond testing: Towards a theory of educational assessment*. London, UK: The Falmer Press.

Gronlund, N. E. and Linn, R. L. (1990). *Measurement and evaluation in teaching* (6th ed.). New York, USA: Macmillan.

Henly, D. C. (2003). Use of Web-based formative assessment to support student learning in a metabolism/nutrition unit. *European Journal of Dental Education*, 7, 116-122.

Hoffman, J. L., Wu, H.-K., Krajcik, J. S., and Soloway, E. (2003). The nature of learners' science content understandings with the use of on-line resources. *Journal of Research in Science Teaching*, 40(3), 323-346.

Justham, D. and Timmons, S. (2005). An evaluation of using a Web-based statistics test to teach statistics to post-registration nursing students. *Nurse Education Today*, 25, 156–163.

Khan, K. S., Davies, D. A., and Gupta, J. K. (2001). Formative self-assessment using multiple true-false questions on the Internet: Feedback according to confidence about correct knowledge. *Medical Teacher*, 23, 158-163.

Kovacs, P. and Rowell, D. (2001). The merging of system analysis and design principles with Web site development: One university's experience. *Technological Horizons in Educational Journal*, 28(6), 60-65.

Narciss, S. (1999). *Motivational effects of the informativeness of feedback*. Paper presented at the annual conference of the American Research Association. Montreal, Canada (ERIC Document Reproduction Services No. ED430034).

Orsmond, P., Merry, S., and Callaghan, A. C. (2004). Implementation of a formative assessment model incorporating peer and self assessment. *Innovations in Education and Training International*, 41(3), 273–290.

Peat, M. and Franklin, S. (2002). Supporting student learning: The use of computer-based formative assessment modules. *British Journal of Educational Technology*, 33, 515-523.

Perrenoud, P. (1998). From formative evaluation to a controlled regulation of learning processes. Towards a wider conceptual field. *Assessment in Education*, 5(1), 85–102.

Sadler, D. R. (1989). Formative assessment and the design of instructional systems. *Instructional Science*, 18(2), 119–144.

Scriven, M. (1967). The methodology of evaluation. In R. E. Stake (Ed.). *Curriculum evaluation. American Educational Research Association Monograph Series on Evaluation* (No. 1). Chicago, USA: Rand McNally.

Sujo de Montes, L. E. and Gonzales, C. L. (2000). Been there, done that: Reaching teachers through distance education. *Journal of Technology and Teacher Education*, 8(4), 351-371.

Sun, L., Bender, W. N., and Fore, C. (2003). Web-based certification courses: The future of teacher preparation in special education. *Teacher Education and Special Education*, 26(2), 87-97.

Velan, G. M., Kumar, R. K., Dziegielewski, M., and Wakefield, D. (2002). Web-based self-assessments in pathology with Questionmark Perception. *Pathology*, 34, 282-284.

Vogel, J. J., Greenwood-Ericksen, A., Cannon-Bower, J., and Bowers, C. A. (2006). Using virtual reality with and without gaming attributes for academic achievement. *Journal of Research on Technology in Education*, 39, 105–118.

Vye, N. J., Schwartz, D. L., Bransford, J. D., Barron, B. J., Zech, L. & The Cognition and Technology Group at Vanderbilt (1998). SMART environment that support monitoring, reflection and revision. In D. Hacker, J. Dunlosky & A. Graesser (Eds.), *Metacognition in educational theory and practice* (pp. 305-346). Mahwah, NJ, USA: Lawrence Erlbaum Associates.

Wang, T. H., Wang, K. H., Wang, W. L., Huang. S. C., and Chen, S. Y. (2004). Web-based Assessment and Test Analyses (WATA) system: Development and evaluation. *Journal of Computer Assisted Learning*, 20(1), 59-71.

Wang, T. H. (2007). What strategies are effective for formative assessment in an e-Learning environment? *Journal of Computer Assisted Learning*, 23(3), 171-186.

Wang, T. H., Wang, K. H., and Huang, S. C. (2008). Designing a Web-based assessment environment for improving pre-service teacher assessment literacy. *Computers & Education,* 51(1), 448-462.

Wang, T. H. (2008). Web-based quiz-game-like formative assessment: Development and evaluation. *Computers & Education*, 51(3), 1247-1263.

Wiliam, D. and Black, P. (1996). Meanings and consequences: A basis for distinguishing formative and summative functions of assessment? *British Educational Research Journal*, 22, 537-548.

In: E-Learning: 21st Century Issues and Challenges
Editor: A.R. Lipshitz and S. P. Parsons

ISBN : 978-1-60456-156-2
©2008 Nova Science Publishers, Inc.

Chapter 2

ASSESSING INTERCULTURAL COMPETENCE IN E-LEARNING PROJECTS

Margarita Vinagre[*]
Nebrija University, Spain

ABSTRACT

This chapter describes how aspects of intercultural communicative competence can be fostered and assessed in on-line collaborative projects. In order to do so, we present the findings of an on-line exchange carried out by the Department of Applied Languages at Nebrija University in Madrid and Dublin City University during the academic year 2006-2007. Students collaborated electronically by e-mail and in wikis, using their native language (L1) and their L2 to interact with a partner and exchange personal, linguistic and socio-cultural information. Data was gathered from a triangulation of instruments, such as e-mail and wiki content, language learning diaries, critical incidents, essays, compositions and self-evaluation questionnaires. On the basis of Byram's (1997) model of Intercultural Communicative Competence (ICC) and the guidelines for assessment of intercultural experience (Byram 2000), we attempted to assess qualitatively whether the different components of ICC can be developed in e-learning environments. Our findings seem to suggest that the instruments mentioned can help us to describe some evidence of development with regard to a) interest in knowing other people's way of life and introducing one's own culture to others, b) ability to change perspective, c) knowledge about one's own and others' culture for intercultural communication, and d) knowledge about the intercultural communication process. Further research needs to be carried out on how best to encourage students to exhibit 'a readiness to suspend disbelief and judgment with respect to others' meanings, beliefs and behaviours' and a 'willingness to suspend belief in one's own meanings and behaviours, and to analyse them from the viewpoint of the others with whom one is engaging' (Byram 1997: 34).

Keywords: E-learning, telecollaboration, asynchronous learning environments, intercultural communicative competence, on-line exchanges

---

[*] Department of Applied Languages, La Berzosa Campus, Hoyo de Manzanares, 28240 Madrid, Spain
E-mail: mvinagre@nebrija.es, Tel: + 34 91 452 11 01 (ext 4542)

INTRODUCTION

The importance of intercultural competence as a learning objective in the foreign language classroom has featured prominently since the 1990's. Byram (1997: 3) suggests that the success of communication does not depend on the efficiency of an information exchange but rather on establishing and maintaining relationships. For this reason, intercultural competence or "the ability to understand and relate to people from other countries" (Byram 1997: 5) has become an increasingly important objective in foreign language teaching. The advent of the Internet has provided us with highly efficient tools (e.g. e-mail, chat, blogs, wikis, forums, etc) which may facilitate the development of intercultural competence in the foreign language classroom. Given the difficulty of achieving this goal within a traditional classroom set-up, it has become necessary to find ways of implementing e-learning projects whose main purpose is to engage students who are linguistically and culturally different in social interaction and telecollaboration. By telecollaboration we mean on-line interaction between language learners and native speakers who engage in collaborative project work, debate and intercultural exchange with a view to learning each other's language and aspects of their culture. Ware (2005: 64) defines it as "a form of network-based language teaching that links students using Internet-mediated communication tools" and according to Belz (2003: 68) "*Telecollaboration* involves the use of Internet communication tools by internationally dispersed students of language in institutionalized settings in order to promote the development of (a) foreign language (FL) linguistic competence and (b) intercultural competence".

Over the years, many researchers have explored how different types of e-learning projects may contribute to the development of intercultural competence in participants (Warschauer & Kern 2000; Furstenberg, Levet, English & Maillet 2001; Liaw 2006; Vinagre 2006b). O'Dowd (2003) explored the potential of computer-mediated communication for intercultural learning and he attempted to identify the characteristics of an e-mail exchange that are conducive to developing intercultural competence. Belz (2003) identified differences in communication patterns that led to tensions and impeded intercultural learning. Müller-Hartmann (2000) analysed the role of tasks in three e-mail projects and his findings stressed the importance of a task-based approach for telecollaborative projects whose aim is the development of intercultural competence. Vinagre (2006a) analysed social interaction and the use of politeness strategies in e-mail intercultural exchanges. She suggested that the abundance of positive politeness strategies which are found in on-line collaborative exchanges as opposed to face-to-face encounters facilitate the creation of a 'sound social space' (Kreijns, Kirschner, Jochems, & Van Buuren, 2004) which fosters linguistic and intercultural development.

All the above-mentioned studies have focused on different aspects of intercultural learning in on-line environments. However, the assessment of intercultural competence is complex and research on this issue is still scarce. In this respect, our aim in this chapter is to contribute to current research by exploring the development of intercultural competence in a telecollaborative exchange between Nebrija University in Madrid and Dublin City University during the academic year 2006-2007. The main objectives of this project were to encourage students to learn each other's language and to compare and contrast two different cultures and two different ways of life as a basis towards understanding each other's 'languaculture'. This term was coined by Agar (1994) to reflect the fact language and culture are inextricably bound together, that is to say, language is shaped by culture and culture is shaped by language use:

> "Language, in all its varieties, in all the ways it appears in everyday life, builds a world of meanings. When you run into different meanings, when you become aware of your own and work to build a bridge to the others, 'culture' is what you're up to. Language fills the spaces between us with sound; culture forges the human connection through them. Culture is in language, and language is loaded with culture...whenever you hear the word language or the word culture, you might wonder about the missing half... 'Languaculture' is a reminder, I hope, of the necessary connection between its two parts..." (Agar 1994: 28, 60)

Thus, we wanted to see whether participants in this exchange were capable of appreciating and learning from each other's 'languacultures'. In order to do so, they would need to go beyond their own personal view-points and be capable of creating 'a third space' (Bhabha 1992: 58) "... [which] has the potential both of revealing the codes under which speakers in cross-cultural encounters operate, and of constructing something different and hybrid from these cross-cultural encounters" (Kramsch 1996: 7). This 'third space', "rather than seek to bridge differences and aim for the universal, [...] seeks to create a dialogic context in which the vital necessity to continue the dialogue ensures a mutual base to explore the sometimes irreducible differences between people's values and attitudes." (Kramsch 1996: 7)

In the next section, Byram's (1997) model of Intercultural Communicative Competence (ICC) and the guidelines for assessing intercultural experience (Byram 2000) are examined in detail. We adopted Byram's model in this study due to its wide acceptance by language teachers and researchers as a representative guideline for the assessment of intercultural competence in telecollaborative projects (Belz 2003; O'Dowd 2003; Liaw 2006; Vogt 2006).

Byram's model of Intercultural Communicative Competence

Byram (1997) proposes a model of Intercultural Communicative Competence (ICC) which comprises linguistic, sociolinguistic, discourse and intercultural components - namely, the partial competences suggested by Van Ek (1986: 35) in his model of communicative ability -, together with the factors involved in intercultural competence. Thus, the model consists of five interdependent principles or *savoirs*: a) attitudes, b) knowledge, c) skills of discovery and interaction and d) skills of interpreting and relating. The interplay of these four principles should lead to the fifth, namely critical cultural awareness. This final component underlies all the others, since it focuses on comparison and evaluation, key abilities for any learner who is to become a truly intercultural communicator.

Attitudes

According to Byram (1997: 33-34), attitudes of "curiosity and openness" are preconditions and anticipated outcomes of intercultural competence, since the success of intercultural communication depends on establishing and maintaining good social relationships. In addition, "a readiness to suspend disbelief and judgement with respect to other's meanings, beliefs and behaviours" and "a willingness to suspend disbelief belief in one's own meanings and behaviours" are crucial in guaranteeing that the negative effects that cultural misunderstandings, preconceived ideas and stereotyping could have on the intercultural interaction are minimised or mitigated in favour of maintaining a friendly relationship. The relevance of these attitudes becomes highly noticeable in on-line projects, where the effectiveness of collaborative learning largely depends "on strategic conflict avoidance and strategic construction of co-operative social interaction" (Vinagre 2006a: 2).

Knowledge

Byram distinguishes between declarative and procedural knowledge "of social groups and their products and practices in one's own and in one's interlocutor's country, and of the general processes of societal and individual interaction" (1997: 58). Declarative knowledge refers to facts and information relating to those social groups, whereas procedural knowledge refers to information about processes of interaction. Declarative knowledge, which is always present to some degree, is not sufficient and needs to be complemented by procedural knowledge on how to act on specific circumstances. Clearly, effective intercultural communication goes beyond a simple "gathering of facts" about one's own and the other's culture and relies heavily on the learner's capacity to develop "underlying understanding, metacognition, and the ability to reflect one's own thinking and respond to experience" (Byram, 1997: 90). All knowledge, however, is relational, that is to say, it is acquired when socialising with one's own social groups.

Skills of interpreting and relating

Byram (1997: 61) defines these skills as the "ability to interpret a document or event from another culture, to explain it and relate it to documents or events from one's own". Therefore, the skills of interpreting and relating refer to the ability to draw on existing knowledge in order to correctly interpret the meaning of a specific cultural product. This knowledge may have been acquired thorough formal or other types of education and it is likely to be knowledge applied consciously. These skills can be distinguished from the skills of discovery and interaction in that they do not necessarily involve interaction with an interlocutor but rather working on documents.

Skills of discovery and interaction

Byram defines skills of discovery and interaction as the "ability to acquire new knowledge of a culture and cultural practices and the ability to operate knowledge, attitudes and skills under the constraints of real-time communication and interaction" (1997: 61). This author also suggests that these skills are "the ability to recognise significant phenomena in a foreign environment and to elicit their meanings and connotations, and their relationship to other phenomena" (1997: 38). Thus, discovery usually takes place though social interaction and these skills are linked to the ability to ask and answer "deep learning" questions, to non-verbal communication and politeness phenomena.

In addition to this model, Byram (2000: 4) offers some guidelines for the assessment of the intercultural experience. These will be presented in detail below, given that we have adopted them, modified in some respects by the model above, as the basis for the analysis carried out in the present study.

INSTITUTIONAL CONTEXT

Setting up the exchange

We set up an exchange programme between students at Nebrija University in Madrid and students at Dublin City University during the academic year 2006-07. The academic profile of the learners from both universities was similar. Most of the students were between nineteen and twenty-one years of age, except for two students who were a few years older. Students at both universities were specialist learners of English and Spanish, respectively, and their level of proficiency in the foreign language was between higher intermediate and advanced. Students worked collaboratively in an e-tandem learning exchange by e-mail and had to carry out two tasks in a wiki-space. The on-line exchange and all the work[1] related to it were worth 20% of the students' final grade in their English and Spanish subjects.

The first step was to assign each of the twenty students a partner, which we did on the basis of the students' similarities in terms of level of proficiency in their target language. Once paired, students had to exchange a minimum of two e-mails a week[2] and discuss a series of topics such as personal information (age, family, pets, hobbies, free time, studies, work, the place where they live, the place where they are from, friends, etc), customs and traditions, music, cinema and television programmes, the educational system, the use of idioms and colloquial expressions, stereotypes, food, festivals, sports, history and politics etc. In addition to their correspondence by e-mail, the students were required to carry out two further tasks in a wiki-space created specially for this project. Each dyad had their own wiki-page in which they were to exchange information, discuss and prepare a topic for an end-of-term oral presentation based on one of the topics discussed with the partner via e-mail and write a final joint essay, half in English and half in Spanish, discussing some 'rich points' in

---

[1] Students had to write a language learning diary on their on-line experience, prepare an end-of-year oral presentation on one of the topics discussed with the partner and write an essay discussing different aspects of both cultures. These last two tasks were completed in the wiki-space.
[2] A copy of all messages was also sent to their instructors.

both cultures. Rich points "are pieces of discourse that indicate that two *languacultures* or conceptual systems have come into contact" (Belz in press). Examples of rich points are bullfighting or fox hunting, understood by some as shows of bravery and courage, whilst others consider them to be cruel sports. Following Neuner (2003), we decided on an intercultural approach in foreign language teaching that focuses on the discussion of cross-cultural experiences, the discussion of stereotypes and negotiation of meaning as we shall explain in the following sections.

METHODOLOGY

In this section, the instruments and methods used in the study are discussed with regard to the assessment of intercultural competence in telecollaborative projects. Our assessment instruments and methods included qualitative analyses of e-mails, wiki-space content, critical incidents which occurred during interaction, language learning diaries and self-evaluation questionnaires. We adopted Byram's (2000: 4)[3] criteria for the assessment of intercultural competence, with some modifications based on Byram (1997), as the basis for these analyses. These criteria and their descriptions are given below:

a) Interest in knowing other people's way of life and introducing one's own culture
   to others
  ▪ I am interested in other people's experience of daily life, particularly those
    things not usually presented to outsiders thorough the media.
  ▪ I am also interested in the daily experience of a variety of social groups within
    a society and not only the dominant culture.

b) Ability to change perspective
  ▪ I have realised that I can understand other cultures by seeing things from a
    different point of view and by looking at my culture from their perspective.

c) Knowledge about one's own and others' culture for intercultural communication
  ▪ I know some important facts about living in the other culture and about the
    country, state and people.
  ▪ I know how to engage in conversation with people of the other culture and
    maintain a conversation.

d) Knowledge about intercultural communication processes
  ▪ I know how to resolve misunderstandings which arise from people's lack of
    awareness of the view point of another culture.
  ▪ I know how to discover new information and new aspects of the other culture
    for myself.

---

[3] Byram's (2000) guidelines include: a) an interest in other people's experiences of daily life; b) ability to change perspective; c) knowledge about another country and culture, and d) knowledge about intercultural communication. There is a fifth criterion, namely "ability to cope with living in a different culture", which we have omitted here since it was not applicable to this study.

Data and discussion

An analysis of the students' e-mails, wiki-space content and language learning diaries revealed examples of the four categories mentioned above. This analysis was carried out by the author and a research student. We have provided examples of the entries in the four categories in Table 1 below:

Table 1. Examples of Categorisation of Students' E-mails and Wiki Content

Category	Examples from students' writing
a) Interest in knowing other people's way of life and introducing one's own culture to others	"Es interesante aprender sobre la lengua que las personas usan en realidad porque es diferente de la del idioma he aprendido en mis libros. Yo se que hay muchas expresiones en inglés diferentes en las DIFERENTES partes del país. Un ejemplo es en Massachussets, toda la gente dice "wicked" para decir "muy muy", en California ellos dicen "hella", pero en Nueva Jersey decimos "mad"; personalmente yo digo "crazy" para expresar esto."[4] [It is interesting to learn about the language that people really use because it is different to that I have read in my books. I know that there are many different expressions in English used in DIFFERENT parts of the country. One example in Massachussets is that everyone says "wicked" in order to say "very very", whilst in California they say "hella"; in New Jersey we say "mad", but personally I say "crazy" in order to express this idea".] "Quizá tenemos algo en común. Me refiero al hecho de que los irlandeses hemos sido conquistado por los ingleses y ustedes por los moros, no es verdad?[Maybe we have something in common. I'm referring to that fact that the Irish were conquered by the English and you were conquered by the Moors, isn't that so?] […]How has the invasion of the 'Moros' influenced life on your people? Have you adopted any of their customs? Have you ever studied Arabic at school or visited your neighbouring country? Are you interested in their music? Do you appreciate their humour?"
b) Ability to change perspective	"The image you described or Irish people is pretty funny and of course is not true, as the Spanish prototypes are not true either in most cases. I think that living in a global and a multicultural world is silly to continuous believing in topics or prototypes. Each country has a mix of people from several countries which make false the prototypes. What do you think?" "A teacher at school once told me that 'if you generalise you are always wrong', and that is what I have discovered with tandem. I have found that many of the stereotypes and preconceived ideas I had about the Irish are not true. There is more to their food than fish and chips and hamburgers, as I thought."

---

[4] Extracts of messages have been left as they were written. Where the original is in Spanish I have translated the information without the students' errors.

Table 1. Continued

Category	Examples from students' writing
c) Knowledge about one's own and others' culture for intercultural communication	"Tanto Irlanda como España son los países del origen católico. En los 6 condados del norte del país las personas no quieren ser llamadas irlandes. Es la misma de las personas de catalan, no,? La mayoria de la gente de esta zona del pais quieren ser separadas del resto del pais. Es a causa de un acontecimiento inmenso en la historia de este pais […]" [Spain and Ireland are both Catholic countries. The people in the six counties in the north (of Ireland) don't want to be called Irish. It is the same with the Catalans, isn't it? Most people in Northern Ireland want to be independent from the rest of the country. This was caused by an important event in the history of this country. […]] "Además de aprender una segunda lengua, se aprende una nueva cultura. No solo tienes capacidad de hablar la segunda lengua, sino también comienzas a participar en sus hábitos, como yo por ejemplo, a las tres cada día pego una siesta ;)" [Besides learning a new language you learn a new culture. Not only can you speak the second language but you also start to take on their customs … like myself, for example, at three o'clock everyday I have a siesta;)]
d) Knowledge about intercultural communication processes	"What do you think about these preconceived ideas? You can say what you think about spain, I am not going to get mad or anything like that…[…] if you want you don't have to talk about your country[5] you can talk about Ireland, but I will prefer if you talk about yours because I could learn lots from your point of view…" "[…] What is your impression of bullfighting-is it not such a crucl art? […] Entiendo que no comprendas el sentido de los toros. Sinceramente, yo soy española pero tampoco le veo sentido. No entiendo que la matanza de un animal sea motivo de diversión pero para mucha gente no significa eso, es algo más intenso, una tradición que ven desde niños y que la viven y sienten con gran intensidad. Espero que te haya ayudado en algo esta información pero como ya te he dicho antes, no a todos los españoles nos gustan los toros." [[…] I can understand that you don't get the meaning of bullfighting. I'm Spanish and I can't see the point of it either. I don't understand how killing an animal can be fun, but it doesn't mean that to many people; it's something more intense, a tradition they have seen since they were children and it constitutes an intense experience for them. I hope that these comments are helpful to you, but, as I mentioned before, not all Spaniards, myself included, like bullfighting]

Most of the examples (205) belong to the category 'interest in knowing other people's way of life and introducing one's own culture to others'. This interest can be inferred from the detailed questions that the partners posed to each other. We are referring here to questions that went beyond enquiring superficially about aspects such as their studies or hobbies. The high presence of instances in this category (more than half of all instances found) may be due to the fact that students were required to discuss a series of topics related to their culture, topics they were then asked to contrast and compare. In order to do so, they had to look for information (in documents, books, on the Internet) and exchange information with their partners. This process could explain the abundance of questions about the other's country and culture after a specific culture-related topic had been introduced. Most questions were duly answered and follow-up questions developing from a conversation were also indicative of real interest in the partner's culture:

---

[5] The student is from Poland, but she is living and studying in Dublin.

"In response to your questions regarding whether or not I knew about the Spanish Armada, I do. It sank off the west coast of Ireland if I am not mistaken, in Sligo. [...] As to whether or not people in the area look Spanish, it's doubtful! They are typically pale skin, blue eyes and 'Irish' looking as I like to call them with strong western accents. You might find it difficult to understand them. Where in Spain is it easiest to understand the natives, not only because of their accents but due to dialogue and the way they use words?"

Another linguistic aspect that showed this willingness to discover different perspectives of their partner's culture was the presence of questions such as "can you tell me what Spanish people are like, what is true in what people say and what is not?" and "what do you think about these preconceived ideas?". In addition, remarks such as "I am very interested in exchange opinions with you", "Quisiera saber mucho tus ideas" [I would very much like to hear your ideas] and "I'd like to know your opinion" also helped to encourage a response from the partner regarding their own or their partner's culture. Finally, students used terms such as 'curious' (5 times), 'curiosity' (1), 'curiosas' (1), and expressions such as 'me intriga' [I'm intrigued, 1] which reflect attitudes of "curiosity and openness", preconditions for the success of intercultural communication and a clear manifestation of intercultural learning.

The second biggest category was "knowledge about one's own culture and other's culture for intercultural communication" (74 instances). Within this category we need to distinguish between the two types of knowledge, declarative and procedural, mentioned above. Declarative knowledge, which is factual, refers to information about the other's country, state and people, whereas procedural knowledge refers to information about the process of interaction, that is to say, how to engage in conversation with people from other cultures.

There were many examples of declarative knowledge. Many students had visited their partner's country before the exchange started and some had spent time in the foreign country either on holiday or as part of their study programmes. Students also looked for information in books and on the Internet when they had to discuss certain topics (such as history and politics) and they felt they did not know much about these matters in either their own or their partner's country. This was important since students were asked to contrast and compare the way things were done in the two cultures. This type of factual juxtaposition and the learning that may derive from it requires extensive declarative knowledge of one's own culture as well as that of the other. In this respect, students were willing to learn about their own culture in order to provide their partner with information, as well as showing their partner how much they knew about the foreign culture. In one particular case, the student was happy to show how similar to the Spanish he was:

"Me encantan los deportes y la música española (de Lolita a Alejandro Fernandez). He vivido en las isla Canarias, Barça, Girona [...]. Hay un montón de cosas que me gustan de España por ejemplo el ritmo de vida, el idioma, la gente extrovertida y el ambiente de los bares ;) [...] Además de aprender una segunda lengua, se aprende una nueva cultura [I love Spanish sports and music (ranging from Lolita to Alejandro Fernandez). I have lived in the Canary Islands, in Barcelona, Gerona [...] There are many things I like about Spain; for instance, the pace of life, the language, its extroverted people and the atmosphere in the bars ;) In addition to learning a language, you learn a culture] [...] I think that you begin to

get more involved in their habits, public holidays and customs. You start to notice
when it's el dia de San Juan for example and things like that, no?"

In this excerpt, the student expresses not only his knowledge of Spanish music and way
of life in general, but having lived in various Spanish cities (two them in Catalonia) he could
actually write some words in Catalan (Barça and Girona) and remember some feast days (el
dia de San Juan).

Since we asked students to contrast and compare the two cultures, we would like to
comment on the reasons that motivated this decision, given that cross-cultural approaches to
culture learning have received a great deal of criticism. Authors such as Guest (2002: 154)
suggest that there are some problems associated with adopting this type of approach in
teaching and learning a second culture. He mentions the risk of oversimplifying the richness
and variety of a culture and reducing it to "caricature". This approach might also encourage
stereotypes "used to exacerbate adversity, and not to encourage mutual respect" and
misrepresent a culture by reducing it to static categories and simple propositions. All this may
result in a failure to reach a deeper understanding of the complex realities behind it. Guest
(2002: 157) suggests that we should:

> "[...] focus on the properties of individuals of character types rather than
> cultures at large. The linguistic dynamics should be adjusted according to the nature
> of the interaction (individual/small groups), and not in order to conform to an
> abstract, generalised, formula ('culture'). Thus, instead of an overtly cultural
> approach it would seem that the method more sympathetic to psychological or small-
> scale interactive models would ultimately be both more accurate and productive".

Therefore, we should move away from the learner as a detached observer of a culture
(understood as static and monolithic) towards a learner who is actively involved in learning
about a culture that is dynamic, through the perspectives of individuals who belong to that
culture. This is precisely the approach that we have adopted in this study, since students in
telecollaboration work in small-scale interactive situations with individuals from the target
culture. In telecollaborative exchanges students contrast and compare different cultural issues
in order to make generalisations that will serve as a starting point for further discussion. Thus,
students remark on "how similar they are under it all" or that "they are both the same",
generalisations that are relevant when 'culture' is understood as a relative concept. Once they
have reached this point they can move on to discussing 'culture as group membership' and
analyse individual variation in 'culture as individual' and 'culture as contested' (Levy, 2007:
108-110). Thus,

> "When an individual learns another language, or moves to live in another
> country, culture may be contested within the individual, as differing belief systems,
> ideas and values meet head to head, and are compared and contrasted both
> consciously and unconsciously through feelings of disquiet and uncertainty. [...]
> This is one reason why learning a language can be such a profound and worthwhile
> experience, because one's core beliefs and values may be challenged, reoriented and
> reset."

Thus, by contrasting and comparing the two cultures we wanted students to observe similarities and differences in order to look for explanations as to their origin whilst challenging their views on their own culture and that of the other.

As regards procedural knowledge, we found that some instances in which the students showed their capacity to engage people in conversation were also connected to their knowledge about the intercultural communication process (i.e. how to resolve misunderstandings in social interaction, category (d) above). This became evident when analysing critical incidents. According to Cushner and Brislin (1996), a critical incident involves a situation concerning cross-cultural misunderstanding. These incidents are particularly interesting in telecollaborative exchanges, since telecollaboration relies heavily on the social interaction that takes place among participants and misunderstandings may pose a threat to the success of such interaction. As Vinagre (2006a: 20) suggests, students in CSCL exchanges who are willing to stress cooperation and friendship between partners, whilst mitigating any threats to each other's face, help to create a highly sociable environment "characterised by effective working relationships, strong group cohesiveness, trust, respect and belonging, satisfaction, and a strong sense of community" (Kreijns, Kirschner, Jochems, & Van Buuren, 2004: 157). Therefore, successful telecollaborative learning depends on establishing and maintaining successful social interaction among participants. If students manage to create a friendly social environment characterised by trust, respect and belonging, the chances of a communication break-down due to misunderstandings are reduced and the chances of successful learning, either linguistic or intercultural, increase. This is partly determined by a more relaxed attitude on the part of the students, who feel free to pose questions and make comments that they would avoid in face-to-face situations. Below, we present an excerpt of a communicative exchange between two students in which a critical incident could have undermined their exchange completely had they not managed to become friendly throughout the exchange:

"El otro día pregunté a una compañera si me podía decir algo sobre vosotros, los irlandeses. Me dijo que teníais fama de beber mucho, de no ducharos a menudo, de no limpiar con frecuencia la casa y de que las chicas irlandesas son muy atrevidas con los chicos. Yo no se sí será verdad o no pero espero que no te ofenda." [The other day I asked a classmate if she could tell me something about the Irish. She said that you drink a lot, don't shower very often, rarely clean your houses and that Irish girls are very forward with boys. I don't know if this is true but I hope you don't get offended by it]

"Regarding what you heard from your friend about the Irish, of course it's not true, and your friend sounds a bit ignorant to be honest. Of course something like that would be offensive, it was just a list of insulting things. It is true that the Irish drink a lot, but of course we bathe regularly and clean our houses. I hope you can see the absurdity of your question. Also, you said "Creo que en Irlanda como en otros sitios de Inglaterra...". Just as a cultural note, never call the Irish English. England had oppressed the Irish for 800 years, and many Irish would take that as the biggest offence of all. I understand if you didn't know, which is why I have explained these things."

"I'm sorry much from the other day, what I said about Irish. I didn't think that I upset you.

I asked my classmate because I wanted to know something about you, but I see that it wasn't a good idea. But I said you that you will tell me things about Irish and for this reason I asked. Excuse me."

"Sí, te diré como los Irlandeses. Una cosa que tu compañera dició que es cierto es que los Irlandeses beben mucho, en general. Pero, como todas lugares en el mundo, cuando beben con moderación, no es una problema. No sé si la gente beben mucho más de la gente de otras países. Mis amigos y yo bebemos en la casa antes de ir a la discoteca, pero no me agrada mucho de las discotecas (¿es la frase correcta?). Prefiero una conversación buena con una bebida agradable- en inglés decimos "over a nice quiet pint". [I will tell you what the Irish are like. One thing that your classmate said and it's true is that Irish people drink a lot in general. However, as in many other places in the world, if you drink in moderation it's not a problem. I don't know if they drink much more than people in other countries. My friends and I drink at home before we go to the disco, but I don't like discos much. I rather have a good conversation over a nice drink-in English we say "over a nice quiet pint"...]

There were a few mistakes in the email you sent me. You wrote "I'm sorry much from the other day", but you should say "I'm very sorry for the other day".(By the way, don't worry about it. It was just a misunderstanding I suppose. But negative things are hard not to be taken in a bad way, so I just wanted to make you aware that the things your classmate said were not true at all. Will we put it behind us?)"

The highly offensive remark made by the Spanish student could have jeopardised this dyad's exchange, since the Irish student could have reacted by being offended and ending the interaction. However, the situation did not escalate because the Irish student realised there was no malice, only ignorance, in the Spaniard's comments, and that she was deeply sorry for them. In their communicative exchange, we can see that they had established a strong bond and it is likely that their previously good relationship was the reason why the offended party, after clarifying the situation, was willing to "put it [the misunderstanding] behind them" and forget about the whole incident.

The category 'ability to change perspective' recorded the lowest number of instances (38). A plausible explanation for this is that students were interested in providing information about their own culture and learning from the partner's culture, but this exchange of information did not necessarily involve a change in perspective. Similar to findings in O'Dowd (2003: 124), there were some students who wanted to "correct misrepresentations" and "fight stereotypes" when they thought their culture was not properly perceived or represented abroad. However, we also came across students who were able to decentre and change perspective. This was reflected mostly in the language learning diaries, where reflection about their own culture and that of the partner was encouraged:

"[My partner] asked me in her last e-mail about "Los Sanfermines". I do not like bullfighting, so I did not know a lot about it, but I looked for information to be able to explain to her about this festivity. This way I also learnt a little bit about my own culture".

"Today, [my partner] wrote me three e-mails...in the first one she explicated me her opinion about bullfighting, after my explanation about "Los Sanfermines". In short, she has the same opinion as I have. She does not understand why the animals has to suffer before they die. She qualifies it as cruelty this kind of "art".

"Today I realize that there is a big rejection against bullfighting in foreign countries. I think it is normal because it is an act of cruelty with the animals. Here we live with it since we are babies, so it is more common. Although, as I said before, I do not like it and I do not understand it. Therefore, I totally understand that foreigners do not understand it neither".

(Three entries from a student's language learning diary)

In other cases, some conclusions based on serious reflection were pointed out by the students:

"Creo que hay mucho prejuicio y ideas preconcebida en esta mundo. Por ejemplo creo que muchas personas creen que los irlandeses beben mucho bebidas alcoholica cuando son en paises diferente...esta idea es bastante verdad pero hay mucho personas irlandeses que viajan para ver las personas diferente, la cultura diferente y las vidas diferente de las personas de la pais. [I think there are many prejudices and preconceived ideas in this world. For instance, many people think that the Irish drink a lot of spirits when they are in a foreign country ...this is quite true. However, there are many Irish people who travel to see different peoples, cultures and lifestyles] I think such judgements are unfair...but we must expect that this is where the world is at today and I feel it is only through such discussion similar to which we are undertaking that progress and understanding will be achieved."

The category 'knowledge about the intercultural communication process' (d) when defined as "I know how to discover new information and new aspects of the other culture for myself" was difficult to identify in isolation, since examples of this category tended to appear linked to the category 'interest in knowing other people's way of life' (a), as shown above. In order to be able to show an interest in knowing other people's way of life, it is necessary to know how to discover new information about the other culture. In a similar way, "knowing how to resolve misunderstandings which arise from people's lack of awareness of the view point of another culture" (category d) also appeared to be linked to an ability to decentre, since this capacity to see things from a different point of view and to look at one's own culture from someone else's perspective clearly facilitated the solving of misunderstandings that arise in communicative interaction.

In addition to the data elicited from the e-mail and wiki-space content and the language learning diaries we also gathered data from a self-evaluation questionnaire specially designed to determine the students' knowledge of the culture and people they were going to work with throughout the semester. They were given the choice of answering the questionnaire in the foreign language or in their mother tongue, thus enabling them to provide clearer and more elaborate answers. The questionnaire was presented to the students as a tool for stimulating serious reflection and raising learner awareness. It included open-ended and closed questions and was administered on-line so that the students could enjoy easy access to it and we could examine the results shortly afterwards. At the end of the exchange period, the participants were then asked to fill in a similar questionnaire and to write a composition in their mother tongue, commenting on their own experience of the project. The data gathered from the students' answers to the questionnaires allowed us to assess whether the project had been a positive and productive experience for the learners, not only from a linguistic point of view but also from a cultural perspective. Thus, 90.9% of the students regarded the exchange as being highly positive and all of them considered that it had helped them to develop their cultural knowledge. We include some of the students' commentaries regarding their experience below:

> I did not know any Americans[6] before this exchange, so the only points of reference I had were films and series. Now I understand many of their forms of behaviour. Even so, I think I still need to learn more about them in order to understand them better.

> A teacher at school once told me that 'if you generalise you are always wrong', and that is what I have discovered with tandem. I have found that many of the stereotypes and preconceived ideas I had about the Irish are not true. There is more to their food than fish and chips and hamburgers, as I thought.

> During this semester [with the project] I also found interesting to discover that although many of us have travelled and lived in other countries we still believe many stereotypes and make all kind of generalisations about other countries and cultures. This is not a "Spanish" behaviour I was surprised to notice that even well educated people (people who travel, who read a lot, etc) have this tendency to believe this stereotypes and sometimes even create them.

In excerpt one and two, the students show an increased awareness of the inaccuracies of stereotyping, whereas the comment in example three refers to key aspects of intercultural learning. While this may not be the "third place" aimed for in intercultural communication, these comments do show some progress in the development of the students' cultural awareness.

CONCLUSION

One of the purposes of this project was to foster the development of the participants' intercultural competence. Students were asked to exchange information about their own cultures and then discuss a series of culture-based topics with their partners. Although we found ample evidence that the students had exercised intercultural competence in categories A (i.e. interest in knowing other people's way of life and introducing one's own culture to others) and C (i.e. knowledge about one's own and other's culture for intercultural communication) this was not the case with categories D (i.e. knowledge about the intercultural communication process) and B (i.e. ability to change perspective).

Thus, most students showed a genuine interest in the other's culture and were happy to provide information about their own culture. However, the majority of them failed to decentre, to relativise their own culture in order to look at the other's culture and their own

---

[6] The partner was American and studied in Dublin.

with objectivity. This meant that, in most cases, students did not change perspective or they failed to integrate the other's perspective into their own. This may have been caused by a fear of 'letting down' their own culture in front of outsiders and a desire to 'defend it' from misinterpretations. Unfortunately, this prevented students from taking intercultural communication a step further.

With regard to this matter, Liaw (2006: 60) mentions that this imbalance in the findings "may suggest that this type of learning environment is conducive to the development of knowledge and attitudes of intercultural competence but not necessarily to the development of empathy and (meta) intercultural skills". Although the connection between this imbalance and the mediated nature of the learning environment is clear, it may be worth carrying out further research to ascertain whether the development of empathy and (meta) intercultural skills can be equally facilitated by telecollaboration. We need to discover how best to encourage students to exhibit 'a readiness to suspend disbelief and judgment with respect to others' meanings, beliefs and behaviours' and a 'willingness to suspend belief in one's own meanings and behaviours, and to analyse them from the viewpoint of the others with whom one is engaging' (Byram 1997: 34). In this respect, it may be worth adopting the Cultura methodology (Furstenberg et al., 2001) in future collaborative exchanges. The aim of Cultura is to develop understanding of another culture through a series of steps. In stage 1, two groups of students from different cultures are required to answer three questionnaires on the Web which have been designed to highlight some basic cultural differences. In these questionnaires students are asked to carry out word associations, complete sentences or react to specific situations all related to topics such as religion, work, politics and so on. Once they have responded to the questionnaires, the answers are then posted on the Internet side by side. Then, in stage 2, students, first on their own and then in their class groups, analyse the responses. At this point students compare and contrast the answers in an attempt to form initial hypotheses to explain the similarities and differences in the answers. In stage 3 the students begin to exchange opinions and to communicate their observations and hypotheses in a forum which is open to all participants. They also ask for information or clarification when required and answer the questions posed to them by their partner group. Finally, in stages 4 and 5, students analyse a broader set of documents ranging from opinion polls to films (e.g. Spanish films and their American re-make versions), press and magazine articles, texts of different kinds written in the mother tongue by authors from different periods and different fields, etc.

Thus, students involved in Cultura,

> "observe, analyze and compare similar material from their respective cultures as they are posted on the Web; exchange viewpoints on these materials in a reciprocal and ever-deepening understanding of the other culture; and study and research and increasing array of material (films, texts, on-line news media) designed to expand their cross-cultural analysis." (Furstenberg et al. 2001: 58)

The aim of this methodology is precisely to allow students to observe similarities and variations between both cultures through the process of juxtaposition. These initial observations will become the starting point for attempting to decipher the meaning behind the differences. However, unlike other approaches, one-to-one contact with partners is delayed and contact with the foreign culture is, at first, indirect and general. This aspect is extremely important, since it allows for the tension of discussing critical topics with the partner to be postponed. It also promotes a data-driven approach that enhances the students' objectivity and, therefore, encourages decentring and understanding "otherness". For all these reasons, we believe that this methodology may facilitate the development of empathy and (meta) intercultural skills in telecollaborative exchanges and it would be of great interest to apply it in future projects.

REFERENCES

Agar, M. 1994. *Language Shock: Understanding the Culture of Conversation*. New York: William Morrow.

Bhabha, H. K. 1992. "Post-colonial authority and post-modern guilt" In L. Grossberg, P. Nelson & P. Treichler (Eds.), *Cultural Studies* (pp.56-66). London: Routledge.

Belz, J. 2003. "Linguistic perspectives on the development of intercultural competece in telecollaboration". *Language Learning and Technology 7* (2): 68-117. On WWW at http://llt.msu.edu/vol7num3/belz/

Belz, J. (in press). "The development of intercultural communicative competence". In O'Dowd, R. (Ed.), *On-line Intercultural Exchange: An Introduction for Foreign Language Teachers*. Clevedon: Multilingual Matters:

Byram, M. 1997. *Teaching and Assessing Intercultural Communicative Competence*. Clavedon, England: Multilingual Matters.

Byram, M. 2000. "Assessing intercultural competence in language teaching". *Sprogforum 18(6),* pp.8-13.

Cushner, K. & Brislin, R.W.1996. *Intercultural Interactions: A Practical Guide*. London: Sage.

Furstenberg, G., Levet, S., English, K.& Maillet , K. 2001. "Giving virtual voice to the silent language of culture. The Cultura project". *Language Learning and Technology 5*, 55-102. On WWW at http://llt.msu.edu/vol5num1/furstenberg/default.html

Guest , M. 2002. "A critical 'checkbook' for culture teaching and learning". *ELT Journal, 56* (2), 154-161.

Kramsch, C. 1996. "The cultural component of language teaching". *Zeitschrift für Interkulturellen Fremdsprachenunterricht, 1* (2). On WWW at http://www.spz.tu-darmstadt.de/projekt_ejournal/jg_01_2/beitrag/kramsch2.htm

Kreijns, K., Kirschner, P., Jochems, W. & Van Buuren, H. (2004). "Determining sociability, social space, and social presence in (a) synchronous collaborative groups". *Cyberpsychology & Behaviour, 7* (2), 155-172.

Levy, M. 2007. "Culture, culture learning and new technologies". *Language Learning and Technology, 11*(2), 104-127. On WWW at http://llt.msu.edu/vol11num2/levy/

Liaw, M. 2006. "E-learning and the development of intercultural competence". *Language Learning and Technology, 10*(3), 49-64. On WWW at http://llt.msu.edu/vol10num3/liaw

Müller-Hartmann, A. 2000. "The role of tasks in promoting intercultural learning in electronic learning networks". *Language Learning and Technology, 4*(2), 129-147. On WWW at http://llt.msu.edu/vol4num2/muller/default.html

O'Dowd, R. 2003. "Understanding the 'other side': intercultural learning in Spanish-English e-mail exchange". *Language Learning and Technology,* 7(2),118-144. On WWW at http://llt.msu.edu/vol7num2/odowd/default.html

Neuner, G. 2003. "Socio-cultural interim worlds in foreign language teaching and learning". In Byram, M (Ed.), *Intercultural Competence* (pp. 15-62). Strasbourg: Council of Europe Publishing,

Van Ek, J.A. 1986. *Objectives for Foreign Language Learning 1: Scope.* Strasbourg: Council of Europe.

Vinagre, M. 2006a. "Politeness Strategies in Collaborative E-mail Exchanges". *Computers and Education,* doi10.1016/j.compedu.2006.10.002.

Vinagre, M. 2006b. "Developing intercultural communicative competence through on-line collaborative exchanges". *III Congreso Online del Observatorio para la Cibersociedad.* On WWW at http://www.cibersociedad.net/congres2006/gts/comunicacio.php?id=336&llengua=es

Vogt, K., 2006. "Can you measure attitudinal factors in intercultural communication? Tracing the development of attitudes in e-mail projects. *ReCall* 18 (2), 153-173.

Ware, P., 2005. " 'Missed' communication in online communication: Tensions in a German-American telecollaboration". *Language Learning and Technology 9,* 64-89. On WWW at http://llt.msu.edu/vol9num2/ware/

Warschauer, M. & Kern, R. (Eds.) (2000). *Network-Based Language Teaching: Concepts and Practice.* New York: Cambridge University Press.

In: E-Learning: 21st Century Issues and Challenges
Editor: A.R. Lipshitz and S. P. Parsons

ISBN : 978-1-60456-156-2
©2008 Nova Science Publishers, Inc.

Chapter 3

E-LEARNING FOR ALL

Evastina Björk***, Stig Ottosson* and Sigrun Thorsteinsdottir**

ABSTRACT

The main focus on e-Learning portals has so far been on technical issues and conformity to SCORM, which initially was developed for people in military training. Other user groups with totally different needs and abilities have so far not received much focus by platform developers, apparently caused by limited knowledge about, for example, disabled or elderly people's life conditions and their need for Internet and related technologies. Quality assurance and how to design platform learning activities to assure long-lasting knowledge achievements by the students taking part in distance learning are additional areas in need of more development and research.

At the same time, a need for e-learning platforms accessible to everybody in society is growing. As elderly (65+) and disabled people now account for around 25 % of the population in Europe and the USA, there is a substantial unexplored market for education providers as well as e-Learning platform producers. Research has started in the field of "Web for All" and the interest for elderly people's Internet habits are intensively discussed among researchers.

One conclusion in this paper is that "e-Learning for All" is possible to obtain. Experiments on how to make examinations on the Internet with high reliability have been done and found difficult but possible to develop. However, it is another issue to prevent students from cheating on tests over the Internet which calls for new technical solutions.

Keywords: E-learning, blended learning, Web for All, web accessibility, examination.

***NHV. Box 12133. S-40242 Göteborg. Sweden. e-mail: eva-stina@nhv.se

*Tervix ICT AB,Theres Svenssons gata 10. S-41755 Göteborg. Sweden.e-mail: so@tervix.com

**SJÁ ehf.. Klapparstigur 28. 101 Reykjavík. Iceland. e-mail: sigrun@sja.is

1 http://www.oecd.org/document/41/0,2340,en_2649_201185_38659497_1_1_1_1,00.html

1.   INTRODUCTION

"Electronic learning" or "e-learning" is a general term used to refer to computer-based learning. E-learning has introduced a whole new set of physical, emotional and psychological issues along with educational issues (Palloff and Pratt 1999).

Before the 1970s, the concept of distance learning referred primarily to correspondence courses that provided materials to read and tests to submit by mail. The scope of distance learning in the 1970s and 1980s included viewing programs on public television or, more recently, on cable access channels, with or without a senior lecturer available for discussions (Delaro 1997). Students sat at home watching hours of videotaped instruction rather than sitting in classrooms doing the same. That meant more accessibility to students unable to attend classes because of scheduling, transportation problems or other restrictions. Distance education implemented in this manner offered limited interaction between lecturers and students but few opportunities for interaction among students.

Current e-learning based distance education efforts are incorporating strategies for delivering content effectively, engaging students in active learning, and offering an approach that is flexible, multi-perspective, experiential, often project based and holistic – which is often referred to as student centered.

1.1. Advantages with e-learning

Key advantages of e-learning are flexibility, convenience and the ability to study at one's own pace at any time and any place where an internet connection is available. The participants can participate and complete coursework in accordance with their daily commitments. This makes an e-learning education a viable option for those who have other commitments - such as family or work – and/or cannot participate easily e.g. due to reduced body function. There are also cost and time benefits with blended learning, not having to commute to and from a place where education is given face-to-face.

Other advantages of e-learning are the ability to chat and exchange information over Internet with fellow classmates independent of metric distance, a greater adaptability to learner's needs, more variety in learning experience with the use of multimedia and the non-verbal presentation of teaching material. Streamed video recorded lectures and MP3 files provide visual and audio learning that can be reviewed as often as needed or wanted. For organizations with distributed and constantly changing learners (e.g. restaurant staff), e-learning has considerable benefits when compared with organizing classroom training.

In a study carried out on students who participated in four e-learning courses weekly written tests on the e-learning portal were shown to be helpful in the learning process meaning that they experienced a better long lasting knowledge (Ottosson 2003).

1.2. Disadvantages of e-learning

1.2.1. Educational related disadvantages

One disadvantage of e-learning is the lack of face-to-face interaction. The feeling of isolation experienced by distance learning students is also sometimes mentioned (Ottosson 2003). On the other hand, it is also known and natural that computer-based-communication encourage students to meet face-to-face simply as it becomes thrilling to meet someone in realty who one has made work with over the Internet. When much group collaboration is required, e-learning can cause lag times in collaborative feedback when for example students check their online agenda to seldom making it impossible to keep within time limits.

1.2.2. Social/cultural and economic related disadvantages

A non-educational disadvantage is that web and software development can be expensive. The development of adaptive materials is also more time-consuming and costly than for that of non-adaptive material. That counts especially for the production on web based material for people with visibility reductions.

Noteworthy is also that the use of the Internet could be a social issue and exclude people with less educational background or because of a financial situation that prohibits an investment in computer technology. The gender perspective is another aspect of Internet use; females can be hindered from using Internet or Internet-related technologies because of to the traditional male oriented contexts in the ICT world (ICT = Information and Communication Technology).

A rather new phenomenon described by Katz and Rice (2002) is that frequent Internet users suddenly can stop to be so. These so called "Internots" showed in their investigation to be 11.5 % of those who had started to use the Internet two years earlier. They found that this group consisted of men under 40 years of age with low educational background and with low income. They were in what is called the "digital divide" being outside the reach of e-learning.

1.2.3. Situational limitations

We all now and then experience situational functional limitations in the use of different Web solutions. Temporary/situational limitations relate to prevailing circumstances, environment, or device making us handicapped without otherwise having a functional disability of any kind. Examples include mobile devices and device limitations, such as having no mouse, or constraining circumstances, such as interacting with a poorly designed website (e.g. a website requiring Javascripts when these cannot be used in places such as on a public library computer or a public hotel computer), etc. Temporary functional limitations include limited use of the hands or eyes as a consequence of an accident. More stationary functional limitations can be visual, auditory, physical, cognitive or a mix of several (which includes language and learning disabilities).

1.2.4. Long lasting limitations

E-learning portals in general have been designed for "ordinary users" (Benktzon 1993) although this group consists of users with large differences in knowledge and skills in using computers and the Web. They have also different skills in using the keyboard, which is a problem not much discussed. An investigation (N 55) (Ottosson 2003) showed, e.g., that only

38 % of the students in an e-learning course in product development had the proper finger setting for typing and that 52 % regarded themselves as slow or relatively slow typists (see table 1).

Typing much without learning the correct finger setting method may in time also cause neck and shoulder problems. Therefore, it seems to be an important question for parents and primary school teachers to teach the young students early to type in a proper way.

**Table 1. Some findings from a questionnary to 55 Swedish students
of which 49 responded (89 %) (Ottosson 2003)**

Question: When you are typing (punching the keyboard), how many fingers do you use?

1–2	3–4	5–6	7–8	9–10
1 (2%)	8 (17%)	10 (21%)	11 (23%)	18 (38%)

Question: Do your regard yourself as a typist who is:

Slow	Relatively slow	Relatively fast	Very fast
2 (4%)	23 (48%)	21 (44%)	2 (4%)

1.2.4 Cheating

Cheating offers an easy way out. Why bother studying hard and doing all those term papers by yourself if you can use somebody else's work? An example of this problem was described on the 13th of November 2003 by BBC News as: "For Anna, 22, a final year student in south-east England, Internet plagiarism is a natural part of undergraduate life. For the past three years, she says, she has been submitting essays bought and copied from the Internet and passing them off as her own. She is currently working on her final-year project and most of the materials in the dissertation are coming off the net. Anna (not her real name) says she cheats because it is easy to get away with it. …. Anna is not alone. Cheating, especially Internet cheating, is increasingly becoming the way of the academic world."

Cheating is not a new phenomenon and in 1928 Hugh Hartshorn and Mark May published a classic study on the nature of character and the effect of character education programs on youth. Using a database of over 10,000 students it was found that moral behaviour was situationally specific and that indirect methods appear to be more effective than direct methods when it come to shaping the character of youth.

With increased distance learning the cheating problem has become a hot issue. The website http://privateschool.about.com/cs/forteachers/a/cheating_5.htm gave in August 2007 the following recommendations on how to catch students when they cheat:

- **Use a PDS (Plagiarism Detection Service) to catch plagiarism.** The service is used by thousands of schools and universities worldwide. Basically PDS compares your students' papers with those in their enormous databases. Similarities are highlighted so that you can review the findings easily. For a look at a rationale for NOT using a PDS read *The Politics of Plagiarism Detection Services*.
- **Lock down your grade program and database.** Hardly a day goes by without some chilling story about hackers breaking into a school's academic database and changing grades. Keep your computer secure by using secure

passwords. Set your screensaver to activate in password protected mode after 2 minutes of inactivity.

1.3. Quality, time and cost aspects on E-learning

In the marketing of e-learning portals and by commercial educational firms today often e-learning is seen as a cost-effective online training. Two other common measures are time and quality issues. Therefore supplier of websites often claim to supply with solutions that save time, reduce costs, and increases quality.

1.3.1. Quality aspects

The quality aspect is often measured in technical terms and conformity to SCORM (Sharable Content Object Reference Model) (see e.g. www.adlnet.org). SCORM is a specification of the Advanced Distributed Learning (ADL) Initiative, which comes out of the US Office of the Secretary of Defense. The military sector in the US identified the possibilities with distance learning and the office of the Under Secretary of Defence for Personnel and Readiness (OUSD PandR) became leaders in the efforts to harness the power of information technologies to modernize structured learning. The Advance Distance Learning (ADL) Initiative now recommends that the ADL Community migrate to the SCORM 2004 3rd Edition.

Training of skills (doing things automatically) was the initial educational principle of SCORM. Therefore, (preferable self assessment) SCORM tests are made after each lesson. As a skill is build up step by step, the soldiers in military training are not allowed to continue to the second step until the first step has been approved. This educational principle excludes the need of final examination tests as the system is built as a self controlling system. SCORM has therefore no principles for examination in theoretical/knowledge based education.

As learning processes are complex, it is a challenge to evaluate the quality of different e-learning solutions when it comes to knowledge generation. When a new solution is introduced, the complexity increases and, as a consequence, evaluation becomes more difficult. So far e-learning has not been validated as an effective way of teaching and learning (de Berredo and Soerio 2007).

1.3.2. Time aspects

There are many time saving aspects of e-learning. The students do not need to transport themselves to the face-to-face education. They do not have to search for the teachers. They can use spare time to study by having access to Internet via broad band or 3G connection. Etc.

1.3.3. Cost aspects

Connected to time is cost for the time not used in an efficient way. However, there are costs for the software and hardware. Taken the cost savings and the spending together, some researchers claim that e-learning has not proven to be an efficient solution for training and education in terms of return on investment (ROI) (e.g. de Berredo and Soerio 2007).

1.4. Scope of the paper

However, as the benefits of e-learning seem to be dominant and in pace with the expanded use of the Internet, an expansion of e-learning can be estimated in all sectors of the society. At the same time, with an expansion the learning materials currently in use will probably have to be adapted to new needs and context of the new Information Society what regards contents, media, deployment, etc. Also new user groups as disabled people and elderly, here called 65+, put new demands on the e-learning portals and internet based information. In this paper, we therefore will discuss these matters as well as quality aspects of e-learning.

2. RESEARCH METHOD

The findings in this paper are based on the authors' practical experience from education of e-learning at the university level, from project leadership of the development of different web solutions (e.g. a new e-learning portal – see Ottosson 2003) and from evaluation of existing web solutions resulting in advice on how to make them more useful also for disabled users and the elderly. The research method is Insider Action Research (Björk 2003, Björk and Ottosson 2007).

3. USABILITY ASPECTS

In theories of Product Development (PD) the starting point is often to listen to the "voice of the customer" to find out the "need" or "customer need". As customers and users quite often are not the same individuals gradually the need to understand or know the users also is spreading. In the latest PD theories the product developers not only need to listen to the customers and to get to know the users. They also need to be one step ahead of the users meaning that they need to formulate "wants" and "wishes" to be able to develop products and solutions for the future (Ottosson 2004, Holmdahl 2006).

As a consequence of this development, usability aspects have got an increased interest and importance for researchers and product developers. Some fingerprints of this are:

> "As the products that we use at work and in our homes become increasingly complex, the usability becomes even more pertinent." (Jordan 1998).

> "Manufacturers increasingly see usability as an area where they can gain advantages over their competitors. This contradicts with the technical side of product development." (Jordan 1998).

> "It is concluded that good user-centered design shortens overall development time and cost by reducing the number of expensive changes late in the process. It also leads to more useful and usable products." (Buurman 1997)

According to ISO (ISO DIS 9241-11) *usability* is "the effectiveness, efficiency and satisfaction with which specific users can achieve specified/particular goals in particular environments". On a deeper level these three terms have the following meanings:

- *Effectiveness*: Is the method or tool proposed effective for reaching the goal? Is it possible to implement the findings in real user environments? What is required to make that happen (e.g. education needs, training needs, expert needs, tools aquisition, organizational change, etc.)?
- *Efficiency:* Is the method or tool proposed efficient to use? Is it tricky to use? Is it time - resource intensive?
- *Satisfaction:* Will the users find the use of the method or tool more pleasant to use than what they experienced before the implementation? Will the users feel that the outcome is more efficient? Will the use of the new method or tool contribute to a better economical result for the individual or will it reduce failure risks in any aspect?

3.1. User characteristics

There are a number of user characteristics that can be predictors of the design for usability. Jordan (1998) has presented some user characteristics that should be considered in the development of new products:

- Earlier experience (of similar products)
- Cultural background (language, traditions)
- Special needs or a disability of some kind
- Age, sex and knowledge

Lack of usability can lead to minor frustration as well as life threatening situations for the individual. Norman (1988) and Magnusson (2001) reported that many people have difficulties with everyday items that cause annoyance and defeats their intended purpose. Unusable products also cost time and money. For example, difficulties in using computers can cost a company 5-10 % of total working time (Jordan 1998). Low levels of usability could mean that users employ just one product function out of several available. A long time needed to learn how to use the product, high service costs, and many customer complaints due to misuse are other results of low usability in products.

What a product communicates to a user is a kind of message of how it should be handled and used. If this message is falsely interpreted, the risk of misuse increases (Wikström 2002). Monö (1997) has described semantic functions aimed at analysing the communication aspects of products and defining a clear product message. In his view a product should:

- describe its purpose, handling and mode of action
- express its qualities
- invite use and reactions
- identify the purpose, type of product, product origin and product category

Products need to have good communicative abilities as, because of cognitive or language difficulties, users may have problems understanding abstract product messages, for example from an instruction manual.

The product developer's ability to empathize, participate and understand user situations is critical for the analysis of how new products especially can support disabled people and offer adequate usability.

3.2. User groups

Users of products can in general be divided into different target groups depending on the aim and the situation. Benktsson (1993) presented a user pyramid to describe the market situation and to illustrate the fact that market segmentation should also deal with different users' abilities to handle a product (see Figure 1). The areas in the user pyramid show in principle the relation between the number of users with different user abilities.

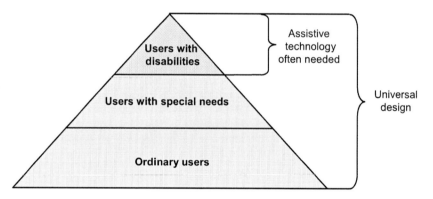

Figure 1. The user pyramid also showing when Assistive technology is needed to support the product although it has a universal design.

Ordinary users are able bodied, capable individuals who are in a position to freely choose what kind of product or service they want or need. If necessary, ordinary users can to some degree adapt themselves both physically and mentally to poor technical solutions.

Users with special needs are individuals who have no recognized physical or mental impairment but who need some special modification of standard products in order to use them properly. For example, elderly people with minor disabilities - such as reduced strength, impaired hearing, etc. - belong to this group.

Disabled users require assistive devices due to severe mobility problems and reduced body functions. The products must have a high degree of both technical and practical functionality; otherwise the products will not work as intended. Disabled users do not have the freedom of choice enjoyed by ordinary users, as they cannot compensate for practical disadvantages in the same way as ordinary users. This group of users is heterogeneous and consists of individuals who have higher individual demands than ordinary users.

It is not relevant or possible to have a strict demarcation between different user groups, as some individuals will fit into more than one group. Although a schematic description shows that users of products consist of groups that differ a great deal in terms of product requirements, it is sufficient for the purpose of the present study to merely distinguish between the three groups.

3.3. Numbers of disabled users

It has been estimated (Arbetsterapeuten 2003) that between 10 and 15 % of the European population belongs to the disabled user group. However, disability statistics tend to reflect users who are registered as disabled. Many disabled people do not consider themselves to be disabled or prefer not to register as such. The consequence of this is that disability statistics only approximate the true numbers and almost certainly underestimated them. According to Michael Paciello (2000) there are approximately:

- 500 million disabled people worldwide
- 8.5 million disabled people in UK
- 52.6 million disabled people in USA
- 37 million disabled people in EU
- 4.2 million disabled people in Canada
- 3.7 million disabled people in Australia

(Temporary disabilities are not included in these statistics.)

Depending on age the rate of disability will differ, which statistics from USA gives a good picture on (see Figure 2).

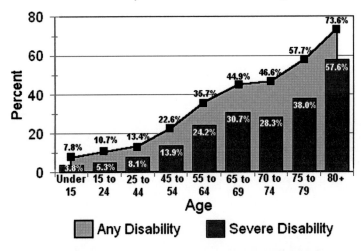

Figure 2. Disability prevalence by age in USA (U.S. Bureau of Census 1997).

In the western world about 20 % of the population has some kind of disability and about 10 % have a severe disability. Figure 3 shows the situation in the U.S. as an example of this.

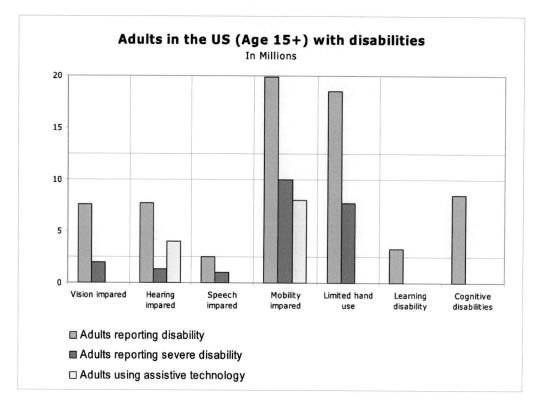

Figure 3. Adults in the US with disabilities (U.S. Bureau of Census 1997).

The barriers in the use of Internet can be grouped in groups with different demands on the web solutions. Some examples of the barriers are:

- **Visual disabilities:** Unsuitable font and size use, too little contrast between background and text, unlabeled graphics, poorly marked-up tables or frames, lack of keyboard support or screen reader compatibility
- **Hearing disabilities:** Lack of captioning for audio, proliferation of text without graphics.
- **Physical disabilities:** Lack of keyboard or single-switch support for menu commands, too small clicking areas
- **Speech disabilities:** Lack of alternatives for voice portals
- **Cognitive or neurological disabilities:** Lack of consistent navigation structure, overly complex presentation or language, lack of illustrative non-text materials, flickering or strobing designs on pages

3.4. Demographic changes

An important part of "Users with special needs" are elderly people. Figure 4 shows what the situation 1996 was in USA.

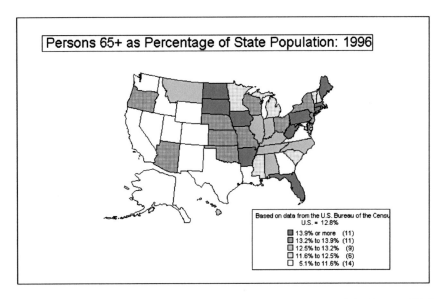

Figure 4. The elderly population state by state in the USA (source: Bureau of the Census 1997b http://www.aoa.dhhs.gov).

In EU during the coming years (until 2020) the proportion of persons aged 50-60 will increase significantly, while the younger members of the work force aged 20-29 will decline strongly (Lutz and Scherbow 2007). Already by 2018, i.e., 20 years from today, there will only be two working-age persons for one person above age 60 (Lutz and Scherbow 2007). Thus, that study showed clearly that massive ageing of the European population structure over the coming decades is a certainty, which seems to be the case also in the US (see figure 5).

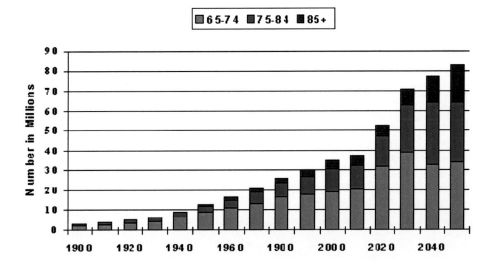

Figure 5. The growth of the older population will be dramatic in the coming decades (source: http://www.aoa.dhhs.gov).

Thus the population of elderly is growing and if the current trends continue the median age will increase in USA (see figure 6) and Europe. In the future the elderly group will make up half of the total population in USA and will continue to live longer. As a result, health care expenditures are expected to rise and more persons could be reporting difficulty performing basic activities such as getting in/out of bed, dressing, and bathing, getting information, participating in different activities in the society, etc.

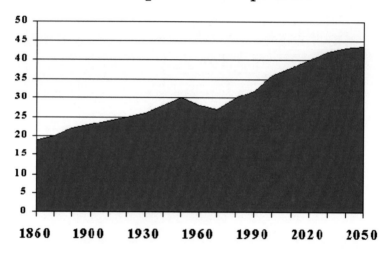

Figure 6. The median age will continue to go up (source: http://www.aoa.dhhs.gov).

3.5. Internet use by people with disabilities

For people with disabilities, the web has become more than a convenience. In many ways it is a means of education, work, shopping, and communicating with others. People with disabilities therefore rely more and more on accessible sites.

In some countries (Australia, Iceland, United States and United Kingdom) it is stated in the regulations to provide e.g. a website with accessible information and functionalities. Except for legal reasons making e-learning accessible for all there are ethical and financial reasons to have "e-learning for All" as an ambition.

However, often ordinary users of Internet and representatives for the society and the industry do not think that people with disabilities are using the web. A number of objections also exist to make useful web sites for people with disabilities why here a citation from http://www.nws.noaa.gov/sec508/htm/myths.htm is given:

Web accessibility is too difficult for the average web designer
None of us were born knowing HTML; accessibility is simply learning a few basic principles that can best be summed up as "don't assume that everyone views your web page in the same way you do." The purpose of our pages is to provide information on designing your pages to ensure that the information isn't lost through incompatible pages.

Accessible web pages take too much time to create

This is the same as saying "it takes too much time to check grammar, spelling, and proof-reading a document". Creating an accessible web page is creating a page that is interoperable, platform independent, and functional for everyone.

An accessible web page is nothing more than plain text

Not true! Web accessibility isn't about making text-only pages. The guidelines generally don't say "don't do that", rather they say "here's how to do that - accessibly". The ALT tag is a good example. ALT allows you to add text to substitute for an image; to make the page accessible you add ALT text, not remove the image from the page. Accessibility isn't taking away from graphics and multimedia - it's enhancing it.

Good assistive technology can solve all accessibility problems

Assistive Technology (or AT) has made tremendous strides in the past several years. Advances in technology and computers hardware and software have opened doors to opportunities for many. However; AT can't read the mind of the web page author and guess what they meant by a particular graphic - that information has to be provided. AT can only work with the information provided - accessibility is nothing more than providing the information in a format that is easily understood.

Web accessibility only helps people with disabilities

To be sure, designing your web pages to meet Section 508 requirements benefits people with disabilities; accessibility also benefits many others (Section 508 is a part of the US Rehabilitation Act of 1973 which requires that electronic and information technology developed, procured, maintained, or used by the Federal government be accessible to people with disabilities. On August 7, 1998, the President signed into law the Workforce Investment Act of 1998, which includes the Rehabilitation Act Amendments of 1998. Section 508 was originally added to the Rehabilitation Act in 1986; the 1998 amendments significantly expand and strengthen the technology access requirements in Section 508.)

3.6. Elderly people and their use of the Internet

Elderly people constitute the fastest growing group of computer users and information seekers on the Internet (e.g. Alpay et al 2004, Eastman and Iyer 2005). Especially those with a lower cognitive age than their chronological age want an active retirement learning new skills (Eastman and Iyer 2005). Noteworthy also is that elderly people (65+) have approximately twice the discretionary income of their children and control 70 % of the net worth of US householders (Eastman and Iyer 2005).

One of the top priorities among the elderly is to seek health information on the Internet. Furthermore, the elderly population is a big consumer population of health services for which the Internet can offer unique opportunities to acquire health care information. The term *telehealth* - defined as "the use of telecommunications and information technology to provide access to health information and services across a geographical distance" (Nickelson 1998) - focuses especially on the twoway interactive audiovisual communications, computers and telemetry to deliver health information and services at a distance (Darkins and Cary 2000).

Three pervasive problems in health care systems have contributed to the growth of *telehealth:*

- Uneven geographic distribution of health care resources
- Inadequate access to health care for certain segments of the population, such as individuals living in rural areas or this who are physically confined
- The spiraling costs of health and rehabilitation services, particularly specialty care

Telehealth holds considerable promise as a tool for reducing inequities in the allocation of health resources, access limitations and escalating costs. However we still lack basic information how and under what circumstances telecommunication mediated services lead to positive psychological and health care outcomes. we also have limited information about the cost effectiveness of *telehealth services.*

More research in the field of elderly and Internet use is important to guide the initiatives needed to ease elderly people into Internet and support means of access. Cognitive, physical and social factors are important to consider for optimizing the access and usage among the elderly population (Lawrence el al 2004). Seniors changing ability demands a holistic perspective in the development of technical tools for better accessibility and to achieve a good usability.

4. WEB FOR ALL

For economical, social and ethical reasons politicians and the industry have started to work towards the development of products that are user-friendly for everyone. This is called Design for All or Universal Design. In the Internet world, an extension of that starts with the term Web for All – which in fact is easier to accomplish than Design for All for other types for physical products.

4.1. Design for All - Universal Design

In recent years the principle of "Design for All" or "Universal Design" has emerged as a perspective to consider in the development of products, systems, services or processes.

> "Universal design is the design of products and environments to be usable by all people, to the greatest extent possible, without the need for adaptation or specialized design" (Mace 1985).

The intent of universal design is to simplify life for everyone by making products, communications, and the built environment more usable by as many people as possible at little or no extra cost. Universal design benefits people of all ages and abilities. However, the perspective "Design for All" seems not to be commonly considered in industry as many managers still think and plan for special target groups in their marketing and development projects. A lot more needs to be done to make industry aware of the big potential in this segment of elderly customers.

Several important aspects must be considered and used as guidelines for design of flexible websites for use by all. First and most important of all is to "know the user" and realize that users are not possible to collect in homogenous groups; they request solutions on an individual basis. Age, experience from usage of computers or other relevant experience, financial situation, and life situation are just a few of all aspects. To these cognitive and physical conditions should be added making the situation complex as they vary widely among individuals. Also to note is the importance of a flexible user interface, which means that the individual user should be able to easily change colors, sizes on the screen to fit to reduced vision or other individual requirements. Often an appropriate training and education are needed using various learning methods and various time schedules for the different goals of the individual user.

4.2. Policies and legislations

The United Nations has stated in the regulation of human rights (1993) that nobody because of race, sexual identity, disability, or political opinion should have limited rights compared to others in society. This means that everyone has the right to an accessible Web, independent of the factors mentioned above and as is technically possible to offer ICT to society, it is a question of initiatives in education and political regulations.

The US is leading this worldwide trend with new regulations and standards. Federal, state and local governments have initiated legislation in the US requiring computer technology to be accessible to people with disabilities. Other countries have established regulations that mandate accessibility at some level, or they are in the process of developing them. In addition, international standards organizations have been working to develop accessibility standards.

Thus, there are several standards efforts in progress by international bodies, such as the European Union (EU), the International Organizations for Standards (ISO), and private groups, such as the American National Standards Institute (ANSI), to foster technological accessibility.

The Web Accessibility Initiative (WAI) of the World Wide Web Consortium (W3C), in partnership with industry sponsors and governments around the world, addresses Web accessibility. WAI provides a repository of the latest Web accessibility guidelines and tools. Other sponsors include the US National Science Foundation; US Department of Education's National Institute on Disability and Rehabilitation Research; European Commission's TIDE Program under Directorate Generale XIII; the Government of Canada, Industry Canada's Assistive Devices Industry Office, Microsoft Corporation; IBM and Lotus Development Corporation; Bell Atlantic, etc.

4.3. Guidelines for creation of a Web for all

To guide how to make Web pages accessible to people with disabilities The World Wide Web Consortium (W3C) (see www.w3.org) has developed interoperable technologies (specifications, guidelines, software, and tools) to lead the Web to its full potential. W3C is a forum for information, commerce, communication, and collective understanding.

Thus, the W3C guidelines explain how to make *Web content* accessible to people with disabilities. The guidelines are intended for all *Web content developers* (page authors and site designers) and for developers of *authoring tools*. The primary goal of these guidelines is to promote accessibility. However, following them will also make Web content more available to *all* users, whatever *user agent* they are using (e.g., desktop browser, voice browser, mobile phone, automobile-based personal computer, etc.) or constraints they may be operating under (e.g., noisy surroundings, under- or over-illuminated rooms, in a hands-free environment, etc.). Following these guidelines will also help people find information on the Web more quickly. These guidelines do not discourage content developers from using images, video, etc., but rather explain how to make multimedia content more accessible to a wide audience.

The WCAG1 Conformity Levels (http://www.w3.org/WAI/WCAG1-Conformance) stipulate three levels of accessibility for people with disabilities:

- Conformance Level "A": all Priority 1 checkpoints are satisfied;
- Conformance Level "Double-A": all Priority 1 and 2 checkpoints are satisfied;
- Conformance Level "Triple-A": all Priority 1, 2, and 3 checkpoints are satisfied;

Thus, the Conformance Levels are designed according to importance so that Triple A is less important than fulfilling Level A. Simply speaking, Conformance Level A has to do with blind users, but so do also Levels Double A and Triple A. The same goes for cognitive impairments, mobility impairments, visual impairments, etc.

According to Paciello (2000) between 95% and 99% of all websites are inaccessible for disabled people (probably WCAG1 Level A). These numbers, however, are varied for example between sectors. E.g. the automotive industry (i.e. car manufacturers) has shown to provide particularly inaccessible websites, often relying heavily on Adobe Flash (sound and movement) and Javascript navigational menus. However, textual websites from archives, library sites etc., often are accessible to a larger audience due to the nature of the content - text is nearly always more accessible than other formats.

An audit of 300 museum, library and archive websites in England and a comparison of 25 international museum websites, was commissioned by City University in 2004 (Petrie et al. 2004). The policy context for the audit was set by the British Disability Discrimination Act, which covers websites and the e-government 2005 policy required for the public sector websites, which states that public Web pages shall meet specified Web accessibility guidelines WCAG1 Level AA. A user panel of blind, partially sighted and dyslexic people could successfully complete only 75.6% of the basic tasks they were asked to undertake on the websites, and 24.4% of these tasks they found impossible to complete. Of the 300 museum, library and archive home pages tested, 125 home pages (41.7%) had no WAI Priority 1 checkpoint violations that automated testing could detect (Petrie et al. 2004). This is higher than would be expected for sectors such as the automotive sector.

How websites are audited can also result in difference between a pass of WCAG1 Level A and a fail. Often automatic testing can yield false results (i.e. a pass where there is a definite fail and a fail when a pass should be awarded to the website. Also, automatic testing cannot detect human errors e.g. in the context (is the language too complex, is it understandable to a wide audience, are ALT texts meaningful; for example, an automatic testing would provide a pass on an ALT text even though the ALT text said 'Blah'). An experienced professional, therefore, should always examine the website to make it accessible for all (Petrie et al 2004).

4.4. Further tips

Photos and graphical pictures that do not also have Alternative (ALT) text (this is seen when the pointer is moved over an image or an image button) is meaningless for blind people.

Pictures with low contrast cannot be recognized by people with poor vision. The reason for poor vision can be clouding of the lens of the eye causing light that passes through the lens to the retina to be scattered. The scattered light causes images to be blurred and visual acuity is reduced. As we age, the lens of the eye also yellows and becomes fixed and unable to focus, the pupil does not dilate very well to changes in illumination, and the retina and cortex become less able to process visual information. Contrast sensitivity decreases, visual acuity drops somewhat, and vision in low light levels suffers.

Large white areas can dazzle some people. Large white areas on the computer screen also often appear more white than on paper while light yellow or light grey backgrounds are better to use. Recommended color combinations are:

- Black on a light grey or white background
- Dark blue on a light grey or white background
- Dark blue on a light yellow background
- Black text on beige-light brown background

People with color deficiencies such as protanopia (color blindness marked by confusion of purplish red and green), deuteranopia (a dichromatism in which the spectrum is seen in tones of red and green) and tritanopia (the spectrum is seen in tones of yellow and blue with confusion of red and green and reduced sensitivity to monochromatic lights) and color blindness can have problems with certain color combinations and information should never be based on color alone e.g. 'click on the red button' (if the red button is identical to the green button). The following color combinations are not recommened:

- Orange/red and green
- Yellow and white
- Red and blue

Recommended letter size is 12 points. Arial or Helvetica are better to use than Times or Times New Roman. Italic text and capital letters should be avoided since these can be difficult for users with reading impairments. Bold text and underlined text should also be avoided.

Pop-ups and other automatic appearing window make the orientation difficult for blind people, users with cognitive impairments as well as for unexperienced users.

Unusual words and long sentences are problematic for people with cognitive disabilities.

Blinking graphics can cause serious problems for people with epilepsy. Frequency from 4 to 59 Hz can start an epilectic attack. Red light is more provocative than blue light.

Photos and graphical pictures that do not also have alternative (ALT) text is meaningless for blind people. Adobe Flash presentations cannot be interpreted by blind people unless especially constructed with accessibility in mind, although it must be noted that very few programmers have the skills to do this and only the latest versions of the best screen readers can handle reading Flash. The same counts in general for PDF files, especially PDF forms which are not accessible at all for blind users. HTML forms should always be used.

4.5. How to Check Web Pages

A number of tools, mostly for checking up Internet Explorer Web pages, exist. Examples are:

http://www.accessify.com/tools-and-wizards/accessibility-checking-favelets.as
With A-Prompt HTML-documents can be tested and corrected:
http://aprompt.snow.utoronto.ca/index.html
CSS-validation service for W3C:
http://jigsaw.w3.org/css-validator/validator-text.html
With Cynthia Says a test of 508 US Standards or the international WAI criterion of the Web Consortium can be checked:
http://www.cynthiasays.com
Color contrast-analyzes can be done with:
http://www.webforall.info/html/deutsch/col_analy.php
HTML Validation Service of the Web Consortium is found on:
http://validator.w3.org
Useful tools for analysis are:
http://getfirebug.com/ (for Firefox)
http://chrispederick.com/work/web-developer/ (for Firefox)
http://www.visionaustralia.org.au/ais/toolbar/ (for Internet Explorer)
http://webxact.watchfire.com/ (automatic testing of web pages based on W3C guidelines)

However, a general word of advice should be to never use automatic tests alone for validating websites. To get a good result, a specialist should always go through each website individually checking the HTML code manually and provide solutions based on that (Petrie et al. 2004).

4.5. E-Learning for all

Our investigations of three popular e-learning portals used in Sweden show that none of them lived up to the criterion of being accessible to all users regardless of functional limitations or disability. By using the rules and tips for Web for All it is, however, possible to make e-learning portals for a wider category than ordinary students. This is truly a challenge for the development of third generation of e-learning portals!

5. QUALITY ASSURANCE FOR E-LEARNING

As the use of e-learning will increase the problem with quality assurance will grow as well. Having all the students in a class, answering examination questions under the control of a personnel ensures that the answers are given by an identifiable individual.

A sharp contrast to this performance is when examination tests are carried out over Internet. When a certain university in Sweden in 2006 gave e-learning courses in economics, the students had to download the examination questions and answer them on line within four hours to get the examination and the university credits. The university had in this case no control over who were actually answering the examination questions as no identification of the person answering was requested or available.

5.1. Identification

The ideal situation of having examination proctors use technology for security can be regained. Thus,with a proctor sitting in a "control room," the student answering examination questions can first with IP telephony - e.g. Skype – dial up the watcher. If the student has a cheap camera on top of her/his computer pointing on her/him, she/he can legitimate her/himself e.g. by showing her/his driver license. We have tested this verification procedure with satisfying results. The problem is so far the logistics for the watcher – if many calls up at the same time there can be a time lag problem.

To increase the safety more a finger print device can be used. We have tested a finger print device that works well and which is safe. The problem in this case is how to make an easy procedure of saving the fingerprints for later recognition. The students also must buy or lend the device, which also can be used for attendance.

5.2. Final examination control

When the identification procedure is done the proctor has to control that the student alone works with the questions and sends in the answers. If the proctor has many students to control she/he needs a program that randomly switches between the students e.g. with a small picture showing the name of the student in the corner of the screen. She/he needs also to be able to see what is going on on the computer screen of the student so that she/he is not communicating with someone else or simply transferring the whole examination to someone sitting elsewhere.

For complete security the use of the computer during the test and the photos taken of each student should be recorded for later controls in suspicious cases.

The software for having proctors monitoring students does not exist today. This is why safe e-examinations cannot be done.

5.3. Continuous examination control

As examination tests at the end of a course is perhaps not the best way to guide learning, an alternative is to break down the examination into many smaller examinations e.g. separated by one week. By letting the students answer and reflect on questions connected to the study material given for each week they will continuously add knowledge, especially as the formulation in their own words of the topics seems to be the most important way to get lasting knowledge. If the students cooperate in answering that is good. Important however is that each of them shall answer the questions in writing. The problem for the teacher is to control that the answers of one student are not copied by other students. To be sure that this is not occurring comparing software of texts can be used.

In a number of tests of this examination model (see Ottosson 2003) it showed that the students liked the schedule to follow. Misunderstandings could be corrected immediately, which is important in the learning process. The students also knew continuously the up-to-date score. Of all the different used e-learning portals on the market in Sweden we have only found one that has this examination module.

5.4. Quick tests

As a complement to the final and continuous examination forms we have also tested a method where the student get a short time to answer basic questions either as alternatives or in short explaining tests. The time for each question should not exceed the time it would take to find out the answers e.g. on Wikipedia (www.wikipedia.com). Typically the time for each question was 10 seconds after which next question appeared.

Some students were stressed by this way of being tested and it is questionable if this testing method is to be recommended

6. CONCLUSIONS

E-learning for all Internet users is possible although it means that the platform makers have to change the way the platforms are designed. This is especially needed to reach 65+ and disabled people. For "Internots," other activities are needed than to re-design the e-learning platforms.

The problem of not knowing who really are taking tests on the Internet is also possible to solve, although different technical solutions are needed.

REFERENCES

Alpay, L.L., Toussaint, P.J., Ezendam, P.M., Rövekamp, A.J.M, Graffmans, W.C., and Westendorp, R.G. (2004). Easing Internet access of health information for elderly users. *Health Informatics Journal*, Vol 10, No 3, pp 185-194.

Arbetsterapeuten. (2003). *Förbundet Sveriges Arbetsterapeuten*. No 02, pp 5-7.

Benktzon, M. (1993). Designing for our future selves: the Swedish experience, *Applied Ergonomics*, Vol 24, pp 19-27.

Björk, E., and Ottosson. S. (2007). Aspects of Consideration in Product Development Research. *Journal of Engineering Design*, Vol. 18, No. 3, pages 195-207

Björk, E. (2003). *A contribution to Insider Action Research Applied on Development of Assistive Products*, PhD Thesis, Otto-von-Guericke-Universität, Magdeburg, Germany

Björk, E., and Ottosson. S. (2007). Aspects of Consideration in Product Development Research. *Journal of Engineering Design*, Vol. 18, No. 3, pages 195-207

de Berredo, R.F., and Soeiro, A. (2007). *A proposal for benchmarking learning objects*, eLearning Papers, www.elearningpapers.eu, Vol 7, N° 3, March 2007, ISSN 1887-1542

Buurman, A. (1997). User-Centered Design of Smart Products. *Ergonomics*, Vol. 40, No 10, pp 1159 – 1169

Darkins, A.W., and Cary, M.A. (2000). *Telemedicine and telehealth: Principles, policies, performance and pitfalls*. New York, USA: Springer

Delaro, J. (1997). *Web school: Interactive distance learning puts college and corporate classrooms online (On line) available: http://www.eyemedia.com/backissues/1997/0897/9708distmain.htm.*

Eastman, J. K., and Iyer, R. (2005). The impact of cognitive age on Internet use of the elderly: an introduction to the public policy implications. *International Journal of Consumer Studies*, Vol. 29, Issue 2, Page 125.

Hartshorne, H., and May, M. A. (1928). *Studies in the nature of character: I. Studies in deceit*. New York, USA: Macmillan.

Holmdahl, L. (2006). *Complexity Aspects of Product Development*. PhD Thesis, Otto-von-Guericke-Universität, Magdeburg, Germany

Jordan, P.N. (1998). Human factors for pleasure in product use. *Applied Ergonomics*, Vol. 29, No. 18, pp 25 – 338.

Katz, J.E., and Rice, R.E (2002). *Social consequenses of Internet use: access, involvement, and interaction, MIT Press,* Cambridge, Mass.

Lawrence, L., Alpay, P.J., Toussaint, N.P.M., Ezendam, T.A.J.M., Rövekamp, W.C., Grafmans, and Westendorf, R.G. J. (2004). *Easing Internet access of health information for elderly users,* Sage Publications, London, Vol 10 (3), (pp 185-194).

Lutz, W., and Scherbow, S. (2007). What Do We Know About Future Change in the Proportions of Children and Elderly in Europe?, Report IR-99-12/March. *International Institute for Applied Systems Analysis*, A-2361 Laxenburg, Austria.

Mace. R.L. (1985). *Universal Design*. in Designers West. (p4).

Magnusson, C. (2001). *Introduktion till designmetodik, rehabiliteringsteknik och design (in Swedish)*, Certec, Lund Technical University, Sweden (www.certec.LTH.com)

Monö, R. (1997). *Design for Product Understanding*, Liber AB, Stockholm, Sweden.

Mortimer, L. (2001). The Devil is in the Details: Converting Classroom Courses to E-Learning. *Learning Circuits*, www.learningcircuits.com

Norman, D.A. (1988). *The Psychology of Everyday Things*. New York, USA: Basic Books.

Ottosson, S. (2003). Dynamic Product Development of a New Intranet Platform. *Technovation - the International Journal of Technological Innovation and Entrepreneurship*, Vol 23, pages 669-678.

Ottosson, S. (2004). Dynamic Product Development – DPD. *Technovation - the International Journal of Technological Innovation and Entrepreneurship*, Vol 24, pages 179-186.

Paciello, M. (2000). *Web Accessibility for People with Disabilities*. R & D Developer Series, ISBN: 1929629087.

Palloff, R.M., and Pratt, K.(1999). *Building learning communities in cyberspace: Effective strategies for online classroom*. San Fransisco, USA: Jossey Bass.

Petrie, H., King, H., Hamilton, F. (2004). *Accessibility of museum, library and archive websites: the MLA audit* (report available for download at http://www.mla.gov.uk/resources/assets/M/mla_web_accessibility_pdf_6541.pdf), City University Centre for Human-Computer Interaction Design, London, UK.

Thorsteinsdottir, S. (2003). *Accessibility, should we care?*, SJA (document available for download at www.sja.is), Reykjavik, Iceland.

U.S. Census Bureau (1997). *1996 Survey of Income and Program Participation*, August-November.

Wikström, L. (2002). *Produkters Budskap, Metoder för värdering av produkters semantiska funktioner ur att användarperspektiv (in Swedish)*. PhD thesis at Department of Product and Production Development at Chalmers University of Technology, Gothenburg, Sweden.

In: E-Learning: 21st Century Issues and Challenges
Editor: A.R. Lipshitz and S. P. Parsons
ISBN : 978-1-60456-156-2
©2008 Nova Science Publishers, Inc.

Chapter 4

WILL E-LEARNING DIE?

Mandy Schiefner[1] and Martin Ebner[2]

[1]University of Zurich, Switzerland
[2]TU Graz, Austria

ABSTRACT

The World Wide Web is currently changing dramatically. The buzzword Web 2.0 describes how we deal with the Internet. "The user is the content" is one of the famous descriptions. Users create their own (learning) content by blogging, podcasting or producing mashups. Of course the innovations summed up with the word Web 2.0 influence the traditional e-learning world.

In this paper we focus on how learning will change in the future. The combination of traditional research work combined with emerging technologies lead to an assumption of the learning behaviour of tomorrow. Will today's teaching soon be a matter of the past? How will a lecture looks like by integrating emerging technologies? We conclude that information anytime and anywhere influences the world of digital natives arbitrarily and causes the death of e-Learning in the present sense. Using computer and mobile technologies for learning purposes will be as normal as writing a letter with pencil.

1. INTRODUCTION

Currently a big change of the user behaviour in the World Wide Web causes a revolution (O'Reilly, 2006). The influence of media in different forms and environments increases rapidly because ordinary Internet user creates content by blogging, podcasting or in wikis. Web 2.0 is not really a big technological change, but helps to bring the first ideas of Tim Berners Lee (Berners-Lee, 1989) realizable: "Anyone can create anything and sharing it with anyone – world wide".

Of course this change will not stop for the area of education and learning. Especially in the field of e-learning it seems that a little bomb exploded and existing concepts and strategies suddenly become a matter of the past. E-Learning 2.0 was defined (Downes, 2005) and shocked the traditional e-learning world.

On the one hand former technological barriers as bandwidth, accessibility and devices have been minimized; on the other hand the usability of web based applications gets better and better. Innovations like the Open Educational Resources Movement[1] (i.e. OECD, 2007) change the concept of (higher) education. With Ajax the next generation of web programming begins; with wikis internet pages are easy to edit and to complement. Blogging as well as podcasting or video sharing has become normal to the everyday life of today's kids. The net generation creates contents, lives in virtual networks and is connected all over the world. Opinion polls pointed out a high acceptance of all new techniques by teenagers (e.g. Lenhart and Madden 2005, Green and Hannon 2007).

The main problem that comes with the revolution of the Web 2.0 is once again the so-called digital gap between digital immigrants (mainly lecturers) and digital natives (teenagers and learners). According Prensky (2001) the use of new media differences exorbitant between these two groups. For our children weblogs, wikis, podcasts belong to their everyday life since birth. For the rest of us these techniques are new; we have to learn and to rethink concepts and workflows. The enormous speed of growing of new techniques leads to an arbitrary problem, which must be taken into account.

In this publication we like to discuss this digital divide and how it will change our learning behaviour in the future. Is microcontent or nanocast a realistic scenario for our children or only hype? Is learning in twenty years comparable to our traditional classroom learning processes? Will informal learning play a more important role, or is face-to-face teaching not replaceable? There are lot of questions, but we should think about appropriate answers that are suitable to the learners of tomorrow and their techniques.

By discussing experiences of current e-learning scenarios of two big traditional European Universities – University of Zurich and Graz University of Technology – the publication concludes what experts in the field of e-learning expect for the future. We take a look into the future of learning: which impact has technology to our education? How will technology change or influence our way to teach and learn?

In the end we try to give an answer to the question "Will e-learning die?" and the result is maybe surprising: YES, we think so. By discussing and strictly reasoning, we hope that the reader of the article will agree to these thoughts and change his personal access to teaching and learning.

2. CHANGES

The availability of the Internet is steadily increasing. Life is going on at the internet: a lots of things from everyday life such as banking activities, booking a holiday trip, and so on are possible at the internet. With an increasing bandwidth it's not only possible to watch TV and films online, but also even to make own live shows by streaming. You don't have to leave your house any longer; you can do nearly everything online. This changes your life and your behaviour tremendous.

The availability of new mobile technologies such as mobile phones, PDAs and so on, implies the use of this technology (Ziefle, 2002) not only in business or private life but also for learning settings (Holzinger et al, 2005a). Technology has impacts on learning settings and learning styles (Holzinger et al, 2005b). If people behave more and more mobile, why shouldn't they learn mobile? Is this the challenge of the future? Why shouldn't we assimilate informal communication, distribution and consumption structures for the learning processes?

But not only technologies are changing. Learning and working processes are changing, as well. Employees, in future mainly knowledge worker, have to be more flexible and mobile. „At the same time, today's and tomorrow's learners will be nomadic and continuously on the move. As learners move from one location to the next, they must be able to use the infrastructure in the different locations to access learning materials. Hence, learning materials must be designed for easy access by the nomadic learners using mobile technology regardless of where they are located and which network infrastructure they are using to access information" (Ally, 2007).

Access to information and learning material is getting more and more independent of time and place. Networking with other people grows by the availability of mobile technologies. Mobile learning can be regarded as a special form of e-learning, which enlarges the freedom of place for learners (Sharples, 2007, p.7).

2.1. New learner

The children of today grow up with Internet and digital devices. For them it's usual to enter the internet to look for news and information. Researchers in the last years tried to identify the differences between teenagers, so called "net generation" (Oblinger and Oblinger, 2005a) or "digital natives" (Prensky, 2001) and so on, and their lecturers. Oblinger (2005) are talking about some different habits of this generation: they search online first (for example in google or wikipedia), only parts of them use traditional forms like libraries. Their primary communication tool is the internet via MSN or Instant Messaging. They meet each other in social networks, they are blogging, creating online content, sharing files and pictures and so on. They are online socialised: multitasking, time shifting and zapping is usual for them.

„Among other differences are their:

- Ability to read visual images—they are intuitive visual communicators
- Visual-spatial skills—perhaps because of their expertise with games they can integrate the virtual and physical
- Inductive discovery—they learn better through discovery than by being told
- Attentional deployment —they are able to shift their attention rapidly from one task to another, and may choose not to pay attention to things that don't interest them
- Fast response time—they are able to respond quickly and expect rapid responses in return" (Oblinger, 2005, p. 2.5)

Green and Hannon (2007) recognized "that the use of digital technology has been completely normalised by this generation and it is now fully integrated into their daily lives. The majority of young people simply use new media as tools to make their lives easier, strengthening their existing friendship networks rather than widening them. Almost all are now also involved in creative production, from uploading and editing photos to building and maintaining websites. However, we discovered a gap between a smaller group of digital pioneers engaged in groundbreaking activities and the majority of children who rarely strayed into this category." (Green and Hannon, 2007, p. 10).

But what is the impact of this net generation on our society? Oblinger and Oblinger (2005) constitute three main changes in societies of the future:

- *Multimodal communication structure*: There are more communication channels available, such as e-mail, chat, instant messaging, sms, twitter, and so on.
- *Culture of «do it yourself»*: Kids are used to make their own things. They choose their own TV program by zapping, they build their own radio program with podcasts, they choose their own information by reading their blogreader. One consequence is that this will influence their way to learn: in future they want to build their own courses, their own personal learning environment (PLE).
- *Culture of choice*: In future you can choose and personalize everything: from your PC desktop to your personal iPod play list, from your own Personal Computer to your own mobile device.

This is often just stereotyping, but it's the effort to describe this new way of technology behaviour. But there is still little empirical evidence for this description.

2.2. New communication structures

As seen above, the work requirements will change, work in multi-disciplinary or multi-professional teams will gets normal. Networks are determining our society structures (Castells, 1996). One effect of globalisation is that working processes are more and more organized in networks, most of them all over the world. This means, that communication is changing, networks are getting important.

Net workers stay informed within new media in new forms: technologies like twitter and jaiku let us stay in contact with our network very easily and very currently. Blogs provide a basis for topical discussions. By the installation of different channels and the combination with mobile technology and blogging systems, it's possible to share information fast, for different target audiences and mobile.

Visual communication with emoticons is getting more and more important, because on the one side most of our communication will be written communication at different input devices. But it seems that there is one communication channel missing, the non-verbal communication. Emoticons are a great chance to integrate non-verbal communication into our writings. On the other side emoticons are fast: with one emoticon you can say a lot, for example "☺". Our mobility needs a fast communication channel to stay informed (Azuma and Maurer, 2007), and emoticons are very easy and quick way to communicate with others.

2.3. New form of content

The last issue that must be pointed out is the kind of information. Till now a typical learning content has been a well-written document with detailed information. Sometimes the help of multimedia expanded it. With other words pedagogues, teachers and programmers created a modern kind of learning content. In fact, the often so-called New Media let the old book appears in new style.

In future teachers will be confronted not only with a new type of learner, with new devices and new communication structures, but also with a new type of content – called microcontent (Leinonen, 2007). Microcontent are very small pieces of information placed on the World Wide Web. Mostly this information chunks make no sense by standing alone. Microcontent needs context or communication behaviour to take place. Research work in this area as well as in the field of nanocast, microblogging or the use of QR-Codes[2] in learning is very rare, so it is very hard to estimate the potential and effect of these new kinds of information distribution in future.

3. FUTURE OF TECHNOLOGY - BASED LEARNING

Considering all arguments it must be pointed out that education in future will change anyway. The question is how and in which way? The enormous speed of technological developments will lead to increasing applications. Due to the fact that the "net generation" is much more familiar with programming the World Wide Web, new data, tools and even programs will grow exponentially.

Bearing in mind that mobile devices including internet connection are at hand by everyone we like to think about what typical lessons of the future will look like? The next two subchapters show which technologies promises a big change of our world of tomorrow and what this means for our educational settings.

3.1. Future technologies and application

Of course it is impossible to make a precise prediction, remembering about 10 years ago nearly nobody used a mobile phone. Today in Central Europe we have at least one per person. The increasing speed of new technologies and web based applications is amazing. According to Moore´s Law (about 1970) hardware is increasing exponentially by doubling every two years. Nevertheless we are expecting some major trends, which will influence our learning environments:

- *Mergence of devices*: In the near future the performance and ability of mobile devices will increase arbitrarily. With other words the key functions of a mobile phone are expanded to make photos, instant messaging, browsing and maybe also job efforts. It is imaginable that our complete work place is just online and we are using clients to connect to this place. For example YouOS is one of the first online

---

2 http://www.jaxo.com/home

Operating Systems[3]. Reading news, watching TV or listening to podcasts with a mobile device will be as usual as doing a phone call today.

- *Widgets and Mashups*: The next generation of internet use is to provide so called Widgets. A Widget is a small third party item, which can easily be embedded into a webpage or on a mobile device. So no further programming is necessary to show for example RSS Readers, statistics or other small applications on our own homepages. Remixing different pieces of online content and providing it on another internet-site is called a Mashup. Reusing, resorting, remixing are the catchwords of the future web. Existing information will be expanded by someone and adapted to his/her personal needs. So the World Wide Web is becoming much more powerful we hardly can imagine, because two components are combined: human creativity and computer batch processing.

- *Surface computing*: Currently the company Apple released the iPhone, the combination of a mobile phone and an iPod. The most interesting feature of this device is the touch screen – Digital Physics is the name of this new way of interaction with a device. Apple's software is tuned to respond to our hand gestures in a way that makes an impression of interaction with the physical object. For example scrolling is represented by striving one finger on the screen from up to down[4]. A similar project called Microsoft Surface[5] will be launched by Microsoft. A simple table with a multi-touch multi-user, touch-and-gesture-activated screen for supporting working with digital materials. A further project is Diamond Touch[6] from MERL. However there is one fundamental change observable: The way how we interact with computers and digital devices. Just by using our fingers and hands but without any input devices, we move digital contents, work and share material.

But what do this mean for education in the 21st century?

3.2. Future education

After pointing out the great improvements from a technical point of view, we have to concentrate on the learner and teacher views.

For example let's think about a typical geographical lecture. The teacher enforces the students to open their books and point at the country or town on an oversized, huge map hanging on a pillar. We are sure that this situation is not a thing of the past; it still describes a typical lesson in elementary schools today.

But in the near future the situation can change dramatically, because first there will be no books anymore. The mobile device of students connects to the internet within seconds and delivers any information; any so called hard fact. Access to information from different sources, from different cultures and languages extend the possibility of teaching in a manifold way. Imagine the teacher only says "Today we are talking (learning) about the country xyz".

---

3 http://youous.com
4 http://www.readwriteweb.com/archives/the_physics_of_iphone.php
5 http://www.microsoft.com/surface/
6 http://www.merl.com/projects/DiamondTouch/

The first child is looking about the population, another one tells about the cities and famous buildings. The next one shouts that there is picture and a video about important cultural aspects of the country. "Oh, the famous actor is born here" the next contribution appeared. A further child is chatting with an inhabitant and asking what is the most famous sightseeing or landmark in his/her town. Someone has already found some historical backgrounds of this country. However, the list of questions and their answers seems to be endless.

Nevertheless there are some very important characteristics:

- *Information chunks and Mashups*: Digital natives are searching for quick information and zapping between a high numbers of websites. Communities are playing a very important role in their daily life. It will not be very surprising when working with small pieces of content will be common. By presenting them to a group the result is much more effective. Different information from different sources and different people combined lead to a big Mashup of information in the classroom. This data has to be integrated to a big knowledge network, like for example a classroom wiki, so that everyone has access to the information of the others. So methods of learning and working together like teamwork, tandems, etc. will play a more important role for educational practice as today.

- *Individualism*: By searching, reading and interpreting information students will do this via their personal environments, with their personal devices and with their personal agents, filter systems and maybe also with their personal programs. This leads to a personalization, which helps to enforce the individualism in a very powerful way.

- *Informal learning*: Learning by listening and reading something without intention will become more and more important. By searching relevant information children read tons of other chunks. They see and listen to the results of their colleagues and recognize the different standpoints and arguments.

- *Problem based learning*: The teacher defines the topic; afterwards he/she confronts the learners with realistic, complex and authentic problems. Searching, reading, interpreting and discussion will lead to a more appropriate learning situation and help the learners to gain a more cross-linked view. Considering also motivational and emotional aspects this can lead to a more in-depth learning.

- *New role of teachers*: In future teachers will have a very new important role; they have to help to survive within the mass of information. In the beginning learners are not able to distinguish which chunk is highly relevant for understanding and which is only a small detail. The main role of a teaching person is to help sorting and structuring learning material and to reflect it. Critical thinking will become a competence, which is getting more and more important. Teachers must have "a wide variety of life experiences and attributes, most centred on the ability to facilitate or connect, and an understanding of social technologies and deep collaboration. [...] There will be many different opportunities for working with kids and communities in a teaching role other than the traditional idea of what a teacher is" (Richardson, 2007).

But these changes require new competencies among teachers and learners. Learning to learn and to validate information from different sources will increasingly become a great challenge for learners and educators in future.

But what does these implications means for traditional e-learning courses? Since about 1995 when the first web-based-training courses were available, e-learning has become popular. A large number of didactical scenarios and technical tools have been developed (Collis, 1998), but many projects showed lacks concerning interactivity (Preece et al, 2002). Enhancing self-regulated learning (Boekaerts, 1999) or active participation of students seems to be impossible. However, from this standpoint all these new technologies will help to improve the current situation. The question is still, if this leads to the end for the classic e-learning in the meaning of the turn of the million.

4. WILL E-LEARNING DIE?

The premises presented in chapter three will influence the learning process. What are the implications for traditional learning institutions, such as school and universities to handle with this new educational scenario? With these changes new ways of learning and interacting with media grow up. Informal learning will getting more and more important, formal learning settings and informal learning will accrete. Computer, digital devices and the internet are ubiquitous so that the 'e' can be neglected. The question «will e-learning die?» can be answered under two different facets: first on a semantic aspect and second on a structural aspect.

4.1. The end of the 'E' on a semantic aspect

E-learning as a concept has had his time. In the early 90's of the last century it was necessary to define and describe the integration of computer technology in the learning process, because it was new. There were no experiences with this learning form before. Experiences had to be made and success factors had to be founded out by teaching, implementation and research.

But time is changing. In our point of view, in a few years, no one will use the term e-learning anymore. Already today there are a lot of existing terms to describe different learning forms for learning with computer or technology based learning: distributed, blended, mobile, distance, informal, and on and on.

But does this imply a new learning theory or a new e-learning wave? Media and technology are a usual part of our life; therefore we don't need a special "e" for the subject we call learning. As Taylor (2007) said: "There's no need to differentiate now between methods of content delivery. The battle is over, and e-learning has won. It's a regular part of the learning mix".

The main focus behind these entire concept is the term «learning». We have to think about the best terms and conditions of learning, with or without media and technology. How can we arrange in-depth learning processes? How can we educate the kids of today? We don't need to separate between learning and e-learning because it's getting usual and ubiquitous.

Learning takes place everywhere. The main focus should be how to support learning, with or without technology. The quality of pedagogy is first dependent on qualitative teaching; media and technology are only the second factors of success. Furthermore the term e-learning is historically intimately connected with instructional design theory, and this doesn't fit to constructivistic and connectivistic learning theories (Neuhaus, 2007, p. 5).

4.2. The end of the 'E' on a structural level

But not only the target group of learning scenarios, technologies and communications styles are changing as said before. There are tremendous changes in the field of e-learning too as we pointed out in chapter three. It's also time to drop the 'e' from a structural perspective: Traditional e-learning courses often consist of Computer or Web Based Trainings (CBT/WBT) or content on learning management systems (LMS/LCMS), like islands at the internet, where students have to go to (Kerres, 2006); fixed courses with fixed content produced by the teacher. Traditional e-learning courses are designed from e-learning experts for learners. Production and contribution these forms of e-learning was too circumstantial. Furthermore this form of e-learning wasn't very successful because the social component was missing, so that Blended Learning, a mix between online learning and traditional learning was seen as a concept so far.

But with Web 2.0 and social software there are some things changing. Users are creating their content and learn in other forms than traditional planned courses; learning in networks and communities is very widespread. Long courses however e-learning or Blended Learning have had their time, learning and further education is now changing. Instead of large e-learning courses small units of learning pieces will be integrated not only in educational settings, but also in usual life. Content is aggregating from different services for learning, like wikis, blogs, VoIP, tagging, etc.. Boundaries between e-learning 2.0 and general learning disappear. Web 2.0 changes learning into "ubiquitous computing" (Kerres 2006), learning and working is possible from everywhere, new learning communities will find each other. If you are connected to the Internet all over time, learning can take place everywhere and at every time. Social aspects of learning processes are more and more relevant, people are learning together in communities of practice, social networks or peer to peer.

Even the role of the author is changing, how Seitzinger (2006) pointed out: "... there seems to be a divergence between the learning content producers and the content users. While producers are trying to force everything into closed systems, the users want to use open systems. (...) We can already see a convergence between these new open media tools and constructivist learning: all three require the users to construct their own content." (Seitzinger, 2006, p. 2). Users are creating their own content in an easy way of doing, bottom-up. Web 2.0 is changing role perception for learners and teachers.

**Table 1: Differences between Web 1.0 and 2.0
according Kerres (2006) and Karrer (2007)**

	Web 1.0 – instruction	Web 2.0 – construction
Learning environment ...	... is an island at the internet with content and tools	... is a portal to the internet with content and tools
Main components	Courseware, LMS, Authoring tools	Wikis, Social networking and bookmarking tools, Blogs, Add-ins, Mash-ups
Ownership	Top-down, one-way	Bottom-up, learner-driven, peer learning
Delivery	At one time	When you need it
Teacher ...	... is creating all resources at the island	... is creating directories, is aggregating resources
Teacher's tasks ...	... teaching – explanation – instruction	... observation – coaching – moderation
Learners ...	... is using the given learning materials	... is setting up his/her own personal learning environment
Learner's tasks ...	... receive – recall – exercise	... decision – action – reflection

This change has effects of the traditional role perception in teaching. Learning and teaching is changing from fixed e-learning courses and ready-mades to constructivist learning environments. Learners are self-directed, are solving real situative problems (Brown, Collins und Duguid 1989)

4.3. Personal learning environment and learning networks

To scope with the problem of the neglected "e", the integration of formal and informal learning processes, with or without media seems to be the solution. The main part is to construct one's own learning space, a setting where the own education and learning process can be haunt.

Personal learning environments and networks like communities of practice for formal learning or the blogosphere for informal learning might be an answer. The goal is to create a personal learning environment and to combine the advantage of technology based learning and social learning. But the main term remains learning.

"The idea of a Personal Learning Environment recognises that learning is continuing and seeks to provide tools to support that learning. It also recognises the role of the individual in organising their own learning. Moreover, the pressures for a PLE are based on the idea that learning will take place in different contexts and situations and will not be provided by a single learning provider. Linked to this is an increasing recognition of the importance of informal learning." (Attwell, 2007, p.1).

Beside Personal Learning Environments learning networks are getting more and more important. The role between teacher and learner blur. Micromentors (Attwell, 2007) that means not a tutor or a teacher but rather peers are involved more and more in the learning process of the individual. As Rudd and Facer (2007, p. 3) said "[...] we need to move away from the institutionalised logic of the school as a factory, to the network logic of the learning community."

Life long learning will become reality, when the learner is connected anytime to the internet and has access to every kind of information: Informal information like information in communities, blogs etc. or formal information, like courses and information from institutions, i.e. schools or universities. Learning environments will exist over institutional boundaries. Learners can aggregate and integrate these different forms of information to their own personal learning environment. Customization of learning material will take place in real-time and focused on problems, individualistic and customized learning material for learning just in time and all over the lifetime.

5. THE DIGITAL WORLD WITH DIGITAL INHABITANTS

Currently we are living in a social world that is changing dramatically. Information is digitalized and supports our daily life. We have to learn how to scope with these changes. And it's a task for everyone, the little schoolboy and schoolgirl and the old woman and her husband. In a society where computers with lots of information will get more and more important, society have to look critical about it and have to build up new competencies.

But what are the implications of this learning scenario for learners and teachers of today? Apart from learning how to use this new technologies (keyword media competences) teachers and learners will have to acquire new and higher ordered competencies as shortly said in chapter three.

Learners first have to learn how to use this new technology. Not once, technologies are changing a lot of time, so they have to learn life long how to use future technologies for learning. But the most important learning task is how to validate new information, how to integrate them to their cognitive space, how to scope with this mass of information. Information literacy will be an important competence. Searching for information and the evaluation of information requires reflection and of course critical thinking. Information competence comprises "filtering of relevant information and integrating of relevant information in prevalent cognitive structures to transform information into knowledge" (Winter, 2001). They have to learn how to trust information, how to guarantee things like authorship. "The ability that is needed to solve problems within non-routine tasks requires competence in finding, handling and creating relevant knowledge" (van Weert, 2006, p. 223).

Teachers have to learn change from their role of knowledge provider to a role of communicator and coach. They don't have to teach hard facts, because they were available at the internet in different forms and sources. They have to help building knowledge by supervising and structuring of learning content. Teaching thinking skills will be a great challenge. Even more lifelong learning will be a requirement for teachers because technologies are changing often and fast. They have to be "up to date" to integrate new developments in technology into their lectures. Recapitulatory, it can be said "according to U-Teacher (2005), a European project on Teacher's professional development in ICT for education, characteristics of a successful teacher are:

- To work effectively in the rapidly changing educational field, teachers should be able to adapt to change, to be flexible, intuitive, innovative and persistent.
- They should also be highly collaborative, demonstrating good interpersonal skills in creating opportunities to communicate and share knowledge, experience and ideas with others.
- Teachers should be problem solvers who are willing to take risks to find solutions to educational issues, and decision-makers who use their experience to motivate students and enhance their learning.
- On the one hand teachers should be enthusiastic, creative, intellectually curious, resourceful and positive, and on the other they should be systematic and well organised, focused, determined and hardworking" (van Weert, 2006, p. 234).

A remarkable point of this last chapter is that until now we wrote anything about technological issues. According to Mark Weiser who has already written in 1991 about his ideas about pervasive computing (Weiser, 1991) we have to bear in mind that mobile devices and internet access will be ubiquitous. Maybe the next step of e-learning is u-learning. However, it must be summarized that the topic is learning and technology is supporting it in manifold ways.

In the end it must be expressed that only critical thinking inhabitants will use and learn with this new technology responsible, sustainable and avoid scenarios like «I, Robot» or Orwells «1984». Technology will influence our daily life as well as our learning behaviour, but in a way we cannot imagine yet. Nowadays nobody is thinking about a pencil for writing and nobody is thinking about using a calculator for doing a calculation and so nobody will think about using a personal internet connected device for getting some information or learning materials. The main difference is that this change will be one of the greatest in the history of the learning mankind. We are very sure that in some years nearly nobody will talk explicit about e-learning – learning and computer are inseparably connected.

REFERENCES

Ally, M. (2007). Mobile Learning. *The International Review of Research in Open and Distance Learning,8* (2). Retrieved from: http://www.irrodl.org/index.php/irrodl/article/view/451/918. [13.08.2007].

Attwell, Graham. (2007). The Personal Learning Environments – the future of eLearning? *eLearning Papers, 2* (1), Retrieved from: http://www.elearningeuropa.info/files/media/media11561.pdf [13.08.2007].

Azuma, J., Maurer, H. (2007). From Emoticon to Universal Symbolic Signs: Can Written Language Survive in Hyperspace?, In: Lindner, M., Bruck, P.A. (Ed.). *Micromedia and Corporate Learning*, 3rd International Microlearning Conference, p.106-122.

Berners-Lee, T. (1989). Information Management: A Proposal. Retrieved from: http://www.w3.org/History/1989/proposal.html [13.08.2007].

Boekaerts, M. (1999). Self-regulated learning: where we are today. *International Journal of Educational Research, 31*, p. 445–457.

Brown, J.S., Collins, A., Duguid, P. (1989). *Situated Cognition and the culture of learning.* In: *Educational Researcher, 18* (1), p. 32-42.

Cambridge, B. (2007). Learning, Knowing, and Reflecting: Literacies for the 21st Century. *International Journal for the Scholarship of Teaching and Learning, 1* (2), 1-7. Retrieved from: http://www.georgiasouthern.edu/ijsotl [17.8.2007].

Castells, M. (2006). *The rise of the network society. The information age*: Bd. Vol. 1. Malden, MA: Blackwell.

Centre for Educational Research and Innovation. (2007). *Giving Knowledge for Free: the emergence of open educational resources.* OECD. Retrieved from: http://213.253.134.43/oecd/pdfs/browseit/9607041E.pdf [27.6.2007].

Collis, B. (1998). New didactics for university instruction: why and how? *Computers and Education, 31* (2), p. 373-393.

Downes, S. (2005). E-learning 2.0. *ACM eLearn Magazine*, October (10).

Green, H., and Hannon, C. (2007). *Their Space: Education for a digital generation.* London: DEMOS. Retrieved from: http://www.demos.co.uk/files/Their%20space%20-%20web.pdf [18.7.2007].

Holzinger, A., Nischelwitzer, A., Meisenberger, M. (2005a). Mobile Phones as a Challenge for m-Learning: Examples for Mobile Interactive Learning Objects (MILOs). In: Tavangarian, D. (Ed.): *3rd IEEE PerCom* p. 307-311.

Holzinger, A., Nischelwitzer, A., Meisenberger, M. (2005b). Lifelong-Learning Support by M-learning: Example Scenarios. *ACM eLearn Magazine, 5* (2005).

Karrer, T. (2007). Understanding E-learning 2.0. In: *Learning Circuits*. Retrieved from http://www.learningcircuits.org/2007/0707karrer.html [13.08.2007].

Kerres, M. (2006). *Potenziale von Web 2.0 nutzen.* In: Hohenstein, A. and K. Wilbers (Ed.) Handbuch E-Learning, München: DWD-Verlag.

Leinonen, T. (2007). *Building the Culture of (e-)Learning in Microcontent Environments*, In: M. Lindner and P.A. Bruck (Ed.), Micromedia and Corporate Learning, 3rd International Microlearning Conference, (p. 24-34).

Lenhart, A., and Madden, M. (2005). *Teen Content Creators and Consumers.* Washington, DC: Pew Internet and American Life Project. Retrieved from: http://www.pewinternet.org/pdfs/PIP_Teens_Content_Creation.pdf [31.7.2007].

Neuhaus, W. (2007). *Web 2.0 und der Kampf der Begriffe.* Berlin, Blog Mediendidaktik - http://www.mediendidaktik.port07.de/docs/neuhaus_2007_04.pdf [13.08.2007].

OECD. (2007). *Giving Knowledge for Free: The Emergence of Open Educational Resources.* http://www.oecd.org/dataoecd/35/7/38654317.pdf [15.08.2007].

Oblinger, D. D., and Oblinger, J. L. (Hrsg.). (2005). *Educating the Net Generation.* Verfügbar unter: http://www.educause.edu/educatingthenetgen. [13.08.2007].

Oblinger, J. L. (2005). Is it age for IT: First Steps Toward Understanding the Net Generation. In D. D. Oblinger and J. L. Oblinger (Hrsg.). *Educating the Net Generation.* (p. 2.1-1.5).

O'Reilly, T. (2006) Web 2.0: Stuck on a name or hooked on value? *Dr Dobbs Journal, 31*(7), p. 10-10

Preece J., Sharp, H., Rogers, Y. (2002). *Interaction Design: Beyond Human-Computer Interaction.* New York, USA: Wiley.

Prensky, M. (2001). Digital natives, Digital Immigrants. *On the Horizon, 9* (5), p. 1-6.

Richardson, W. (2007). *The Future of Teaching.* Retrieved from: http://weblogg-ed.com/2007/the-future-of-teaching/ [13.08.2007].

Rudd, T., Sutch, Dan., and Facer, K. (2007). *Towards new learning networks*. : Futurelab.

Sharples, M. (2007). *Big Issues in Mobile Learning*. Report of a workshop by the Kaleidoscope Network of Excellence, Mobile Learning Initiative, University of Nottingham, 2007.

Seitzinger, J. (2006). *Be constructive: Blogs, Podcasts, and Wiki as Constructivist Learning Tools* (eLearning Guild) Learning Solution e-magazine.

Tayler, D. H. (2007). *It's Time to Drop E-learning*. Retrieved from: http://www.trainingzone.co.uk/cgi-bin/item.cgi?id=170224 [13.08.2007].

Van Weert, T. (2006). Education of the twenty-first century: New professionalism in lifelong learning, knowledge development and knowledge sharing. *Education and Information Technologies, 11* (3-4), 217-237.

Winter, U. (2001, 04. Oktober). *Kampf gegen die Informationsüberflutung: Neue Wege zur Herausbildung von Informationskompetenz bei Mitarbeitern und Bibliotheksnutzern.* Retrieved from: http://www.db-thueringen.de/servlets/DerivateServlet/Derivate-994/winter.html [24.7.2005].

Weiser, M. (1991). The computer for the twenty-first century. *Scientific American, 265* (3) p. 94-104.

Ziefle, M. (2002). The influence of user expertise and phone complexity on performance, ease of use and learn ability of different mobile phones. *Behaviour and Information Technology, 21*(5) p. 303-311.

In: E-Learning: 21st Century Issues and Challenges
Editor: A.R. Lipshitz and S. P. Parsons

ISBN : 978-1-60456-156-2
©2008 Nova Science Publishers, Inc.

Chapter 5

SELF-REGULATION IN MATHEMATICAL E-LEARNING: EFFECTS OF METACOGNITIVE FEEDBACK ON TRANSFER TASKS AND SELF-EFFICACY

Bracha Kramarski[*]

ABSTRACT

This study compares two mathematical e-learning instructions supported by different forms of feedback: E-learning with metacognitive feedback (EL+MF), and e-learning with result feedback (EL+RF). Metacognitive feedback was based on the IMPROVE self-questioning strategy (e.g., Kramarski and Mevarech, 2003), and result feedback included correctness of the solution.

The participants were 62 ninth-graders who practiced mathematical problem-solving through interactive tasks accessible on the Web. Results showed that EL+MF students significantly outperformed the EL+RF students in procedural and transfer problem-solving, and used more conceptual arguments when providing mathematical explanations. Furthermore, at the end of the study the EL+MF students exhibited more self-efficacy in learning mathematics in a computer-based environment.

Keywords: E-learning, metacognitive feedback, math, self-efficacy, transfer

INTRODUCTION

Rapid advances in computer technologies have facilitated the development of electronic tools and resources that have, in turn, expanded the opportunities to empower student-centered learning alternatives. Although at face value the potential of these opportunities is

[*] School of Education, Bar-Ilan University, Ramat-Gan 52900, Israel, E-mail: kramab@mail.biu.ac.il

compelling, the extent to which learners develop conceptual understanding is not at all certain (Land, 2000). Research shows that students are usually not in fact "mindfully engaged" when it comes to learning with advanced computer technologies. Research discusses how poor self-regulatory skills often get in the way of students' learning with the typically highly student-centered designs utilized in advanced technology environments (e.g.,. Winters and Azevedo, 2005, and Land, 2000). One of the main challenges we currently face as instructional designers of these environments is how to support students learning to manage their own cognitions.

The purpose of this research is to evaluate the effectiveness of metacognitive support in assisting students in self-regulation on mathematical e-learning. Prior to explicating the design of the study a brief overview of mathematical knowledge definition and self-regulation utilized in the study is given.

Mathematical knowledge

Research in the area of mathematical education has largely emphasized the importance of promoting it as an integral part of doing mathematics. According to mathematical standards (NCTM: National Council of Teachers of Mathematics, 2000, PISA: Program for International Students Assessment, 2003), mathematical knowledge requires the attainment of abilities to use procedural and conceptual knowledge. Students are required to construct conceptual conjectures, develop and evaluate mathematical arguments, and select and use various types of representations. PISA assesses students' knowledge in relation to the content, process, and context in which mathematics is used. They emphasize the importance of problem solving real-life tasks. Real-life tasks employ realistic data, are based on a wide range of mathematical knowledge and mathematical skills, and often ask solvers to use different representations in their solutions (PISA, 2003). Research of NCTM standards has moved beyond identifying their elements to focusing on the conditions under which they can be optimally enhanced in the classroom.

In recent years, the role of self-regulation of learning in education has elicited much interest. (e.g., Kramarski, Mevarech, 2003; Pintrich, 2000; PISA, 2003; Schraw, Crippen, and Hartley, 2006; Veenman, Van Hout-Wolters, and Afflerbach, 2006; Zimmerman, 1998). Students with strong self-regulation skills are better learners. These learners utilize learning resources more appropriately, make better use of learning strategies, and are more attentive when they don't understand something (Schraw, 1998).

Self-Regulation of learning

Self-regulation of learning (SRL) refers to a cyclical and recursive process which utilizes feedback mechanisms so students understand, control and adjust their learning accordingly (e.g., Butler and Winne, 1995).

The process involves a combination of four areas for regulation during learning: cognitive strategy use, metacognitive control, motivational beliefs, and context condition (Pintrich, 2000). Cognitive strategies take the form of simple problem-solving and critical thinking strategies. Metacognitive processing refers to knowledge and control of cognitive skills. The motivational component refers to students' beliefs in their capacity to learn, values for the task and interest. Finally, context refers to evaluation and monitoring changing task conditions. Researchers (e.g., Schraw, Crippen, and Hartley, 2006) believe that the role of metacognition is especially important because it enables individuals to monitor their current knowledge and skill levels, plan and allocate limited learning resources with optimal efficiency, evaluate their current learning state, and update products through internal feedback. According to Butler and Winne (1995), the internal feedback serves a multidimensional role in aiding knowledge construction.

However, research indicated that the cognitive and metacognitive components are usually insufficient in promoting student achievement; students also must be motivated to use the strategies as well as regulate their cognition and effort.

Self-efficacy, a theoretically grounded motivation construct, may be a particularly valid concept to examine in the context of learning with e-learning. Self-efficacy, defined as an individual's self-perception of their capability to meet situational demands (Bandura, 1997), has been routinely shown to be positively related to students' direction, vigor, and persistence of behavior in a wide variety of domains (e.g., Pajares, 1996; Pintrich and Groot, 1990).

This study is guided by the following question: How can metacognitive support in e-learning construct mathematical knowledge and self-efficacy of secondary school students?

Metacognitive support

A number of researchers have argued that there are some key factors to improve metacognition through classroom instruction: (a) defining specific processes and strategies used by students to improve academic achievement, (b) including a description of why and how students select a specific self regulatory strategy, approach or response within learning, and (c) utilizing feedback mechanism for students to monitor their learning and adjust accordingly. They emphasize the importance of extensive practice followed by explicit guidance in the use of strategies (e.g., Azevado, and Cromley, 2004; Kramarski and Mevarech, 2003; Schoenfeld, 1992; Schraw, Crippen, and Hartley, 2006).

Current research has focused on the role of self-questioning strategy as a metacognitive internal feedback mechanism (e.g., Ge and Land, 2004; King, 1994; Mevarech and Kramarski,1997; Schoenfeld, 1992). Such strategy might include different kinds of self-questioning based on different cognitive and metacognitive purposes. Mevarech and Kramarski (1997) designed the IMPROVE method that encourages students' to be actively engaged in self-regulation of learning by using four kinds of questions: Comprehension, connection, strategy use, and reflection.

Comprehension questions are designed to help learners understand the information of the task or problem solving (e.g., "What is the problem?"; "What is the meaning of?"). Connection questions are designed to prompt learners to understand deeper-level relational structures of the task by articulate thoughts and elicit explanations (e.g., "What is the difference/similarity?"; "How do you justify your conclusion?"). Strategy questions are designed to prompt learners to be aware of selecting the appropriate strategy (e.g., "What is the strategy, and "Why?"); and reflection questions play an important role in helping students to self-monitor their problem-solving processes and consider various perspectives and values regarding their selected solutions (e.g., "Does the solution makes sense?"; "Can the solution be presented in another way?").

Generally speaking, research reported positive effects of supporting metacognition by self-questioning students' learning outcomes. Ge and Land (2003) found that students who received a combination of different types of self-questioning in English literature problem-solving performed significantly better than those who did not receive such questions in the processes of problem representation, developing solutions, making justification, monitoring and evaluating. Kramarski and Mevarech, (2003) found that self-questioning based on the IMPROVE method in mathematics problem-solving enhanced students mathematical reasoning and guided their self-monitoring in problem-solving processes.

However, most studies based on self-questioning examined the effects on content domains such as reading comprehension (e.g., Palincsar and Brown, 1984), science (e.g., Davis and Linn, 2000), mathematics (e.g.,Kramatski and Mevarech, 2003), and general problem-solving (e.g., King, 1994) that does not integrate e-learning (e.g., Ge and Land, 2003). We believe that there is a need for systematic research to determine the benefits of self-questioning as a metacognitive feedback strategy embedded in mathematical e-learning. We argue that supporting students with explicit metacognitive feedback in e-learning should help students: Access and interact with the content functionality, allow them to think about the deeper concepts and structure of disciplinary relations, and enable them to solve transfer tasks in various contexts: real-life and formal. Furthermore, we assume that metacognitive feedback can strengthen students' motivation and capability to persistently behave in a wide variety of domains which, in turn, will enhance self-efficacy in mathematical e-learning (e.g., Bandura, 1997; Pajares, 1996; Pintrich and Groot, 1990).

Past research on feedback in computer-based learning environments has shown differential effects of feedback strategy on students learning. It was found that corrective feedback helps immediate learning, whereas guided and metacognitive feedback help in gaining deep understanding and developing the ability to transfer knowledge (Azevado and Bernard, 1995; Kramarski and Zeichner, 2001; Moreno, 2004). We believe that obtaining knowledge about using mathematical e-learning embedded with feedback either with metacognitive self-questioning strategy (EL+MF) or result feedback based on corrective answers (EL+RF) helps educators and researchers to gain insight to students' mathematical knowledge and self-efficacy.

The purpose of the study is three-fold: (a) To investigate effects of mathematical e-learning embedded with feedback either with metacognitive self-questioning (EL+MF) or result feedback based on corrective answers (EL+RF) on procedural problem-solving tasks; (b) to examine students' ability to transfer problem-solving tasks with regard to mathematical explanations under these instructions; and (c) to compare the differential effects of both instructions on self-efficacy.

METHOD

Participants

Participants were 62 (boys and girls) ninth-grade students (age mean = 14.3) who studied in two classes within one junior high school in central Israel. Each instructional approach was assigned randomly to one of the classes. The composition of students was similar in terms of socioeconomic status as defined by the Israel Ministry of Education.

Measures

The study utilized two measures for the pretest and posttest: (a) Mathematical test; and (b) self-efficacy questionnaire.

(a) Mathematical test

A mathematical pretest and posttest (26-items) was designed for the linear function unit. The test was adapted from the studies of previous research (Leinhardt, Zaslavski and Stein, 1990; Kramarski and Mevarech, 2003). The test includes two components: the first (12-items) refers to students' ability to solve procedural tasks. Such tasks demand basic skills based on a formal context to which the students were exposed in their e-learning practice (e.g., computing the slope with a formula; analyzing the structure of graphs). The procedural tasks on the posttest were different from the tasks on the pretest. The second component (14-items) refers to problem-solving of transfer tasks. These items were more complex, demanding higher order skills and were based on tasks that the students were not exposed to in their e-learning practice. The tasks were presented in two kinds of context: Real-life and formal. Students were asked to find connections between various functional representations (e.g., algebraic, table, graph), draw conclusions, and make algebraic generalizations based on a given graph. The transfer tasks on the posttest were similar to the tasks on the pretest. The Cronbach Alpha reliability coefficient for each component of the questionnaire was .86; .85 (respectively, for procedural and transfer knowledge).

Scoring: Each item on the test for the procedural and transfer tasks was scored from 0 (not responding, or wrong response) to 1 point (correct answer). The mathematical explanations were scored by summing the explanations (0-7). In addition, the quality of mathematical explanations was analyzed based on three criteria of arguments: logical-formal (e.g., using mathematical terms or generalization rules); procedural (e.g., calculation example); and no-arguments (e.g., no mathematical explanations).

(b) Self-efficacy questionnaire

The self-efficacy scale from Motivated Strategies for Learning Questionnaire (MSLQ, Pintrich et al., 1991) was used to measure participants' self-efficacy on the pre/post test. This scale consists of eight self-report questions (e.g., I believe I will receive an excellent score on the posttest after learning a function unit with this computer program). The Cronbach's alpha for the self-efficacy scale was .91.

Scoring: Each item was scored on a 5-point Likert scale ranging from almost never (1) to almost always (5).

INSTRUCTIONS

General instruction

Both in the EL+MF and EL+RF instructions the linear function unit was taught four times a week during five weeks according to the junior high school mathematics curriculum developed by the Israel Ministry of Education. Students in both instructions practiced the same problem-solving interactive tasks that were accessible to the students on the Web. Students were asked to work in pairs – solve the tasks, discuss methods of providing mathematical explanations, and send the solutions by e-mail to the teacher. The teacher encouraged students to participate in e-learning, and explained its effects on problem-solving. APPENDIX A provides an example of a mathematical task presented in both instructions.

Metacognitive feedback

EL+MF students were exposed to metacognitive feedback based on the IMPROVE self-questioning strategy as discussed earlier (Mevarech and Kramarski, 1997; Kramarski and Mevarech, 2003). The metacognitive feedback included four categories of questions: (a) comprehending the problem (e.g., **"What is the problem"**?); (b) constructing connections between previous and new knowledge (e.g., "What is similar/different between the problem-at hand and the problems you have solved in the past? and WHY?"); (c) using appropriate strategies for solving the problem (e.g., "What is the strategy for solving the problem and WHY?"); and (d) reflecting on the processes and the solution (e.g., "Does the solution make sense?"; "Why is it a good explanation?").

The questions were presented on the screen and printed on a worksheet.

During the first meeting, the teacher discussed with the students the nature of IMPROVE method and its impact on learning mathematics. They were informed that metacognitive self-questioning would help them better understand and remember mathematical topics which, in turn, will affect their confidence in learning mathematics.

The teacher provided examples of tasks in various difficulty levels embedded with metacognitive self-questioning, and demonstrated how to answer such questions. Students were asked to think aloud about the questions, discuss them with peers, and provide written responses.

Result feedback

Students in this learning instruction were not exposed explicitly to self-questioning. At the end of solving the task a computer-generated result feedback was provided by giving a grade as to the correctness of the answer.

Procedure

Participants were 62 (boys and girls) ninth-grade students that were assigned randomly to two e-learning instructions: EL+MF and EL+RF. Students' in both groups studied the linear function unit during five weeks. During practice students in the EL+MF environment were supported by metacognitive feedback based on the IMPROVE self-questioning strategy (Mevarech and Kramarski, 1997; Kramarski and Mevarech, 2003), whereas students in EL+RF environment were exposed to result feedback.

Mathematical knowledge and self-efficacy were assessed by measures of pre- and post-test. The mathematical test assessed students' procedural and transfer knowledge in real-life and formal context. The self-efficacy questionnaire assessed students' beliefs in their ability of problem-solving in computer-based learning environments.

RESULTS

Table 1 presents the mean scores and standard deviations of students' problem-solving of procedural tasks and transfer tasks with regard to mathematical explanations.

Table 1. Means and standard deviations on procedural and transfer tasks in real-life and formal context with regard to mathematical explanations by instruction and time

	EL+MF n=32		EL+RF n=30	
	Pretest	Posttest	Pretest	Posttest
Procedural tasks[1]				
M	.52	.68	.54	.56
SD	.23	.28	.26	.27
Transfer tasks				
Real-life context[1]				
M	.45	.80	.61	.75
SD	.21	.17	.23	.18
Mathematical explanations[2]				
M	1.97	4.24	2.86	3.74
SD	1.22	1.21	1.68	1.65
Formal context[1]				
M	.44	.84	.61	.81
SD	.29	.19	.27	.18
Mathematical explanations[2]				
M	1.71	4.63	2.69	3.47
SD	1.61	1.41	2.24	1.97

Note: Range, [1]0-1; [2]0-7

The first purpose of our study was to investigate students' (EL+MF and EL+RF) problem-solving skills of procedural tasks. We performed a one way ANOVA on prior and post mathematical problem-solving of procedural tasks. The findings indicated no significant differences between the two instructions on prior mathematical problem-solving $F(1.60) = 2.78$; $p>.05$. However, ANOVA on the post-test indicated significant differences between the instructions on solving procedural tasks $F(1.60) = 14.13$; $p<.001$. At the end of the study the EL+MF students outperformed the EL+RF students in problem-solving procedural tasks (Effect-size: ES = 0.44). We calculated effect-size as the difference between means in proportion to the total standard deviations of the post-test (SD=0.26).

The second purpose of our study was to investigate students' (EL+MF and EL+RF) problem-solving transfer tasks of real-life and formal contexts with regard to mathematical explanations. We performed a two-way analysis of variance (instructions (2) by time (2), with repeated measures of the second factor) on solving transfer tasks pertaining to each context. This time repeated measures were performed because of the fact that the transfer tasks were the same for the pre- and post-test.

Findings indicated significant differences for the main effect of time on solving transfer tasks $F(1,60) = 67.44$ and 74.19, $p<.001$, and mathematical explanations $F(1,60) = 46.26$ and 55.94, $p<.001$, respectively for each context. Additionally, we found significant interaction between the effects of instructions and time on solving transfer tasks $F(1,60) = 5.47$ and 3.59, $p<.01$, and for providing explanations $F(1,60) = 14.96$ and 9.92, $p<.001$, respectively for each context.

Table 2. Effect-sizes (ES[1]) on improvement problem solving of transfer tasks in real-life and formal context with regard to mathematical explanations by instruction

ES	EL+MF n=32	EL+RF n=30
Transfer tasks		
Real-life tasks	1.59	1.42
Explanations	1.57	0.56
Formal tasks	1.43	0.71
Explanations	1.52	0.51

Note: [1]We calculated effect sizes on each post-test measure as the difference between pre/post-test means as a proportion of the total standard deviation of the pre-test (SD=0.22, 1.45, 0.28. 1.93 respectively).

Effect-sizes (Table 2) indicated that at the end of the study the EL+MF students improved their ability to solve transfer tasks and to provide mathematical explanations regarding real-life and formal context. In particular, the EL+MF students improved their ability to solve transfer tasks more in real-life context than in formal context. Furthermore, they provided correct explanations on both types of the transfer tasks more often.

Further analysis on the quality of mathematical explanations indicated that by the end of the study more EL+MF students provided logical-formal arguments than the EL+RF students, 65% and 44%, $t(60) = 3.67$, $p<.05$ respectively, whereas no significant differences were found between the two environments on procedural arguments, 17% and 16%, $t(60) = 0.76$, $p>.05$ respectively.

The third purpose of our study was to compare students' (EL+MF and EL+RF) self-efficacy regarding problem-solving in e-learning. Figure 1 presents the means of self-efficacy by instruction and time.

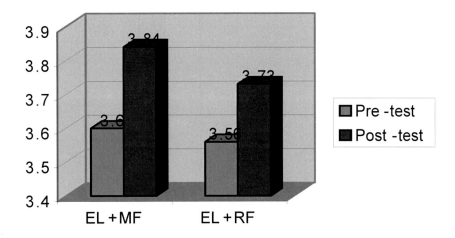

Note: SD for pre-test = 0.55; 0.57, and SD for post-test = 0.55; 0.49 respectively for EL+MF and EL+RF.

Figure 1. Means of self-efficacy by instruction and time.

We performed a two-way analysis of variance (instructions (2) by time (2), with repeated measures on the second factor) on self-efficacy. The findings indicated significant differences for time $F(1,60) = 9.61$, $p<.01$, and interaction between instructions and time $F(1,60) = 3.41$, $p<.05$. At the end of the study the EL+MF students improved their self-efficacy more than the EL+RF students (ES= 0.43; 0.30).

DISCUSSION

We found that students exposed to metacognitive feedback based on the IMPROVE self-questioning strategy in e-learning (EL+MF), significantly outperformed the EL+RF students in procedural and transfer problem-solving tasks with regard to mathematical explanations in various contexts: real-life and formal. In particular, they succeeded more in solving problems of real-life context that require high order skills (PISA, 2003). Moreover, at the end of the study the EL+MF students provided significantly more conceptual arguments based on logic-formal conclusions during the solution process, and exhibited a higher level of mathematical self-efficacy in computer-based learning.

The findings raise some issues and implications for further discussion regarding the role of metacognitive feedback and transfer knowledge.

Metacognitive feedback

There are several possible reasons for the beneficial effect of metacognitive support on mathematical e-learning. First, it seems that making disciplinary strategies explicit in e-learning with IMPROVE tools can encourage students to think about the steps they need to

Second, our findings may be derived from the fact that students who used metacognitive self-questioning strategy actively monitor, control and update products through internal feedback. This process might help students shift their attention from problem-based features (i.e., goals and rules of the problem) to a processing level (i.e., whereby they consider strategies, make sub-goals and evaluate moves). Perhaps, such process enhanced EL+MF ability of problem-solving, and self-efficacy for learning unlike students who were not exposed to such support (EL+RF).

Our findings support previous research regarding differential effects of feedback types on learning (Kramarski and Zeichner, 2001; Moreno, 2004). For example, Moreno found that when students are exposed to multimedia with the use of an explanatory feedback to guide novice students in the process of meaning making promote deeper learning than those that present identical materials using corrective feedback alone. The explanatory feedback group produced higher transfer scores. Mental load rating scales provided evidence that the explanatory feedback was effective due to reductions in cognitive load.

Further research is needed to investigate more deeply students' performance under different conditions of feedback embedded in e-learning.

Transfer knowledge

The findings indicate that students who were exposed to metacognitive feedback (EL+MF) were better able to transfer their knowledge from solving formal tasks which was taught in both classrooms to real-life tasks which was new to all students. As conceptualized by Cooper and Sweller (1987) three variables contribute to problem-solving transfer. Students must master strategies for problem-solving, develop categories for sorting problems that require similar solutions, and be aware that novel problems are related to previously solved problems. It is possible that the metacognitive IMPROVE self-questioning strategy led them to reflect more efficiently on the solution of the transfer tasks because of the opportunity to: (a) look at the big picture (e.g., connection questions); (b) know what to do (e.g., comprehension questions); (c) find how and when to do (e.g., strategy questions); and (d) make thinking visible (e.g., reflection questions). Moreover, as students master metacognitive problem-solving strategies, they allocate less working memory to the details of the solution and instead devote cognitive resources to identifying connections between novel and familiar problems, and to planning their work (Schraw, Crippen and Hartly, 2006). Similar findings, reported by other researchers, indicate that metacognitive support is effective in developing problem-solving ability because it enables one to link the quantitative knowledge to the situational knowledge. When the two types of knowledge are joined, a mental representation is constructed which supports mathematical reasoning (Ceci and Roazzi, 1994; Hoek, Eeden and Terwel, 1999; Kramarski, Mevarech and Liberman, 2001).

Our findings extend other findings in non-technology environments which indicated that self-questioning had a cognitive effect on students' reasoning and their ability to promote transfer of new knowledge (e.g., Davis and Lin, 2003; Kramarski, Mevarech, 2003; Kramarski, Mevarech and Arami, 2002). Our conclusions provide evidence consistent with other research findings, that eliciting elaborated responses through self-questioning prompts are effective in facilitating high-level cognitive processing (e.g., King, 1992).

Practical implications and future research

The study points towards the positive effects of supporting e-learning with metacognitive feedback to promote mathematical knowledge (procedural and transfer) and self-efficacy. Our findings strongly lead to recommending supporting self-regulation of learning (SRL) as a powerful instructional technique in promoting mathematical knowledge (e.g., PISA, 2003; NCTM, 2000).

We recognize the need to understand more about how mathematical knowledge and self-efficacy emerge in advanced computer-based learning embedded with different metacognitive feedback such as combining self-questioning with human tutor feedback via e-mail or other online communication media (Azevedo, Cromley., 2004). The study suggests the need to design question prompts adapted to individuals with different competence and self-efficacy levels in mathematics, especially in the context of computer-supported learning environments (Ge, Chen and Davis, 2005). Some other kind of support can be provided by directing students' attention in a dynamic format to important aspects of activating a problem schema, eliciting their explanations, and promoting self-monitoring and self-reflection before, during and at the end of the problem solving process.

We also suggest that the self-regulation components can be examined in different ways through observations, interviews, and "thinking aloud" techniques (Veenman, Van Hout-Wolters, and Afflerbach, 2006).). Such techniques might reinforce findings regarding the effects of using metacognitive feedback on mathematical knowledge and self-efficacy.

In conclusion, our study contributes to our understanding the nature of metacognitive feedback through self-questioning utilized as a scaffolding strategy, especially in supporting mathematics and self-efficacy in e-learning environments.

REFERENCES

Azevedo, R., and Bernard, R.M. (1995). A meta-analysis of the effects of feedback in computer-based instruction. *Journal of Educational Computing Research, 13*(2), 111-127.

Azevedo, R., and Cromley, J. G. (2004). Does training of self- regulated learning facilitate student's learning with hypermedia? *Journal of Educational Psychology, 96*(3), 523-535.

Bandura, A. (1997). Self-efficacy: The Exercise of Control. NY, USA: Freeman/Times Books/Henry Holt and Co.

Butler, D.L., and Winne, P.H. (1995). Feedback and self-regulated learning: A theoretical synthesis. *Review of Educational Research, 65*(3), 245-281.

Cecil, S. J., and Roazzi, A. (1994). The effects of context on cognition: Postcards from Brazil. In J. S. Sternberg and R. K. Wagner (Eds.). *Mind in context: Interactionist perspectives on human intelligence.* England, UK: Academic Press, 74-100.

Cooper, G., and Sweller, J. (1987). Effects of schema acquisition and rule automation on mathematical problem solving transfer. *Journal of Educational Psychology, 79,* 347-362.

Ge, X., Chen, C.H., and Davis, K. A. (2005). Scaffolding novice instructional designers' problem-solving processes using question prompts in a web-based learning environment. *Journal of Educational Research, 33*(2), 219-248.

Ge. X., and Land, S.M. (2003). Scaffolding students' problem-solving processes in an ill-structured task using question prompts and peer interactions. *Educational Technology Research and Development, 51*(1), 21-38.

Ge. X., and Land, S.M. (2004). A conceptual framework of scaffolding problem solving processes using question prompts and peer interactions. *Educational Technology Research and Development, 52*(2), 5-22.

Davis, E.A., and Linn, M.C. (2000). Scaffolding students' knowledge integration: Prompt for reflection in KIE. *International Journal of Science Education, 22*(8), 819-837.

Hoek, D., van den Eden, P., and Terwel, J. (1999). The effects of integrated social and cognitive strategy instruction on the mathematics achievement in secondary education. *Learning and Instruction, 9,* 427-448.

King, A. (1991). Effects of training in strategic questioning on children's problem-solving performance. *Journal of Educational Psychology, 83*(3), 307-317.

King, A. (1992). Facilitating elaborative learning through guided student-generated questioning. *Educational Psychologist, 27*(1), 111-126.

King, A. (1994). Guiding knowledge construction in the classroom: Effects of teaching children how to question and how to explain. *American Educational Research Journal,* 31(2), 338-368.

Kramarski, B., and Zeichner, O. (2001). Using technology to enhance mathematical reasoning: Effects of feedback and self-regulation learning. *Educational Media International, 38*(2/3), 77-82.

Kramarski, B., Mevarech, Z. R., and Liberman, A. (2001). The effects of multilevel- versus unilevel-metacognitive training on mathematical reasoning. *Journal for Educational Research, 94*(5), 292-300.

Kramarski, B., Mevarech, Z. R., and Arami, M. (2002). The effects of metacognitive training on solving mathematical authentic tasks. *Educational Studies in Mathematics, 49,* 225-250.

Kramarski, B., and Mevarech, Z. R. (2003). Enhancing mathematical reasoning in the classroom: Effects of cooperative learning and metacognitive training. *American Educational Research Journal, 40*(1), 281-310.

Kramarski., and Mizrachi, (2006). Online discussion and self-regulated learning: Effects of instructional methods on mathematical literacy. *Journal of Educational Research. , 99*(4), 218-230.

Land, S.M. (2000). Cognitive requirements for learning with open-ended learning environments. *Educational Technology Research and Developments, 48,* 61-78.

Leinhardt, G., Zaslavsky, O., and Stein, M. K. (1990). Functions, graphs, and graphing: Tasks, learning, and teaching. *Review of Educational Research, 60,* 1-64

Mevarech, Z. R., and Kramarski, B. (1997). IMPROVE: A multidimensional method for teaching mathematics in heterogeneous classrooms. *American Educational Research Journal, 34,* 365-394.

Moreno, R. (2004). Decreasing cognitive load for novice students: Effects of explanatory versus corrective feedback in discovery-based multimedia. *Instructional Science, 32,* 99-113.

National Council of Teachers of Mathematics. (2000). *Principles and standards for school mathematics.* Reston, VA: Author.

Palincsar, A., and Brown, A. (1984). Reciprocal teaching of comprehension fostering and monitoring activities. *Cognition and Instruction, 1,* 117-175.

Pajares, F. (1996). Self-efficacy beliefs in academic settings. *Review of Educational Research, 66*(4), 543-578.

Pintrich, P. R., and De Groot, E. V. (1990). Motivational and self-regulated learning components of classroom academic performance. *Journal of Educational Psychology, 82*(1), 33-40.

Pintrich, P.R. (2000). The role of goal orientation in self-regulated learning. In M. Boekaerts, P. Pintrich, and M. Zeidner (Eds.), *Handbook of self-regulation* (pp. 451-502). San Diego, CA: Academic Press.

Pintrich, P.R., Smith, D.A.F., Garcia, T., and Mckeachie, W.J. (1991). The manual for the use of the Motivated Strategies for Learning Questionnaire (MSLQ) (Tech. Rep. No. 91-B-004). Ann Arbor: University of Michigan, School of Education.

PISA. (2003). *Literacy Skills for the World of Tomorrow.* Further results from PISA 2000. Paris.

Schoenfeld, A. H. (1992). Learning to think mathematically: Problem solving, metacognition, and sense making in mathematics. In D.A. Grouws, *Handbook of research on mathematics teaching and learning* (pp. 165-197). New York: MacMillan.

Schraw, G., (1998). Promoting general metacognitive awaewness. *Instructional Science, 26*(1-2), 113-125.

Schraw, G., Crippen, K.J., and Hartley, K. (2006). Promoting self-regulation in science education: Metacognition as part of a broader perspective on learning. *Research in Science Education, 36*, 111-139.

Veenman, M. V. J., Van Hout-Wolters., B. H. A. M., Afflerbach, P. (2006). Metacognition and learning: Conceptual and methodological considerations. *Metacognition and Learning, 1*, 3-14.

Winters, F.I., and Azevedo, R., (2005). High-school students' regulation of learning during computer based science inquiry. *Journal of Educational research, 33*(2), 189-217.

Zimmerman, B. J. (1998). Academic studying and the development of personal skill: A self-regulatory perspective. *Educational Psychologist 33*, 73-86.

APPENDIX A

Example of a mathematical task provided in e-learning (EL+MF vs. EL+RF)

Students in both instructions were exposed to the same mathematical task. They were asked to look at the graph, calculate the slope, and explain the property of the slope in each section line. Students that were exposed to metacognitive feedback instruction (EL+MF) were prompt to solve the task with self-metacognitive questions (e.g., "What is the problem all about?"; "Why is it a good explanation?"). They were also asked to answer in writing the metacognitive questions. However, students in EL+RF instruction were asked to find the solution without explicit metacognitive strategy use. They received only computer-generated result feedback by giving a grade as to the correctness of the answer.

In addition, students in both instructions were asked to send the solution by e-mail to the teacher.

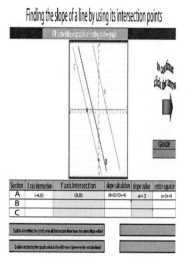

Metacognitive self-questioning:	
Comprehension	What is the problem?
Connection	What is similar/different?
Strategy	What is the strategy? Why?
Reflection	Does the solution make sense?
	Why is it a good explanation?

Figure 2.Example of a task provided in EL+MF instruction.

In: E-Learning: 21st Century Issues and Challenges
Editor: A.R. Lipshitz and S. P. Parsons

ISBN : 978-1-60456-156-2
©2008 Nova Science Publishers, Inc.

Chapter 6

THREE CHALLENGES FOR LIFELONG E-LEARNING: PERSONALIZATION, QUALITY AND OER

Dejan Dinevski[*]
University of Maribor, Slovenia

ABSTRACT

"Free and open learning for all everywhere at all times" is a noble aspiration written in global strategies and heard so many times from the highest political levels. It should lead towards a "better world", but the research and experiences shows that there are several obstacles in the way. The relationship of "lifelong learning" and its technology foundation "e-learning" is explored in the chapter. Directions of e-learning technology development for efficient lifelong learning are identified and some guidelines for major research tracks are suggested.

Personalization is a key technology succes factor for wide implementation of e-learning. Personalization can make the ICT based e-learning platform friendly and even intimate which is a critical aspect to overcome the so called "technology barier". The personalized e-learning system will be able to respond to the individual learning styles, explicit and implicit preferences, role and the existing level of knowledge. Personalization will be achieved without or with as little user intervention as possible with tracking their usage data and history. "Cognitive-based personalization" is based on monitoring learner behavior in a real time, and predicting what the user would like to do next - finally leading to the "whole-person personalization" which seeks to understand the deep-seated psychological sources.

The quality of an e-learning educational offering depends not only on products, such as learning material or services, but also on the interaction of the learner with contents, tasks, tutors and other learners. E-learning quality is a broad concept which has yet to develop unified guidelines. Several issues for this development are described and questions to be anwered are identified.

Open educational resources (OER) in e-learning are the future source of information for lifelong learners. Open source and open standards are defined as the basis of the "open educational resource movement" that is beginning to form on a global level at the

---

[*] dejan.dinevski@uni-mb.si

dawn of the 21st century. Several good practices, ideas and existing initiatives are presented and the vision of the future of open educational resources is introduced.

INTRODUCTION

From the political declarations of UNESCO, the European Commision and other relevant organizations it is not hard to conclude that the ultimate goal of educational policy is: "free lifelong learning for all everywhere at all times". "How to get there?" is a critical question that has to be adressed by the lifelong learning researchers in 21st century.

To become a lifelong learner in a knowledge-based society one has to posses some essential competencies: self-direction and creativity, critical thinking and problem-solving skills, collaborative team-work and communication skills. Does it lead to a need for a "pre-lifelong learning" to achieve those competencies?

One of the common denominators of all the visions for the future of lifelong learning is that it should be based on information and communication technology, more specifically, on modern e-learning principles and practices. E-learning provides a key to make lifelong learning more effective, efficient and pervasive. In this text we are investigating which are the most significant directions of e-learning research and development in order that lifelong learning on the basis of e-learning becomes a reality.

Let us quote just one reference for now which hits the core of the idea behind lifelong learning:

> "Globalisation, new technologies and demographic developments constitute an enormous challenge; one of the answers to this problem is the access to lifelong learning." Ján Figel, Commissioner for Education, Training, Culture and Multilingualism, European Commission (presented at http://ec.europa.eu/ education/programmes/elearning/index_en. html, accessed on 17th of March, 2007).

WHAT IS LIFELONG LEARNING AND WHAT DOES E-LEARNING HAVE TO DO WITH IT?

"Lifelong learning" is the frequently used term which is, on the other hand, very general and thus not exact. Since the term is used as a strategic measure in the most important political declarations of the European Union (EU), the most thoughtful definitions, presented also in this chapter, are published by the European institutions and learning networks. The affirmed aim of the EU written in the famous "Lisbon declaration" is to become "the world's most dynamic and competitive knowledge based society by 2010". Though sometimes disproved, education and training have become major points of attention in the policy decisions and programs since both are the means to boost up the economic growth and aid the greater social cohesion. Furthermore, the lifelong learning with four major objectives (personal fulfillment, active citizenship, social inclusion and employability/adaptability) is seen as a key element of the strategy devised in Lisbon. Let's not refer only to the political agenda – from the practical point of view of the individual the most conclusive seems to be the following statement (Tamkin, 1997): "Lifelong learning is an essential survival tool and we should all be doing it."

The related terms of lifelong learning and university continuing education both describe very broad ideas. They are consequently very expansive and not consistently defined. In fact the problem is that there are too many definitions of the terms including the ones from UNESCO, Council of Europe, European Commission, EUCEN (European Universities Continuing Education Network), etc.

In our context the most relevant definition for lifelong learning is the one from the Communication of the European Commission, titled "Making a European Area of Lifelong Learning a Reality" (2001) which says that it is all purposeful learning activity undertaken throughout life, with the aim of improving knowledge, skills and competences within a personal, civic, social and/or employment-related perspective. This includes all forms of learning: formal (courses and examinations), non-formal (without examinations) and informal (without either courses or examinations). In this policy document the concept of "European lifelong learning area" (which reflects the earlier one of a European research area) is the area where citizens can move freely to "learn, work and make the most of their knowledge and skills to meet the aims of the EU to be more prosperous, tolerant and democratic". The spirit of the referenced Communication is captured in the on the first page: "When planning for a year, plant corn. When planning for a decade, plant trees. When planning for life, train and educate people".

Since some comparisons in European and North American understandings and actions on (e)learning are made in this text, let us quote one more prosaic citation, taken from the author coming from the U.S. Army, being at the same time a founding Chair of IEEE Learning Technology Task Force (Schoening, 2002): "Give a man a fish and he'll eat for a day. Teach him to fish and he'll eat for life. Teach students to learn and they'll excel in the 21st century."

Usually people understand LL more practically and with deeper meaning as presented by (Lockwood, 2001) "Lifelong learning is a continuous process that motivates and empowers individuals – it assists them to acquire new knowledge, skills and understandings that can be applied confidently in new circumstances and environments. These flexible and adaptable people will be the key to empowering communities, especially rural and remote communities, as they face the challenges of the 21st century. The challenges, arising mainly from the shift from an industrial and service economy to a knowledge-based economy require people who can adapt to change by learning new skills and acquiring new knowledge."

Lifelong learning area

Lifelong learning in its definition covers the whole education area: initial education, basic continuing education and university continuing education. All the listed components are graphically represented in the Fig. 1. According to some writers the usage of lifelong learning term is so all-encompassing that it is in danger of losing all meaning (Coffield, 2004).

For the »continuing education« (CE) we will refer to EUCEN (Osborne and Thoma, 2003) which states that it is »any form of education, both vocational and general, resumed after an interval following the continuous initial education«. This includes: full-time and part-time programmes for older adults leading to qualifications; courses taken for vocational reasons or for love of the subject; courses leading (but not necessarily) to credits, diplomas and degrees; courses taken by graduates (but not always so). The definition is rather hazy, but it has been generally used by the authors describing the continuing education in Europe. On the other hand the term "university continuing education" is not frequently used in the EU official documents where lifelong learning is used instead (in almost identical meaning). Synonyms for general understanding of continuing education are also "adult education" (used for example in Finland) or "permanent university education" (used in Spain) and also "post-experience education". Almost all agree that UCE is education for adults returning to university education after a break following their initial education but sometimes it is limited to vocational educational activities. Let's mention here that also the related terms like "adult student", "part-time student", "higher education" and "further education" are not understood in one universal way, but depend on the society, tradition and culture of the country.

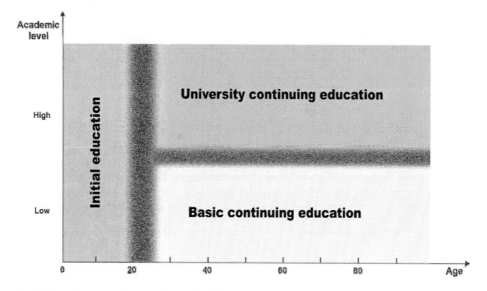

Figure 1. Lifelong learning (the whole area), initial and continuing education

Not to remain on the technical level – what about the significance of the continuing education? A descriptive portrayal of the university continuing education is presented by Taylor (Taylor, 1990) where it's central concerns are classified as:

- individual and cultural education for personal growth and understanding
- facilitating the pleasure of intellectual discovery and debate
- civic and collective education to meet the needs of the community and to enhance democratic structures
- developing adult students critical faculties
- disseminating the core value of university education
- awareness of scientific, environmental and social issues
- developing effectiveness and capability through intellectual and specialized skills
- generally bringing together the expertise and values of the university and the life experience and real life issues of the regional community.

University and lifelong learning

Universities, as the main creators of knowledge, deserve a special place in lifelong learning system. University continuing education (UCE) is a motor of a high level lifelong learning and as such it is already mentioned in the previous paragraph; several political documents are actually speaking about UCE, but saying lifelong learning instead.

The roles of the Universities in continuing education are (Dinevski and Vesenjak D., 2004):

- provider and supporter of continuing professional development
- developer and organizer of universities' degree education, when operating with adults and employees
- distributor of high level knowledge and developer of methods of knowledge dissemination
- developer of e-learning, network based working methods and virtual university concept

Universities have many competitors in providing continuing education. Besides the interuniversity competition there are other institutions that regularly carry out education, like companies, chambers of industry and commerce, commercial consultancies, non-governmental organizations, professional associations and summer universities. Nevertheless, universities do have important advantages when meeting competition. They have the established structure and university label, underlying research, academic staff, high quality standards and especially stability and continuity. On the other hand small course-providing companies are more flexible and can respond quickly to the needs of the market.

Historically, because of different concepts it is not possible to establish the beginning of UCE, but in general UCE in started between the 16th and 19th centuries. In Western European universities, rapid development started to occur as departments with specific responsibility for CE began to be formed within universities. These departments generally arose because of initiatives taken by national governments and reflected the effect of significant government funding. In some countries laws have been passed requiring their universities to become more open. These oblige the universities to help anyone, regardless of their age or social background, to increase and refresh their knowledge (for example France).

Even though continuing education or lifelong learning provision in universities has often been subsidized and even regulated by law (education legislation together with labor law and social legislation) they have been relatively unsuccessful in competing with the private providers which is very much against the interests of the universities. Taking part in continuing education allows them to create close and regular links between their academic staff and practicing members of their professions. This in turn allows the universities to update their knowledge of the application of their subjects, update their teaching go full-time students to reflect the current attitudes of their professions, and possibly to attract funds for research or development work. European Centre for the Strategic Management of Universities states (Becher, 1993) that continuing education enables universities to play a more significant role in their region's economic and social development and meet their moral obligation to make available state-of-the-art knowledge to all parts of society.

EUCEN reports that many European universities provide CE but there are large variations in this provision from one country to another. The reference (Osborne, Thomas, 2003) contains extensive reports on EU countries. In Finland (that is mostly used as an example of exceptionally successful and developed CE) a considerable number of CE programmes are on offer. These have been divided operationally by the Government into voluntary education, employment education and personal education. These forms are clearly distinguished by the Government and all receive funding. The development has been so extensive that not only do all the Finnish universities now have at least one centre responsible for CE; some have up to ten.

It is evident that e-learning is going to be the foundation of the efficient and cost-effective UCE. The comprehensive analysis of technological, organizational and pedagogical aspects of e-learning and open and distance education in universities is presented in (Dinevski and Plenković, 2003) where also the common barriers of its introduction at the university level are explored.

Organizational Forms of Continuing Education within Universities

Brennan (2002) provides an assortment of practices within UCE in universities, describing a range of organisational structures using case studies from Spain, Portugal, Finland, France, Norway, Belgium, Lithuania and the United Kingdom. His model is shown in Table 1 and is often used as a reference for organizational forms of lifelong learning. Let's note here that the model E is the authors' prediction for the future dominant model that was not yet observed.

Independently of the organizational model within the university it is often emphasised (for example Edwards, 1993) that the challenge of lifelong learning in 21 century will be met only by linking the academia an business sectors. Only strong co-operation between the two can form the framework for wide and efficient lifelong learning provision.

Table 1. Organizational structures for university continuing education (Brennan, 2002)

Model	Form
A	University continuing education delivery through a separate department, centre or company, with or without expertise brought in from subject departments.
B	University continuing education delivery as above and by a range of subject departments with a number of functions for university continuing education (e.g. development, monitoring, quality assurance) carried out by the university continuing education department.
C	University continuing education delivery entirely devolved to subject departments but with strong central support through a range of functions e.g. strategic leadership, development, monitoring, quality assurance, promotion.
D	University continuing education delivery devolved to subject departments with little or no central support, co-ordination or monitoring.
E	University continuing education delivery through a consortium of institutions each contributing particular expertise towards collaborative university continuing education programmes.

THE ROLE OF E-LEARNING IN LIFELONG LEARNING

"Technology can make lifelong learning a reality" (Regan, 1998) is in a nutshell presented the North American point of view. With electronic tools, people can (theoretically) learn virtually anytime and anyplace they choose without obstacles in place, time and social status. Is it really so simple?

Let's just clear up some terminology. "E-learning" can be seen as complete information technology support to learning processes. UNESCO uses the term "open and distance learning", but in the latest professional literature the term "e-learning" has been progressively dominant. "eLearning" is a unique term and the name of programmes and action plans of the European Commission. There are many terms used in professional literature, for example in the references (Lockwood, 2001), and (Keegan, 1991) like "Open", "Distance", "Flexible", "Interactive" or "Distributed learning". Each of the terms has its own (sub)meaning but it can be stated that the "e-learning" comprise all the listed terms. The term that was used for more than a century, and which is the predecessor of e-learning, is "distance education". Although the terms are often used interchangeably, they somewhat differ in their meaning. We won't go into terminology distinctions but will use the "e-learning" except in the citations. The e-learning is not seen as a shift from the traditional to open learning, but rather as a support to conventional learning processes with the use of modern information technology and distance educational methods. Modern implementation of e-learning in educational institutions can be considered as the result of the convergence process of distance and conventional education (Dinevski and Brodnik, 2005).

E-learning in higher education

In 2002 UNESCO's "Policy Paper for Change and Development in Higher Education" urged higher education institutions to make greater use of the advantages offered by the advancements of communication technologies so that »each university should become an open university offering possibilities for distance learning and learning in various points in time« (Moore and Tait, 2002). According to the same report open and distance learning was (in 2002) one of the most rapidly growing fields of education, and its potential impact on all education delivery systems has been greatly accentuated through the development of Internet – based information technologies, and in particular the World Wide Web.

As more recent reports demonstrate clearly, the pace of e-learning and "open and distance learning" is still accelerating, and it is likely to occupy a growing part of the landscape in higher education. E-learning at the tertiary levels shows a two-fold development pattern. On the one hand, numerous single model open universities have emerged to absorb large number of new learners, while, on the other hand, increasing number of traditional universities have begun to offer their programmes also through distance education. The further development of information and communication technologies together with new pedagogical practices has reinforced this trend.

While North American universities are widely and systematically implementing e-learning into their daily practice, Europe developed a twofold development pattern. The UK Open University has set the standards for a particular type of university institution, the open universities. Big open universities have been established in Spain (Universidad Nacional de Educacion a Distancia), Germany (Fernuniversitaet), Netherlands (Open Universiteit), Portugal (Universidade Aberta), Austria Danube University of Krems and the most recent one in Greece. In Finland the Open University is decentralized – all the universities are funded to provide Open University services and they collaborate with one another, and with a number of other educational institutions throughout the country. In other countries the dual mode types of universities represent the dominant model.

In recent years, the European Union has consistently increased e-learning and distance education components of its educational programmes, and has included open and distance learning explicitly even in its Maastricht Treaty back in 1992. E-learning is strongly presented in policy documents of the European Commission. In 2003 the Commission adopted a proposal for a specific eLearning Programme which in 2007 merged with other educational programmes into the "Lifelong Learning Programme" with almost 100% increase of the overall budged when compared to previous years.

In a policy paper published by the European Open and Distance Learning Liaison Committee, it was noted that "a new vision of ICT for learning is needed at policy, management and grass roots practice level if a new window of opportunity is to be found for ICT to become really interesting to innovators in the learning system". Furthermore, a new policy paper published in May 2006 identified "the knowledge gap on learning innovation" as a major problem. (European ODL LC 2004 and 2006)

Innovations in the lifelong learning processes

E-learning has a major impact on thinking and practice through the whole educational system, regarding such critical matters as how students learn, how they can best be taught, and how educational resources might more efficiently be organised to deliver the instruction that is needed.

In the book where the role of "Net Generation" is explored (Tapscott, 1998), the new ways of learning for the new generation are presented.

The new learning process brings up the following shifts:

- From linear to hypermedia learning,
- from instruction to construction and discovery,
- from teacher-centered to learner-centered education,
- from absorbing material to learning how to navigate and how to learn,
- from school to lifelong learning,
- from one-size-fits-all to customized learning,
- from learning as torture to learning as fun, and,
- from the teacher as transmitter to the teacher as facilitator.

Tapscott's research leads him to conclude that the "Net Generation" is a force for educational transformation. They process information differently than previous generations, learn best in highly customizable environments, and look to teachers to create and structure their learning experience. Furthermore, the importance of understanding the behavioral patterns of the network generation exceeds merely appreciating that they are comfortable working online. A crucial element for successfully delivering virtual courses entails transforming the educational experience so that it is meaningful to the information-age learner.

An American study published under the title "Thwarted Innovation" (Zemsky / Massy 2004) concludes that despite massive investments in ICT-supported education only little impact has been achieved with respect to changing teaching practices. The study found that wider use is made of systems for managing courseware (Blackboard, WebCT) and simple, mostly PowerPoint-based "e-lectures". A profound change in teaching styles did not take place, despite numerous projects that explored and showcased novel approaches. The authors conclude: "eLearning will become pervasive only when faculty change how they teach – not before."

DIRECTIONS OF E-LEARNING TECHNOLOGY DEVELOPMENT FOR LIFELONG LEARNING

Users/learners of lifelong learning services to be offered by universities and other educational institutions are expected to be mostly adults with different levels of background knowledge and different levels of ICT skills. Therefore it is crucial that the e-learning platforms are operating in friendly, easy to use and robust environment. On the other hand the didactics will have to be designed in such a way that the learning process is motivating for the learner and that it supports the knowledge generation. As far as the high quality access is concerned there is a new technology coming up, namely the m(mobile)-learning which promises to make the learning possible practically anywhere and anytime.

In majority of e-learning programs offered today, the burden for learning is placed wholly on the shoulders of the learner. When "e-students" go to a course web site, they enter a menu of activities: announcements, documents, assignments, external links, communications, and tools. Students are expected to navigate this material on their own, without much support. They are generally offered email links to faculty and other students, but not much more. "Collaborative learning" is trying to solve this situation creating a virtual social space that must be managed for the teaching and learning needs of the particular group of people inhabiting that space. Such a common space is very important for the motivation and effective learning of continuing education students that lack the social component of traditional student's environment. Such a system also allows for something that is often overlooked in the e-classroom: recognizing and acknowledging the most valuable contributors. All these qualities are beneficial to the adult learner who is using the information technology as the means of interaction with the faculty, teachers and fellow students.

From the perspective of ICT itself a new vision can be found in the current development and usage of "social software" based tools and services that are highly supportive of e-learning practices and processes. Social software, such as Weblogs, Wikis, RSS-based content syndication, social book-marking, podcasting, etc., shows several positive effects within the realm of education. Wider adoption for educational and lifelong learning purposes could have a big innovative impact as these tools and services are ideally suited to learner-centred as well as collaborative approaches in developing competences required in our knowledge society. Software-based tools, services and multimedia allow for the emergence of innovative educational practices when used in didactically sound ways. There really exists a knowledge gap in how to use digital resources intelligently in learning innovation, but this gap will be best closed by teachers with the right professional attitudes through sharing within communities of practice experiences and lessons learned.

Will Richardson, author of "Blogs, Wikis, Podcasts and Other Powerful Web Tools for Classrooms"(Corwin Press, 2006), in an article published in the George Lucas Educational Foundation's "Edutopia Magazine", writes: "The good news for all of us is that today, anyone can become a lifelong learner. (Yes, even you.) These technologies are user friendly in a way that technologies have not been in the past. You can be up and blogging in minutes, editing wikis in seconds, making podcasts in, well, less time than you'd think. It's not difficult at all to be an active contributor in this society of authorship we are building. As usual, many of our students already know this. (...) In an environment where it's easy to publish to the globe, it feels more and more hollow to ask students to 'hand in' their homework to an audience of one. When we're faced with a flattening world where collaboration is becoming the norm, forcing students to work alone seems to miss the point. And when many of our students are already building networks far beyond our classroom walls, forming communities around their passions and their talents, it's not hard to understand why rows of desks and time-constrained schedules and standardized tests are feeling more and more limiting and ineffective." (Richardson 2006b)

When describing technology for learning we have to mention the Web 2.0 which can be distinguished from the Web 1.0 version with respect to several technological as well as behavioural features (O'Reilly 2005). It has also inspired parts of the education community among others. The following are some elements that are more widely understood to form part of the Web 2.0 and to be of interest for an "e-learning 2.0" (Gesser, 2007):

- Social Software for easy publishing and sharing of ideas, content and links: In particular Weblogs, Wikis, Social Bookmarking, and content sharing websites such as Flickr. Increasingly also collaborative authoring and other interactions in real time: For example, Writeboard, Writely, SynchroEdit and others;

- Collaborative filtering: Discovery of "most interesting" resources through filtering techniques, but also ongoing conversations, recommendations and cross-linking of resources in social networks; | Open APIs of Web service applications (e.g. Google Maps API, Flickr API) for creative re-use (e.g. mashups) of services and content;

- Many services based on RSS [Really Simple Syndication] feeds, which are used to continually update websites as well as the personal libraries of end-users with information about, and a link to, available thematically relevant content (which can also be pod- or videocasts);

- The content on Web 2.0 websites will also often be licensed as open content (e.g. Creative Commons).

PERSONALIZATION IN E-LEARNING

"Personalization" is a means to overcome one of the most important barriers for the lifelong learner, namely her/his friendliness and intimacy experience when in interaction with ICT based e-learning platforms.

Efficient personalization of e-learning is one of the key success factors for wide implementation of e-learning to variety of target groups. Successful teachers know that they can make a big difference in the classroom with personalized attention, particularly in recognizing how individuals may need to learn in different ways. Good instructors intuitively manage key human factors (e.g. will, happiness, dislike, fear, striving, frustration, satisfaction, anger, passion) to promote learning. Online these factors may be easily overlooked. To optimize the learning processes in the online environment, the e-learning providers should collect and analyze information about how individuals learn in a given situation be able to produce personalized solutions based on the findings. Personalization helps learners to improve the learning ability and to understand their own optimal learning methods which results in better management of their learning processes.

In all learning models and especially in e-learning the motivation is crucial. The necessary technology component of e-learning itself seems to make (some) learners feel uncomfortable. The variety of new technology features, services and functionalities may limit rather than stimulate the critical motivation in learners. The personalization of the e-learning platform offers the learning organizations a method for enhancing the learners' intimacy through their web site, which is, without any doubt, an additional motivation factor for the learner to whom the computer represents a major learning media. The technology providers will be forced to offer both highly sophisticated and at the same time "simple to use" e-learning functionalities. One of the major solutions to combine these two directions is the personalization of the e-learning technology platform.

Web interface personalization

In February 1999, the Gartner Group stated that, "matching direct or inferred reader requests through content personalization will be the most dramatic development in the Internet...through 2002, and will help differentiate the Web as a new medium." Clearly this is an important technology, and is being applied in many Internet systems in use today. Studies, for example (Greer and Murtaza, 2003) reports that relative advantage, compatibility, ease of use, and trialability significantly impacts the intended use of the personalization features on a web site. On the other hand visibility, image and result demonstrability were found not to have a significant impact on intent to use the personalization features on a web site. The study also found that the personalization features should be easy to use and should exhibit some advantage to the users to ensure adoption and use.

Three aspects of a Web site affect its utility in providing the intended service to its users. These are the content provided on the Web site, the layout of the individual pages, and the structure of the entire Web site itself (Mulvena et al., 2000). The relevance of each of the objects comprising a Web page to the users' needs will clearly affect their level of satisfaction. The structure of the Web site, defined by the existence of links between the various pages, restricts the navigation performed by the user to predefined paths and therefore defines the ability of a user to access relevant pages with relative ease. However, the definition of relevance is subjective. It is here that there is a potential mismatch between the perception of what the user needs, on the part of the Web site designer, and the true needs of users. This may have a major impact on the effectiveness of a Web site.

Basic personalization technology

Personalization technology involves software that learns patterns, habits, and preferences. Personalization is a toolbox of technologies and application features used in the design of an end-user experience. Features classified as "Personalization" are wide-ranging, from simple display of the end-user's name on a Web page, to complex catalog navigation and product customization based on deep models of users' needs and behaviors. Similarly, personalization technologies range from commonplace use of databases, cookies, and dynamic page generation, to esoteric pattern matching and machine-learning algorithms, rule-based inferencing, and data mining (Kramer et al., 2000).

As far as the technological process is concerned, personalization can be considered a three-step process in which customer information (their preferences, behavior, and profile) is taken as input, business rules are evaluated, and customized content is generated as output (Votch and Linden, 2000). Some special features of the personalization of e-learning services, which goes beyond the scope of this text, are presented in (Dinevski, 2004). An example for implementation of the personalization features that are especially appropriate for e-learning systems is presented in (Dinevski et al., 2003).

The users of the e-learning portal can be more productive if the portal is following their needs and interests. There are several common "personalization" solutions. For instance, for the purpose of the role division, one is provided, after authentication, with specific content and outlook. This "personalization" is driven by fix role categories of the users (teacher, learner, administrator etc.). Segmented personalization uses demographics, geographics, psychographics, or other information to divide or segment learning populations into smaller, identifiable and manageable groups for personalization. Basically, this is not a part of personalization but authentication, or better, security service. However, it raises a notion about user segmentation in general and personalization provision for them. Authentication is important but not required for identification of users. Personalization is performed according to some kind of profiles, whether aggregated or individual. We also have to distinguish between registered users and anonymous users and treat the latter as potential customers with triggering some special "program" to retain them. They should be offered by relevant content (and possibly presentation) as soon as possible. We have to take into account that the personalization ideal is constrained also by a today's hardware and a need to provide personalization in real-time. The goal should be to achieve personalization without or with as little user intervention as possible with tracking their usage data (whole-person personalization as presented below).

Higher levels of personalization

Very challenging is "cognitive-based personalization" which uses information about learning preferences or styles from a primarily cognitive perspective to deliver content specifically targeted to differing learner attributes. As an example, some learners prefer linear content handling and others random presentation with hyperlinks. Some authors distinguish between "left" and "right" thinking style when browsing the e-content. The background of different cognitive styles is well presented in (Fiorina et al., 2004) or (CHOU H. W. and WANG Y. F. 1999). This type of personalization generally works by collecting data, monitoring learning activity, comparing that activity with other learner behavior, and predicting what the user would like to do or see next.

A comprehensive and complete mode of personalization which, at this point in time, exists mostly on the experimental level, and is going to be a hot research subject in the following years is so called "whole-person personalization" (Devedžić, 2006) which seeks to understand the deep-seated psychological sources (more than the conventional cognitive-based prescriptions) impacting differences in learning behavior, make predictions about delivering content, and deliver content specifically to help the learner achieve learning objectives and more importantly, improve learning ability and enhance online learning relationships. As the individual learns, the system also learns as it collects data, tracks progress, and compares responses and common patterns to improve responses, i.e., it becomes more precise over time. In its most sophisticated form, whole-person personalization requires real-time personalization to modify responses to a learner based on a changing perception throughout the learning experiences, as it occurs (like an instructor in the box).

As another future orientation in personalization research it is worth to point out the "Learning Orientation Model" presented in (Martinez, 2002) which is an adult learning model that considers key sources for individual learning differences. In the last ten years discoveries in the neurosciences have revealed the extraordinary complexities of brain activity when interacting dynamically with the learning environment and situation. These discoveries highlight more than the cognitive element. They explore the dominant power of emotions, intentions, and social factors on learning, and the very human variability of learning. The challenge is to use this research for instructional design, and create methodologies and strategies to personalize learning. To achieve this requires adapting and providing online learning that supports individual differences economically and efficiently. The Learning Orientation Model portrays characteristics, influences, and relationships between three key construct factors: (1) conative (emotions) and affective (intentions) intrinsic motivational aspects, (2) self-directed strategic planning and committed learning effort, and (3) learning autonomy. Combined, these three factors greatly influence an individual's general approach to learning. This model offers explanations for fundamental learning differences, and suggests specific strategies for accommodating learning needs for audiences differentiated by learning type. The Learning Orientation Model describes four dominant learning types. The four learning orientations are (a) transforming learners, (b) performing learners, (c) conforming learners, and (d) resistant learners. Learning orientations are an effective way to segment the audience according to higher-order psychological factors (e.g., affective, conative, and social outlooks). These factors foster how we develop, manage, and sometimes override our cognitive learning preferences, strategies, and skills.

QUALITY IN LIFELONG LEARNING

American Society for Quality, Education Division developed an interesting approach to measure and certify the "self-directed lifelong learning" process (Schoening, 2002). Its fundamental concept is that the ISO-9000 approach to quality management, already being developed by leading schools, can be extended to individual learning. Self-directed Lifelong Learning is actually a set of interrelated processes. Since Quality Assurance has proven to be an effective approach to improving any process, on any scale, of any size organization this should be true even for a one-person organization, which a learner is considered to be in this approach.

Self-directed or self-managed learning doesn't just happen; it must (as the name implies) be managed. This requires the learner to have a Quality Management System. A typical learner would have a system to manage the following:

- Establishment of learning goals, objectives, and overall life directions
- Identification of customers (teachers, parents, self, future spouse/family, future school, future employer)
- Definition of key processes (study for test, write report, lead team project, completed research paper, prepare/present presentation, research career opportunities, establish learning requirements, design learning experience.)
- Execution of processes (where the actual learning takes place)
- Maintenance of records (of processes followed)
- Continual improvement of the system
- Completion of regular self-audits of overall system

The working group of American Society for Quality, Education Division (Schoening, 2002) imply that a learner can achieve ISO9001:2000 registration, which will assure schools, employers and other stakeholders of his/her capability to manage his/her own learning processes. Although this could be a realistic approach for some groups of lifelong learners, it has, by the opinion of the author, small potentials for broad lifelong learning society.

Quality in E-learning

The market for e-learning content has not taken off as has been predicted by analysts time and time again. One of the main reason for this is it is very difficult for "learning customers" to assess the quality of the puzzling array of courses and programs offered on the Internet. Even if the customers choose brand names such as well known universities providing tried and tested content, all too often the didactical quality or the technical implementation of the offerings is disappointing.

How to define the "quality in e-learning"? This is actually a broad concept which has no unified guidelines. In the publications on e-learning the quality is often mentioned as one of the most important issues, but it is rarely described what the authors had in mind when using this term. Clearly, the quality of an e-learning educational offering depends not only on products, such as learning material, or services, but also on the interaction of the learner with contents, tasks, tutors and other learners.

Being the cofounder of the "European Foundation for Quality in eLearning" (EFQUEL - http://www.qualityfoundation.org/), its conclusions will be recognized in the following explanation of the quality in e-learning. One of the common views in the debates with some of the cited authors in the last four years was the agreement that the "learner orientation" is the central one when referring to quality, but the other perspectives (teachers, learning institutions, government, parents, etc.) must not be neglected.

From the learner's point of view the quality can be described as the ability to provide a learning experience which is tailored to the learners needs in the frame of the existing context conditions, e.g. the university or workplace (similar to the quality definitions which view quality as 'fitness for purpose'). Nevertheless one has to add right away that so far, it is unclear which learner variables/characteristics have which impact on e-learning. Quality in this sense is more than just an evaluation at the end of a course. It is a comprehensive concept which concerns all areas of e-learning. It is a concept which builds the foundation for all provision of e-learning, and which is based on all processes of e-learning provision.

According to (Ehlers, 2007) we have to answer several questions here: the first one that we are asking in the scope of this concept is: Who has to be involved in the quality development process? The participating group of persons, the stakeholders, would be obviously the teachers themselves and the students, learning in the course plus parents, employers, school management, government and also some others. It is important to take into account the views and perspectives of relevant actors and weigh their participation.

The second question would be: What is the object of quality development? Let's say that the most imperative object of quality development (by far not the only one) is a new learning program. A program is a complex construct of objectives, materials, methodologies, organization and structure. The ISO reference Framework (ISO SC36, Information Technology for Learning, Education, and Training, 2004) is breaking down the processes necessary to develop an e-learning program. When taking a look to the set of matters (Fig.2) one can see that the space of quality is clearly multidimensional. A concise operationalization is therefore necessary to isolate certain objects (e.g. the course structure, materials, learning objectives, etc.) in order to enter into a straight negotiation process about how these processes should be carried out properly.

In a next step we would then have to answer the question: How is quality defined for each process step? This question relates to possible quality models, e.g. pedagogical instruction design models or technical- or business models. At this stage quality development needs norms and values which show 'good' quality. These can be specified in criteria catalogues or other published guidelines. The last step of this process is a "negotiation" where all stakeholders present their view and perspectives. Questions of responsibility have to be clarified in this process and a consensus has to be made. According to the model from Ehlers and Pawlowski (Ehlers and Pawlowski, 2004), quality development takes place as a sequence of four steps which involve (a) a needs analysis, (b) a decision process, (c) a realization phase and (d) an incorporation phase. In this profoundly defined Quality development space there are 4 dimensions of quality: experience, analysis, innovation and knowledge. Please consult the cited reference for a detailed presentation of this model.

- 1 Needs Analysis
- 1.1 Initiation
- 1.2 Stakeholders definition
- 1.3 Definition of objectives
- 1.4 Demand analysis

- 2 Framework analysis
- 2.1 Analysis of the external context
- 2.2 Qualifications
- 2.3 Resources (Budget, Schedule)
- 2.4 Environment

- 3 Design / Conception
- 3.1 Learning objectives
- 3.2 Concept of the contents
- 3.3 Didactic Concept / Methods
- 3.4 Roles
- 3.5 Organizational Concept

- 3.6 Technical Concept
- 3.7 Design Concept
- 3.8 Media concept
- 3.9 Communication concept
- 3.10 Test / Evaluation

- 4 Development / Production
- 4.1 Content realization
- 4.2 Design realization
- 4.3 Technical realization
- 4.4 Media realization

- 5 Implementation
- 5.1 Testing
- 5.2 Change Control
- 5.3 Activation
- 5.4 Technical Environment
- 5.5 Organization
- 5.6 Service concept

- 6 Learning Process / Realization
- 6.1 Administration
- 6.2 Learning activities
- 6.3 Support of learning activities
- 6.4 Review of Competency Level
- 6.5 Support of transfer

- 7 Evaluation
- 7.1 Evaluation planning
- 7.2 Performance evaluation
- 7.3 Data Analysis

- 8 Optimization / Improvement

Figure 2. All processes necessary to develop a new e-learning program according to ISO (document SC36 published in 2004).

As a concluding remark we could say that quality "mark" in e-learning cannot be assessed in the evaluation phase at the end of a course, but quality development rather has to be viewed as a key aspect, occurring in every single development and delivery process of e-learning courses and programs.

Quality of electronic learning material (e-content)

In the whole concept of quality presented in the previous chapter one aspect deserves a more thorough treatment. Namely in the practice of lifelong learning the quality of e-content it is very often the only quality issue. This happens when the learner is "exposed" only to the developed e-content (without the interaction of learning institution, teacher or mentor) found in some of the open content initiative databases or just anywhere else in the web space. Though the quality of the learning process in this case is repeatedly argued about, this is a reality; today this is still the most widespread way of lifelong learning.

In the process of e-content quality evaluation two basic aims are generally followed: 1. To assist the users of different materials treasuries in the selection of appropriate material and 2. To motivate authors for the production of higher quality materials through awarding quality labels.

On the basis of authors' experience with the evaluation of hundreds of e-content units in the scope of national evaluation system (presented in Dinevski et al., 2006) and consulting several institutional e-content quality assessment procedures, the evaluation of the following e-content elements is suggested:

1. Technical implementation and compatibility evaluation

Those elements of e-materials are to be focused upon that specifically determine the quality of production, installation, upgrading, and uninstallation in different systems and environments: availability of learning materials, installation / use preparation, registration, starting the programme / environment / use of material; uninstallation / end of use, interoperability;

2. Production quality evaluation

The quality of the production of e-material is considered, not only regarding technical excellence, but also the use of techniques and technologies for reaching the aim of the e-material (text quality, graphics quality, quality of visual presentation, use of multimedia ...): legibility and clarity of the text, grammatical correctness of the text, consistent use of styles, clarity and organization of presentation on the screen, good use of frames, hyperlinks, lists;

3. User interface evaluation

Planning a user interface is a demanding task and its quality is crucial to the success of e-material. E-learning interface is specific in the fact that in order to ensure quality it has to enable both the view of the learner and the educator. Therefore the following points are evaluated separately: orientation, possibility of tracking, navigation, additional navigation / organization services, support.

4. Content and didactical value evaluation

Didactical quality is probably the most important point in the view of education. We are aware that this part of quality assessment is the least comprehensive and will have to be upgraded. Here the evaluation focuses upon learning content, that is, connections between learning aims, content, methods, and the learner. E.g. the description of the aim of use of learning material, definition of the learning aims, the conformity of learning aims and the content of the learning material, presentation and clarity of the topic regarding the support of the learning process, use of diverse learning methods, the possibilities of testing and implementing knowledge, possibilities for evaluation and high-quality self-evaluation of the newly acquired knowledge.

OPEN EDUCATIONAL RESOURCES IN E-LEARNING

At present a world-wide movement is developing which promotes unencumbered open access to digital resources such as content and software-based tools to be used as a means of promoting education and lifelong learning. This movement forms part of a broader wave of initiatives that actively promote the "Commons" such as natural resources, public spaces, cultural heritage and access to knowledge that are understood to be part of, and to be preserved for, the common good of society. (Barnes et al., 2006)

To relevantly describe the meaning of the Open educational resources movement for lifelong learning we have to introduce the Open source and Open standards first.

Open source model

The Open Source (OS) model as defined by Open Source Initiative (OSI - http://www.opensource.org/) has a lot to offer. It's a way to build open standards as actual software, rather than paper documents. It's a way that many companies and individuals can collaborate on a product that none of them could achieve alone. It is proved (the references are listed at the mentioned OSI web page) that OS generally means higher security and higher reliability. The real-world evidence shows that OS also brings robustness, clear flexibility and higher quality if compared to closed software in general. In the "Bazaar-mode" development as described in the highly cited and excellent source on OS philosophy "The Cathedral and the Bazaar" (http://www.catb.org/~esr/writings/cathedral-bazaar/) one can expect higher development speed and lower overhead.

What is the relationship between open source software and open standards? Open source software is based on open distribution of the source code that forms the software's foundations. This means that any technically competent programmer can examine the inner works of the source code, and potentially make changes to the operation to the software. Open source software is typically provided free of charge or with a nominal distribution cost. Open standards are transparent descriptions of data and behavior that form the basis of interoperability. Interoperability is the ability of different software systems to exchange information in such a way that they can both act in equivalent ways on the information, leading to equivalent user outcomes. In practice, interoperability means that users are not locked to any one software system – they can substitute a standards-compliant system for another standards-compliant system. Open standards can be implemented by commercial systems and open source systems alike.

In the 1990s open source software had success in horizontal applications, or applications that are useful in many different industries. These applications include operating systems, web servers, enterprise resource planning and customer relationship management. But open source has had less impact vertically, in applications specific to one single industry, such as e-learning. In addition, open source software tended to focus on rapid innovation rather than the slower consensus-building approach which is typical of open standards.

Open source software has become mainstream today. Applications such as the Firefox Web browser, Apache Web server, Linux operating system, MySQL database platform, and PHP programming language continue to gain popularity. Most importantly, these applications often equal or even surpass the quality of well-known commercial, proprietary software.

Open source and open standards in e-learning

E-learning technology went trough intense early development without standards or open source software; e-learning standards were initially developed without widespread vendor adoption or open source software examples.

While open source software has both historical and philosophical roots within universities, e-learning was not one of the major focus areas of the early open source software movement. The early development of e-learning technology was based on the rise of the web and the widespread adoption of e-learning software and courses, especially Learning Management Systems such as WebCT and Blackboard in the education sector, and Saba,

Click2Learn, and others in corporate training. On the other hand there are early attempts to create open standards for e-learning software and content, driven by specification organizations such as IMS Global Learning Consortium, AICC and ADL, and relevant committees of international standards bodies such as the IEEE LTSC. Despite the potential relevance of these open standards for the proprietary e-learning systems, the consistent adoption of e-learning standards by LMS vendors was slow, particularly in the education sector.

When advocating OS in e-learning applications most of the readers will search for the benefits of the "customers" instead those of developers. What is the main advantage that the OS applications brings to the educational and training institutions? Generally the benefits of open source in e-learning are (Dooly, 2005): low initial cost, flexibility and customizability, extensive active user communities, multi-platform capabilities, adherence to standards and tendency to use and link to other open source software.

The past decade have seen wider adoption of standards by e-learning vendors, especially in corporate training through the adoption of the Shareable Content Object Reference Model (SCORM) from ADL, which builds on work from IMS and AICC. At the same time, there are a number of solid open source software development initiatives, especially in the LMS market like Moodle, OpenUSS, Ilias, Claroline, Dokeos and many others including the Sakai project in the US which is a good example where a consortium of universities is working together to develop a learning environment.

Open source software is already being used by educational institutions not only for basic IT infrastructures but also for educational applications such as Learning Management Systems (LMS), Learning Content Management Systems (LCMS), course authoring tools, tools to create media elements such as animations, audio, and video clips, browsers and players to present content and courseware libraries.

Recent empirical evidence comes from the OSS Watch Survey 2006, conducted by the University of Oxford's Research Technologies Services, with 103 ICT managers responding from UK Higher Education and Further Education institutions. The survey found that more than three quarters (77%) consider open source options when engaging in IT procurement exercises. The most important reasons for choosing OSS are an expected lower total cost of ownership (74%), lower likelihood of getting "locked in" by a software provider (63%), better interoperability with other products (59%), and the possibility to migrate data better across systems (52%). The use of OSS is most common for database servers (62% of institutions), Web servers (59%) and operating systems (56%); most institutions that use OSS on their servers rely on in-house support for the OSS. Of particular interest are the results regarding the use of Virtual Learning Environments, of which the two proprietary systems Blackboard and WebCT and the open source VLE Moodle were considered in the survey. In the Higher Education institutions there is a greater presence of the proprietary systems (WebCT 20%, Blackboard 17%) than the OSS Moodle (9%). However, 56% of the Further Education institutions make use of Moodle, while Blackboard is used by 21% and WebCT by 3%.

Open educational resources movement

The term Open Educational Resources (OER) has been introduced and promoted in the context of UNESCO's aim to provide free access to educational resources on a global scale. The term was first adopted by UNESCO in 2002 in the final report of the Forum on the Impact of Open Courseware for Higher Education in Developing Countries, to refer to "the open provision of educational resources, enabled by information and communication technologies, for consultation, use and adaptation by a community of users for non-commercial purposes". (UNESCO 2002).

With regard to this definition, it is important to note that "resources" are not limited to content, but comprise "three major areas of activity: the creation of open source software and development tools, the creation and provision of open course content, and the development of standards and licensing tools. The outputs of all three may be grouped together under the term Open Educational Resources (OER)." There are also much broader interpretations of Open Educational Resources (OER). For example, the OECD's Centre for Educational Research and Innovation (CERI) states on the webpage of their OER survey that this would comprise "Open courseware and content; Open software tools; Open material for e-learning capacity building of faculty staff; Repositories of learning objects; Free educational courses".

The most descriptive and practical definition comes from the cited report (Gesser, 2007) which tries do define it with the statement that it is based on the following core attributes:

- that access to open content (including metadata) is provided free of charge for educational institutions, content services, and the end-users such as teachers, students and lifelong learners;
- that the content is liberally licensed for re-use in educational activities, favorably free from restrictions to modify, combine and repurpose the content; consequently, that the content should ideally be designed for easy re-use in that open content standards and formats are being employed;
- that for educational systems/tools software is used for which the source code is available (i.e. Open Source software) and that there are open Application Programming Interfaces (open APIs) and authorizations to re-use Web-based services as well as resources (e.g. for educational content RSS feeds).

The definition is concluded by the very brave statement: It is expected that adherence to the principles outlined above can bring about tremendous benefits for education and lifelong learning in a knowledge society, not least of which is to eliminate many inefficiencies and bottlenecks in the current provision of e-learning opportunities. For the detailed set of discovered benefits of OER as seen from the viewpoints of educational networks, teachers and students please consult the report itself.

It is pretty obviously that pedagogical model is not a key point in the OER as such. The discussion of OER has often been dominated by technical and management considerations rather than the perspectives of educational practitioners. To achieve the ambitious goals of the presented lifelong learning philosophy the didactics and pedagogy must be deeply involved into the practical solutions. This subject requires a wide and integral aproach that exceeds the scope of this paper. Obviously serious research will have to be invested in the direction of pedagogical models in lifelong learning.

Open educational resources idea and initiatives

With reference to the OER movement, the William and Flora Hewlett Foundation justifies their investment in OER as follows: "At the heart of the movement toward Open Educational Resources is the simple and powerful idea that the world's knowledge is a public good and that technology in general and the Worldwide Web in particular provide an extraordinary opportunity for everyone to share, use, and re-use knowledge. OER are the parts of that knowledge that comprise the fundamental components of education – content and tools for teaching, learning and research."

There is an established understanding that easy access to educational resources is required to promote lifelong learning by active learners of all ages. Also the role of such access in reducing social inequalities, fostering social inclusion of migrants, and supporting education in developing countries is often acknowledged. (Halimi 2005). No doubt that open access to resources is an important element in educational innovation; on the other hand it is also clear that it doesn't solve all the problems. The decisive factor is that open educational practices are fostered by the appropriate institutional culture and mindset and supportive environment, including easily accessible and shareable tools, services and content.

There are a variety of "Open questions" on this subject among which the most important is: Who (and why) will create and provide educational content? The answer to this question is not easy. Probably the public and politics must answer it (and not the publishers).

Today, one can find several repositories of learning and teaching resources that are accessible freely by anybody. They are of several kinds but mostly project based with a lot of volunteering work invested. The amount of the learning material us usually very low and the diversity is limited.

Other type of repositories is in a way "public", but not free for all. The most important are those initiated by national Ministries of Education or other political initiatives. The special place has the European SchoolNet (EUN), which is a collaboration of ministry departments and national educational networks throughout Europe. The initial idea of the EUN, which was started in 1996, was a "bottom-up" process with the EUN as a central access point to educational resources from the national and regional networks. This included the idea that in the emerging digital environment educators would themselves increasingly create and provide content to a common pool of teaching and learning materials. Over the following years the EUN, and the national educational networks, learned that there are considerable barriers to an effective participation of educators in pooling educational resources. Consequently, the approach shifted towards a more "top-down" approach, which over the years has been massively supported through project-based EU funding. Today, the core longer-term initiative of the EUN is the European Learning Resource Exchange (LRE), which will be accessible to all interested Ministries of Education participating in the EUN and other public and private sector owners of educational content repositories. Important ongoing work is the creation of the LRE Application Profile, which provides a set of metadata elements and vocabularies that are to be used by all participating learning object repositories.

The MIT Open Courseware initiative, which started in "early" 2001, was one of the first and the most well-known all over the world as a single institution effort for open content (in March 2006 about two thirds of MIT professors had their courses online). In higher education, the "MIT broadened" Open Courseware Consortium with over 100 participating universities from all over the world seems to have reached a critical mass for a serious breakthrough. There are also several other excellent repositories initiatives, like the US-based Connexions platform which has about 200,000 unique visitors per month who come from over 150 countries.

The special place among the "big plans" deserves the Google Print Library Project which has the ambitious aim of digitally scanning millions of books from the collections of major American libraries and making them searchable online via Google's search engine.

On a global level an encouraging example is the recent establishment of the Global Learning Objects Brokered Exchange (GLOBE) initiative, which is a collaboration of ARIADNE (Europe), Education.au (Australia), eduSource Canada, MERLOT (USA) and NIME (Japan).

To come to the big repositories of high quality content which will be free for all, still a lot of answers have to be answered and finding them will be one of the major research trends in lifelong learning and e-learning in the following years. Clearly open content itself (though high quality one and even localized for the end user) is not enough for effective lifelong learning. Before addressing useful open content, tools and licenses, one must consider the pedagogical approaches in which these resources could make a difference, i.e. by being used in innovative forms of teaching and learning.

The nature of open content

Open digital content has some fundamental differences when compared to the published commercial content. The roles of all the stakeholders in learning processes are different when open content is used as a learning material. Though there are several licensing, accessibility and copyright solutions for open content, we can draw some general principles of its lifecycle (creating, using, modifying, sharing, licensing, controlling quality and managing): Open content obviously has many authors, including professional authors, teachers and also learners and is therefore in the constant improvement process. Open content quality control is in the hands of learners and teachers (and is conducted simultaneously with the learning process) instead of instructional experts. The learning units are constantly evolving with various granularity of interlinked material, variety of micro content from different content feeds is present and updates are frequent. Wikis, Weblogs, RSS feeders and aggregators, are the authoring tools together with content acquisition and creativity tools which results in different formats and usually poor metadata structures. The creation of rich metadata will remain costly and OER initiatives will need to strike the right balance between the achievable richness of metadata and the costs they incur (e.g. due to the need to employ skilled personnel).

Open content licensing is a separate story, where the leading role is that of "Creative Commons" (CC). As a response to "open content unfriendly" commercial "all rights reserved" license, the non-profit organization Creative Commons provides an easy to use mechanism for choosing and attaching to a creative work one of six standardized CC licenses from the most liberal "Attribution" to more restrictive (but still open) "Attribution–NonCommercial–NoDerivatives". Creative Commons licenses have already been "ported" into several legal jurisdictions around the world and are in the process of integration into many others (http://creativecommons.org/worldwide).

The vision for the future of open educational resources

In the excellent recent publication "Open Educational Practices and Resources" (Gesser, 2007) the vision for the situation in "Open educational resources in e-learning in 2012" is presented approximately like this:

Educational institutions from primary schools to universities and lifelong learning providers will foster and support open learning practices that help equip teachers, students and workers with the competences, knowledge and skills to participate successfully in the knowledge society. Educational institutions and teachers will understand their key role in a knowledge society much better, and will be encouraged to employ and experiment with innovative educational practices making use of a rich pool of open resources. The current dominant paradigm of teacher- and subject-centred learning in formal education will have given way to a learner-centred, competency-based paradigm. In particular, learning communities and collaborative approaches will flourish, making use of a new generation of easy-to-use Web-based tools and information services (e.g. Wikis for collaborative work on study projects, Weblogs for sharing ideas and comments, RSS feeders and aggregators for receiving current "real world" information, etc.). Open and easy access to e-content repositories of academic and educational institutions, public sector information agencies, libraries, museums and other cultural institutions will allow for making use of information sources as needed to carry out creative projects and study work. As a rule, all educational material as well as research publications, the creation of which has been publicly (co-)funded, will have to be published under an appropriate open content license. With respect to Open Educational Resources, teachers will not be simple "end-users", as they understand the importance of continuous questioning, evaluation and improvement of educational practices and resources. As members of communities of interest in different disciplines and subjects, they will share experiences, lessons learned and suggestions on how to better foster the development of students' as well as their own competences and skills.

CONCLUSION

It is more or less evident that the lifelong learning in general and the university continuing education will continue to experience the consistent expansion in the future. Being on the top of the political agenda, lifelong learning is presented as an answer to the challenges of globalization, new technologies and demographic developments. But to reach the goal presented in the introduction: "free lifelong learning for all everywhere at all times", several questions will have to be answered and lifelong learning processes will still have to undergo a vast development in several areas. All-encompassing lifelong learning will be very difficult to achieve even for the most developed North American and European societies.

There is practically no doubt that the foundation of lifelong learning provision is going to be the information technology and e-learning together with the emerging mobile learning technologies. E-learning has a major impact on thinking and pedagogical practice through the whole educational system. It creates new means of communication and even social relations between students and teachers and as a consequence new ways of knowledge transfer, for example, collaborative learning are evolving. As several shifts of the learning process are identified, one can conclude that the influence of e-learning on education in general will be very extensive.

As far as technology development of e-learning is concerned we are still very much in the experimental stage of creating virtual e-learning environments. Much still needs to be learned about designing successful learning solutions. Nevertheless, the web offers a useful technology and environment for personalized learning, especially because learners can be uniquely identified, content can be mass customized, and subsequent progress can be monitored, supported and assessed. Technologically, researchers make progress in realizing the personalized learning dream. The missing link is the instructional design perspective that understands the impact of emotions and intentions and embraces a truly personal understanding of how individuals want or intend to learn differently. From the perspective of ICT itself a new vision can be found in the current development and usage of "social software" based tools and services (Web 2.0) that are highly supportive at e-learning practices and processes. Social software, such as Weblogs, Wikis, RSS-based content syndication, social book-marking, podcasting, etc., shows several positive effects within the realm of education. Wider adoption for educational and lifelong learning purposes could have a huge innovative impact as these tools and services are ideally suited to learner-centred as well as collaborative approaches in developing competences required in our knowledge society.

A systematical and standardized approach to quality issues in e-learning is one of the critical steps of lifelong learning development. Clearly, the quality of an e-learning educational offering depends not only on products, such as learning material or services, but also on the interaction of the learner with contents, tasks, tutors and other learners. E-content quality is the most important from the lifelong learning perspective.

Author believes that the most important e-learning development directions, in order to come to the lifelong learning reality, are open access to learning, open source software, open standards, and open educational resources. To come to the big repositories of high quality content which will be free for all, still a lot of answers have to be answered and finding them will be one of the major research trends in lifelong learning and e-learning in the following years. Clearly open content itself (though high quality one and even localized for the end user) is not enough for effective lifelong learning. Before addressing useful open content, tools and licenses, one must consider the pedagogical approaches in which these resources could make a difference, i.e. by being used in innovative forms of teaching and learning.

REFERENCES

Barnes, P., Bollier, D., Rowe, J. (2006). *The Commons Rising*. Tomales Bay Institute http://onthecommons.org/files/Commons_Rising_06.pdf, accessed 1.1.2007.

Becher, T. (1993). Meeting the Contract. The Role of European Universities in Continuing Education and Training, Brussels. *European Centre for the Strategic Managmenet of Universities*, p. 11.

Brennan, M. (2000). Organisational structures: European University Continuing Education: The Managers' Handbook. Liège. *EUCEN*,2000, p. 51-104.

Chou, H. W., and Wang, Y. F. (1999). Effects of learning style and training method on computer attitude and performance in World Wide Web page design training. *Journal of Educational Computing Research*, vol 21, p. 325-344.

Coffield, F. (2004). Breaking the Consensus; Lifelong Learning as Social Control. *British Educational Research Journal*, 25, 4, pp 479-99, p. 487.

Dalziel, J. (2003). Open standards versus Open source in e-learning. *Educause Quarterly*, Vol 4, 2003.

Devedžić, V. (2006). *Semantic Web and Education*. New York, USA: Springer US.

Dinevski, D., Ojsteršek, M., Plenković, M. (2003). Information technology platform for e-learning implementation. The 10th International Scientific Conference, Opatija, 28th-30th June 2003. *Society and Technology*, 2003, Rijeka: Sveučilište, pp. 148-158.

Dinevski D., Plenković, M. (2002). *Modern University and E-learning, Media Culture and Public Relations*, Croatia, 2, pp. 137-146.

Dinevski, D. (2004). Personalization of the e-learning systems in the service of the learner, The proceedings of the Third EDEN Research Workshop, march 2004, Bibliotheks- und Informationssystem der Universitaet Oldenburg - Verlag, pp. 536-542.

Dinevski, D., Brodnik, A. (2005). Lifelong *learning technology innovations for efficient adult education*. Florjančič, J. and Paape, B. W., editors. Personnel and management : selected topics. Frankfurt am Main: P. Lang, pp. 135-144.

Dinevski, D., Jakončič-Faganel, J., Lokar, M., Žnidaršič, B. (2006). *Quality Assessment Of Electronic Learning Material*. Conference Knowledge management in organizations KMO 2006, Maribor, Slovenia 13.-14. June 2006.

Dinevski, D., Vesenjak Dinevski, I. (2004). The concepts of University lifelong provision in Europe. *Transition studies review*, Springer Verlag Wien, Vol. 11, No. 3., pp 227-235.

Dooly, B. J. (2005). Open Source E-Learning: Alternatives to Proprietary Tools, Systems, and Courseware. *Brandon Hall Research*, Sunnyvale, CA.

Edwards, C. (1993). Lifelong learning, Communications of the Association for Computing Machinery, New York, USA, Vol. 36, Iss. 5, p. 76.

Ehlers, U.D. (2007). *Towards greater quality literacy in a eLearning Europe, eLearning Papers* • www.elearningpapers.eu, Vol 2, N° 1 • January 2007 • ISSN 1887-1542.

Ehlers, U.D., Pawlowski, J.M. (2004). E-Learning-Quality: A Decision Support Model for European Quality Approaches, In: Fietz, G., Godio, C., Mason, R. eLearning for international Markets. Development and Use of eLearning in Europa. *Bielefeld*.

European Commision. (2001). *Making a European Area of Lifelong Learning a Reality*. COM Brussels, Commision of European Communities, p. 9.

European ODL Liaison Committee. (2004). *Distance Learning and eLearning in European Policy and Practice: The Vision and the Reality.* Policy Paper approved by the Member Networks; released 17 November 2004, http://www.odl-liaison.org/pages. php?PN=policypaper_2004 , accessed 1.1.2007.

European ODL Liaison Committee (2006). Learning Innovation for the Adapted Lisbon Agenda. *Policy Paper.* http://www.odl-liaison.org/pages.php?PN=policypaper_2006 , accessed 1.1.2007.

Fiorina, L., Colombo, B., Bartolomeo, A., Antonietti, A.(2004). *The Influence of Thinking Style and Modelling Hints on Personalisation of Hypertext Browsing.* The proceedings of the Third EDEN Research Workshop, march 2004, Bibliotheks- und Informationssystem der Universitaet Oldenburg - Verlag, pg. 543-548.

Gesser, G., ed. (2007). *Open Educational Practices and Resources.* Published by Open e-Learning Content Observatory Services project, Salzburg, Austria, ISBN 3-902448-08-3.

Ghosh, R. A. (2006). Economic impact of open source software on innovation and the competitiveness of the Information and Communication Technologies (ICT) sector in the EU, MERIT 2006, http://ec.europa.eu/enterprise/ict/policy/doc/2006-11-20-flossimpact.pdf, accessed 1.1.2007.

Greer T. H., Murtaza M. B. (2003). Web personalization: The impact of perceived innovation characteristics on the intention to use pesonalization, The Journal of Computer Information Systems. Stillwater: Spring 2003. Vol. 43, Iss. 3; pg. 50

Halimi, Suzy (2005). *Lifelong learning for equity and social cohesion: A new challenge for Higher Education.* In: McIntosh, Christopher (Ed.): Lifelong Learning and Distance Higher Education. Commonwealth of Learning /UNESCO 2005, pp. 11-22, http://www. col.org/colweb/webdav/site/myjahiasite/shared/docs/PSeries_LLLDHE.pdf

Hedge, N., Hayward, L. (2004). Redefining Roles: university e-learning contributing to lifelong learning in a networked world, E-learning, Vol. 1, No. 1, ISSN 1741-8887, *Symposium Journals*, 2004

Henry P. (2001). E-learning technology, content and services. *Education + Training*, Vol. 43, No. 4, MCB University Press, USA.

International Organization for Standardization / International Electrotechnical Commission: ISO/IEC, FCD 19796-1. *Information Technology — Quality Management, Assurance and Metrics-Part 1: General Approach, Online accesible*: http://jtc1sc36.org/doc/36N0771. pdf. Download 2007-03-01, accessed 1.1.2007.

Keegan D. (1991). *Foundations of Distance Education. Second edition.* Routledge Education, London and New York, USA, (p. 7).

Kramer J., Noronha S., Vergo J. (2000). *A user-centered design approach to personalization.* Association for Computing Machinery. Communications of the ACM. New York, USA: Vol. 43, Iss. 8; pg. 44.

Lockwood F. (ed), Gooley A. (ed) (2001*). Innovation in Open and Distance Learning.* Kogan Page, London,.

Masie E.(2000). *Portals, Portals, Everywhere!, Education at a distance.* Vol. 14, No. 2, Riverside, CA, USA.

MECA-ODL – *Methodological Guide for the Analysis of Quality in Open and Distance Learning delivered via Internet* (2003), ISBN: 84-921190-9-8, Available online at: http://www.adeit.uv.es/mecaodl/, download 1.3.2007.

Moore M.M., Tait, A. (2002). *Open and Distance Learning – Trends, Policy and Strategy Considerations*, UNESCO Division of Higher Education, Paris.

Moore, M.M., Tait, A. (2002). *Open and Distance Learning – Trends, Policy and Strategy Considerations*. UNESCO Division of Higher Education, Paris, (p. 88).

Mrtinez, M. (2002). What is personalized learning? *The eLearning Developers' Journal*, Online accesible at: www.elearningguild.com, accessed 1.1.2007.

Mulvenna M. D., Anand S. S., Buchner A. G. (2000). Personalization on the Net using Web mining, Association for Computing Machinery. *Communications of the ACM*, New York, USA, Vol. 43, Iss. 8; pg. 122.

O'Reilly, Tim. (2005). *What is Web 2.0: Design Patterns and Business Models for the Next Generation of Software* (30 September 2005), http://www.oreillynet.com/pub/a/oreilly/tim/news/2005/09/30/what-is-web-20.html, accessed 1.1.2007.

Osborne, M., Thoma, E. (eds). (2003). *Lifelong learning in a changing continent*, NIACE, England and Wales, p. 4.

OSS Watch Survey 2006 (2007), http://www.oss-watch.ac.uk/studies/survey2006/survey2006report.xml, accessed 1.1.2007.

Regan, E.A., (1998), Lifelong learning and performance: Linking academia and Business, *Office Systems Research Journal*, Springfield 1998, Vol. 16, Iss. 2, p. 43.

Richardson, Will. (2006). Blogs, Wikis, Podcasts and Other Powerful Web Tools for Classrooms. Thousand Oaks, CA: Corwin Press

Richardson, Will. (2006b).*The New Face of Learning*. What happens to time-worn concepts of classrooms and teaching when we can now go online and learn anything, anywhere, anytime? (October 2006), http://www.edutopia.org/magazine/ed1article.php?id=Art_1648andissue=oct_06 , accessed 1.1.2007.

Schoening. (2002). Creating Lifelong Learners through Quality Assurance. *J. Educational Technology and Society* , 5(1), ISSN 1436-4522

Stephenson J. (2001). *Teaching and Learning Online*. Kogan Page, London.

Tamkin, P. (1997). Lifelong learning: a question of privilege? *Industrial and Commercial Training*. Guilsborough: Vol. 29, Iss. 6; p. 184.

Tapscott, D. (1998). *Growing Up Digital: The Rise of the Net Generation*. New York, USA: McGraw-Hill.

Taylor, R. (1990). University Liberal education; a "Great Tradition"? *Adult Learning*, Vol 1, No. 9, pp. 243-245.

UNESCO. (2002). *Forum on the impact of Open Courseware for higher education in developing countries*. Final report. Paris: UNESCO.

Votch V., Linden A. (2000). Do You Know What 'Personalization' Means? Gartner Group Research Note, May 18, 2000.

Zemsky, R., Massy, W. F. (2004). *Thwarted Innovation. What Happened to e-learning and Why*. A Final Report for The Weatherstation Project of The Learning Alliance, http://www.irhe.upenn.edu/Docs/Jun2004/ThwartedInnovation.pdf, accessed 1.1.2007.

In: E-Learning: 21st Century Issues and Challenges
Editor: A.R. Lipshitz and S. P. Parsons

ISBN : 978-1-60456-156-2
©2008 Nova Science Publishers, Inc.

Chapter 7

GUIDING THE DESIGN OF E-LEARNING PROGRAMS: A DESIGN FRAMEWORK FOR CREATIVE LEARNING EXPERIENCES

Sylvia M. Truman[1]

Knowledge Media Institute, The Open University, United Kingdom

ABSTRACT

A question that has gained widespread interest is 'how can learning tasks be structured to encourage creative thinking in the classroom through technology?' Contemporary applications of learning theories towards educational technology design are influenced by constructivist and constructionist learning approaches. This chapter draws upon theories of learning and creativity to provide a design method to encourage creative thinking in the classroom. It is suggested here that learning theories may provide insights towards understanding the creative process. Extending upon this, a generative framework for creative learning is presented which exists as a design support tool in planning lesson materials for the classroom and the design of educational software. An example of how this framework can be applied in the design of educational technology is provided through the instantiation of the framework in a collaborative music composition task.

1. INTRODUCTION

In some instances traditional pedagogy has been concerned with pre-packaged lesson materials delivered from the teacher to the student. Such an approach concerns itself with the passive absorption of knowledge, later tested through examinations. Although this may equip

---

[1] Correspondence to: Knowledge Media Institute, The Open University, United Kingdom
e-mail: s.m.truman@open.ac.uk

students to pass examinations, they may face difficulty when applying concepts to authentic practice (Brown et al., 1989).

With growing advancements in technology, learning programs are commonly used in today's classrooms, however, technology is often misconstrued as a medium for disseminating knowledge to students as opposed to providing a virtual space in which the student is an active participant, exploring a domain for themselves. In order to provide meaningful learning experiences it is important to consider aspects of learning theories in the design of educational technology. This chapter focuses upon constructivist and constructionist perspectives on learning. These perspectives suggest learning is not solely an individual process as people naturally interact with others and their surroundings, and that learning is the outcome of these interactions (Vosniadou, 1996). From a constructionist point of view it is important for students to be actively engaged in personally creating a product meaningful to themselves and others (Papert, 1993; Harel, 1991). Similarly to learning, creativity also involves the active construction of new ideas and content within the social context of other members of the field. A number of scholars have suggested there exists a strong relationship between learning and creativity (i.e. Guilford, 1950; Karnes *et al.,* 1961; Torrance, 1981). Guilford (1950) states that creativity can be considered a sub-type of learning.

Creativity is a phenomenon which was typically characterised by the 'lone genius myth' (Sampson, 1993). Scholars advocated that creativity defies definition due to its multifaceted and complex nature (i.e. Torrance, 1988). Many have argued that creativity resides only within certain 'gifted' individuals (i.e. Ripple, 1989). Contemporary research suggests this is not the case, and it is now widely accepted that every individual possesses creative potential, albeit to differing degrees (Runco & Bahleda, 1986; Sternberg, 1985). Historically, creativity research has focused upon stage models of the creative process as initially proposed by Wallas's four-stage model (Wallas, 1926). Wallas described creativity as progressing through the phases of preparation, incubation, illumination and verification. Preparation concerns immersing oneself in a domain and developing a curiosity about a particular problem (Getzels, 1964). Within this stage an individual will consciously accumulate knowledge and draw upon influences from previous experience. During the incubation phase, conscious thought pertaining to the problem is rested and left to the unconscious mind (Claxton, 1998). Finally, illumination occurs when one experiences a sudden flash of insight (Wallas, 1926) or sudden inspiration (Poincare, 1913). Verification concerns forming judgments pertaining to the creative artefact produced. Wallas noted that during the creative process, an individual could return to earlier phases. This has been supported by subsequent research (i.e. Patrick 1937, Patrick, 1938; Rossman, 1931; Hadamard, 1945).

2. BACKGROUND MOTIVATION: THEORIES OF LEARNING

2.1. Learning theories

Different learning paradigms hold opposing perceptions towards learning. Whereas behaviourism sought to investigate which inputs produced certain outputs of the learning process, cognitivism was concerned with information processing models which focused upon why particular inputs produced certain outputs. Both approaches appear to downplay the contexts in which learning occurs. This has led to more contextualised approaches towards learning such as constructivist and constructionist approaches (Tavangarian *et al.*, 2004). These perspectives offer a more experiential based approach, situating learning in appropriate contexts for the student (Rogers, 1969; Schank, 1995; 1999; Brown *et al.*, 1989). If learning is not situated in a context appropriate to the material being learned, a number of problems may arise. Brown *et al.* (1989) assert that although learning abstract, de-contextualised concepts in the classroom equips students to pass examinations, they may encounter difficulty when applying concepts in authentic practice (Baccarini, 2004). Secondly, students may rely upon particular features of the classroom context in which the task itself may have become embedded. This differentiates the task from authentic activity in the mind of the student. It is therefore emphasised here that learning should be set in a context appropriate to the concepts to be learned.

2.1.1. Contextualised approaches towards learning

Learning is not solely an individual process as people constantly interact with others and their surroundings (Frank, 2005). Learning as a social process is advocated by the Vygotskian School of constructivist learning theory. This school of thought emphasises learning as the outcome of interactions between social agents and the environment (Vosniadou, 1996). Based upon observational scientific studies of learning, Constructivism is associated with cognitive psychology owing to the view of the student constructing their own meanings by actively participating within a domain for themselves (Forrester & Jantzie, 2001; Honebein *et al*, 1996). These theoretical insights emphasise that learning involves the construction of meaning. Therefore, we can define 'learning' as the construction of meaning.

According to the constructivist paradigm, important aspects of learning are as follows: learning is contextual in that one should not learn isolated facts as by nature people learn in relation to what they already know (Schank, 1995). Secondly, one needs knowledge to learn as it is not possible to assimilate new knowledge without having a previous knowledge structure, therefore, the more a student knows, the more they can learn. Efforts to teach must provide direction in association with the student's level of prior knowledge. Thirdly, learning is a self-regulated process as individuals learn at a different rates depending upon their prior knowledge and experience (Bandura, 1986). For the purposes of this body of work, the remainder of this chapter will focus upon constructivist and constructionist learning paradigms.

2.2. Constructivist approaches

Constructivism contrasts with objectivism. From the objectivist perspective, it is assumed that knowledge needs to be transmitted to the student so they can acquire the necessary skills and facts (Tam, 2000). The constructivist approach argues learning is an active process as although information can be acquired through traditional methods, understanding cannot be imparted this way (Schank, 2002; Tam, 2000). Table 1 identifies the core learning principles of constructivism.

Table 1. Core learning principles of constructivism

LEARNING PRINCIPLES	EXPLANATION
Learning is an active process in which the student uses sensory input and constructs meaning out of it.	Learning is not the passive acceptance of knowledge which exists out there. It involves the student engaging with the world. Learning takes place when a student attempts to make sense of the world in which they exist (Raskin, 2005; Von Glaserfeld, 1995; Piaget, 1926; Vygotsky, 1978).
People learn by interacting with the world	Knowledge is perceived as residing in the mind therefore, learning is the consequence of personal interactions with the external world.
People learn as they construct meaning	Learning involves constructing meaning.
Language is fundamental to learning	Students organise their thoughts to communicate ideas which subsequently aids the process of learning (Vygotsky, 1978).
Learning is an individual and social activity	Integral aspects of the learning process include interactions with others and the external environment (Von Glaserfeld & Steffe, 1991). We may learn concepts from others which we may not have discovered by ourselves until later (Vygotsky, 1978).
Learning is contextual	It is important to learn in a context appropriate to the learning material. This is especially important when concepts need to be applied in authentic practice (Brown et al., 1989).
One needs knowledge to learn	It is not possible to assimilate new knowledge without having a previous knowledge structure. The more a student knows, potentially the more they can learn. Efforts to teach must provide direction in association with the student's level of prior knowledge.
Time is important to the process of learning.	Learning is not instantaneous, significant learning takes time.
Learning is a self regulated process	Every individual learns at a different rate depending upon their prior knowledge, experience, intrinsic characteristics and environmental factors imposed on them (Bandura, 1986; Vygotsky, 1978).
Motivation is a key component in learning	Not only is it the case that motivation aids learning, it is essential for learning especially with regard to one's desire to learn (Bandura, 1986; Hein, 1991; Vygotsky, 1978)

With regard to table 1, the points of the constructivist paradigm are clear. Learning is viewed as an individual and social activity in which interactions with others and the external environment are conducive to significant learning (Frank, 2005; Dewey, 1916). Students learn as they learn constructing meaning for themselves through active participation.

2.2.1. Variants of constructivist learning theory

There are a number of variants within constructivism each with a differing emphasis of focus, although these are not mutually exclusive. Table 2 provides an overview of the main issues which will be discussed in this chapter owing to their relevance to the proposed study.

Table 2. Main issues of constructivist learning theory

Issues	Description
Issue one	Learning by constructing meaning internally
Issue two	Social Learning
Issue three	Learning in context
Issue four	Exploratory learning (i.e. learning by doing)

The above issues are discussed in the following subsections.

2.2.1.1. Issue one: learning by constructing meaning

A fundamental theory of development is Piaget's Genetic Epistemology Theory (Piaget, 1972). Piaget's theory focuses upon the development of cognitive structures in children resulting from their personal experiences with their surrounding environment. The theory identifies four developmental stages that children progress through from birth to the age of fifteen. Piaget's work highlights a number of principles describing the development of cognitive structures. Piaget's theory emphasises that learning occurs through reflection. This point has also been highlighted by a number of scholars (i.e. Schon, 1983; Dreyfus & Dreyfus, 1986). Piaget advocates the continuing development of schemata through concepts of assimilation and accommodation and the four stages of intellectual development. These stages are: sensori-motor, pre-operational, concrete operational and formal operations.

With regard to the developmental stages defined by Papert, the sensori-motor stage occurs within the first two years of life. It is suggested that during this time a child will learn the immutability of certain objects existing in their environment (Piaget, 1972). This stage is concerned with sensori-motor action such as sucking, grasping and moving around in the environment to develop an understanding of limits and potentialities of objects existing in the physical world. Piaget suggested that during the pre-operational stage the child moves away from the primary focus of motor actions and begins to form an understanding of aspects symbolically. It is thought that at this stage the child becomes more 'conscious' of the objects they interacted with whilst in the sensori-motor period. During the ages of eight to eleven the child enters the concrete operational period. At this point the child is able to make deductive inferences. These deductions have limitations imposed upon them as they are limited to events which have been observed (Forman, 1980). Within the final stage the child is able to derive deductive inferences from other deductions through the use of operations as the content of thinking.

Reflecting upon the above, important aspects of learning derived from genetic epistemology are:

- Sources of knowledge
- The process of equilibration
- Types of knowledge
- Levels of knowledge

The process of equilibration refers to the way in which a child progresses from one developmental stage to the next through a process of equilibration (Phillips, 1981). During this process the child constructs their own understanding of the world by organising their knowledge as derived from their personal experiences. The process of equilibration allows the child to construct inferences related to their expectations of newly encountered situations. The process of equilibration concerns three steps. Firstly, a disturbance occurs resulting from a conflict between what is expected and what actually occurs. Secondly, the regulation step is reached whereby regulations are used to reduce the disturbance arising from step one. Lastly, adaption occurs allowing the child to adapt to their surrounding environment. The adaption process involves the interaction of two sub-processes referred to as 'assimilation' and 'accommodation'. According to Piaget (1972) the adaption process is vital to learning.

Assimilation allows new scenarios to be interpreted by their relation to existing cognitive structures (i.e. subsuming to an existing schema). Accommodation involves changing the cognitive structure to allow the child to make sense of their environment (i.e. creating a new schema to contain the information). There are a number of implications for education arising from genetic epistemology theory.

Reflecting upon Piaget's work, there are a number of implications for education. Firstly, development can be facilitated by placing the student in learning scenarios which require adaption by means of assimilation and accommodation processes. Secondly, learning materials should be directed at an appropriate developmental level for the student. Piaget's theory of genetic epistemology has proven to be a key contribution to constructivist theory from which subsequent theories have evolved. Piaget's work has been applied to the educational method of constructionism as captured in the following statement by Papert (1999):

> "Children are not empty vessels to be filled with knowledge (as traditional pedagogy has it), but active builders of knowledge – little scientists who are constantly creating and testing their own theories of the world".

Extending upon the above, a number of scholars have suggested that a student's skills and knowledge can be enhanced by learning in collaboration with peers (i.e. Vygotsky, 1978; Crawford, 1996; Hausfather, 1996). This notion is of particular interest to this chapter and is further discussed as follows.

2.2.1.2. Issue two: social learning

Numerous scholars have emphasised that social interaction is paramount to cognitive development as learning occurs through interacting with others. This is thought to enhance the integration of newly acquired concepts into the mental structure of the learner (Derry, 1999; McMahon, 1997; Vygotsky, 1978; Driscoll, 1994). Whereas Piaget implies that development has an end point in the stages of development, Vygotsky (1978) suggests that development is a continual process too complex to be defined in a series of stages. Vygotsky further suggests that this continual process is dependent upon social interaction aiding cognitive development which he refers to as the 'Zone of Proximal Development' (ZPD). The ZPD centres on developing a student's skills through guidance or collaboration.

Vygotsky proposed the ZPD to define the relationship between learning and development. The theory emphasises that learning tasks should be aligned with the developmental level of the student. Vygotsky suggests the mental development of a student is determined by two levels: the 'actual developmental level' and the 'zone of proximal development'. The 'actual developmental level' refers to the level of development of a student's mental function as a result of already completed development cycles. The 'zone of proximal development' refers to the distance between what is currently known and what can be known by the student. Vygotsky (1978) offers a description of the zone of proximal development as follows:

> "It is the distance between the actual development level as determined by independent problem solving and the level of potential development as determined through problem solving under adult guidance or in collaboration with more capable peers…..profound thinkers never entertained the notion that what children can do with the assistance of others might in some sense by more indicative of their mental development than what they can do alone".

According to Vygotsky, learning occurs within the ZPD, forming a bridge between what the student knows today and what they are capable of knowing tomorrow. This reflects the theory's focus upon social interactions and cultural contexts in which shared experiences occur (Crawford, 1996).

According to the theory, learning scenarios directed at a student's actual developmental level will prove ineffective. Instead it is suggested that learning tasks should be targeted a higher developmental level, slightly above the student's level of competence. This is regarded as beneficial as the student would be more likely to rise to the challenge, possibly exhibiting higher levels of motivation. This has many implications in terms of collaborative learning. According to the theory, if students with differing levels of ability work collaboratively, development is dependent upon the social interaction. In order for effective cognitive development to occur, students involved in collaborative learning should be situated at different developmental levels (Driscoll, 1994, Hausfather, 1996).

There are a number of implications for education arising from social development theory. Firstly, learning should be a reciprocal experience for both student and teacher (Hausfather, 1996). The role of the teacher should be that of collaborator and guider as opposed to disseminator of knowledge (Tavangarian *et al.,* 2004). Secondly, it is important for teachers to engage and motivate students in their learning and to provide learning tasks in which the student's level of knowledge is increased. The concept of the ZPD advocates that discrepancies between the student's progress and the solution are identified, and that the teacher should provide guidance where appropriate. This is important as the teacher needs to be mindful of the student's developmental level in order to modify their level of guidance in response to the student's performance. Thirdly, it is equally important that assessment methods consider the ZPD to effectively target the student's actual development level and their level of potential development. This is especially important as two students may possess the same level of actual development, but may differ in terms of their potential development. Finally, learning tasks should be designed to encourage interactions between the student, peers and teacher.

Many social learning theories have been influenced by the work of Vygotsky. This taxonomy of constructivism emphasises the construction of social contexts in which collaboration with others can build a sense of community. This is an important consideration as no classroom is an isolated box, rather a classroom is part of a wider community (Jaworski, 1996). The establishment of a learning community has many advantages. Firstly, both students and teachers are actively learning. Secondly, learning scenarios can be provided in which students can construct new situation-specific understandings by extending upon prior knowledge through collaborative learning (Ertmer & Newby, 1993). Through collaborative discussions, new perspectives can be negotiated leading to the development of shared understandings (Voigt, 1989). This aspect is emphasised here as individual students will bring to the group different perspectives based on their own past experiences.

2.2.1.3. Issue three: learning in context

The constructivist approach asserts that knowledge arises from the activity, culture and context in which it is situated (Brown *et al.,* 1989; Wozniak & Fischer, 1993; Lave, 1998; Lave & Wenger, 1991). A fundamental theory arising from this perspective is 'cognitive apprenticeship' (Brown *et al.,* 1989). 'Cognitive apprenticeship' emphasises the importance of initiating a student into a community of practice. This approach enables students to acquire skills and knowledge in contexts which reflect the way in which knowledge can be used in real-life situations (Bruckman, 1998). Theories encompassed within this taxonomy consider 'culture' as the mediator of learning for students and teachers (Derry, 1999; Wilson & Myers, 2000; McMahon, 1997). In any given subject domain, the culture in which the domain is immersed will to an extent define what is to be known within that area. This approach seeks to embed learning in activity utilising the social and physical context in which learning takes place.

In traditional classroom-based learning, abstract concepts are taught independently from the context in which they can be applied. Numerous scholars have sought to provide a solution to this by proposing theories of learning which involve learning by actively participating within a domain (Rogers, 1969; Schank, 1995, 1999). Brown *et al.* (1989) extend upon the notion of enculturation through a useful metaphor, which is to consider 'knowledge' as a set of tools. Brown *et al.* state that tools and knowledge can only be understood through their use. Secondly, using both tools and knowledge entails changing the student's view of the world. Finally, both involve adopting a belief system relevant to the culture within which they are used. Learning how to use these tools is dependent upon what the tools can be used for which is determined by the context of activity within that community. Subsequently, the activity is shaped by the perceptions and beliefs held by that community. Three important factors are emphasised in theories concerning situated cognition and apprenticeship these are: activity, concept and culture. These factors are inter-dependent as one cannot exist in the absence of the other two. A downfall of traditional classroom based learning is that although students are provided with opportunities to use tools (i.e. knowledge) of a domain, they are not provided with the opportunity to enter into the culture that uses them.

Students joining and working within communities will adopt certain behavioural types and belief systems common to that group, and over time the student will act in accordance with the norms and beliefs common to the community (Brown *et al.,* 1989). This approach emphasises that students should be provided with authentic practices to facilitate their learning by socially interacting with others in activities similarly to that of craft apprenticeship. There are a number of implications for education arising from this approach.

The beneficial implications for education arising from this approach include collective problem solving. Secondly, collaboration with peers may assist students with confronting ineffective strategies and individual misconceptions. Thirdly, the role of the teacher is that of a guider and coach. Literature suggests that apprenticeship begins via the provision of scaffolding by the teacher, who aligns learning material with the developmental level of the individual student (Vygotsky, 1978). As the student's confidence increases within the subject area, they move towards more autonomous learning, actively participating within a domain for themselves (Johnson & Dyer, 2005). The student will then reach a stage of reflection within which they are able to articulate what they have learnt and the student is able to generalise. Finally, teachers must empower students to continue learning independently. Through situating learning in appropriate contexts, students can learn through their own experiences

2.2.1.4. Issue four: learning by doing

Trial and error are important concepts within the natural process of learning. Unfortunately classrooms do not always provide adequate room for error and learning failures. Schank (1995; 2002) states that during childhood much of what is learned is through mistakes. Throughout this early stage failures in areas such as language learning are generally accepted as intrinsic to the learning process. This emphasises the connection between conscious and non-conscious knowledge as 'learning by doing' concerns the acquisition of unconscious knowledge (Schank, 1995). In order to provide an overview of learning by doing, it is necessary to explain 'scripts'. According to Schank (1995), 'Scripts' contain information related to past experiences and situations. Scripts are acquired by learning them though instances such as expectation failure. Expectation failure allows an individuals understanding of a situation to be modified. This modification occurs either by relating the situation to a previous experience, or by creating a new case. 'Learning by doing' focuses upon the acquisition of new micro scripts which are often unconscious. It is these 'micro-scripts' which guide the skills of an individual's ability. Owing to these aspects 'learning by being told' is not as effective as it is difficult to explain concepts to others who do not possess the same micro scripts.

Learning goals are equally important as if there is no clear goal, the learner will not become motivated to overcome any failure to attain the goal (Schank, 2002). Rogers (1969) also emphasises the importance of this in his experiential learning theory. Roger's theory asserts that students should be provided with learning scenarios in which they can learn significant and meaningful concepts through their own experiences. Similarly to Schank, Rogers also suggests that students should reflect upon their own learning to add meaning to the educational experience allowing them to assess whether they have acquired what they wanted to know. The importance of reflexivity in learning has since been emphasised by numerous scholars (i.e. Schon, 1983; Reynolds, 1965; Dreyfus & Dreyfus, 1986; Argyris & Schon, 1978).

There are a number of implications for education arising from theories of learning by doing. Firstly, as this approach is more synonymous with the natural process of learning, concepts learned through this method will be more meaningful to the student. Secondly, 'learning by doing' seeks to place learning tasks in appropriate contexts for the student, however, the path of exploratory learning may not always be clear for the student. In this instance it is important for the teacher as a facilitator to intervene and offer guidance to the student in overcoming their difficulties. This also raises implications for the role of the teacher as they will be required to encourage explanation, exploration and generalisation whilst being mindful of the differences in student's approaches toward learning. Finally, 'learning by doing' allows the student to reflect upon their own learning experiences.

2.3. Extending upon constructivist learning theory

Constructivist learning theory concerns the mental construction of knowledge. This has been extended upon through constructionism. Constructionism is an educational method based on constructivist learning theory (Papert, 1993). Regarded as the second dimension of constructivism, constructionism concerns learning by building something tangible in the real world (Jonassen, 1994). Papert (1993; 1999; 2002) states that students gain a more in-depth understanding through learning scenarios which allow them to construct something tangible, which can then be critiqued and used by others. This approach also allows students to learn effectively in more contextualised scenarios by working on a given task as opposed to merely absorbing delivered facts. The distinction between *'constructivism'* and *'constructionism'* is detailed in table 3.

Table 3. Distinctions between constructivism and constructionism

Dimension	Explanation
Constructivism	The idea that knowledge is something you construct in your head (Piaget 1972; Lave & Wenger, 1991).
Constructionism	The idea that the best way to do the above is to build something tangible, something which exists outside of your head (Resnick *et al.*, 1996; Harel, 1991; Papert, 1993).

(Adapted from Papert, 2002)

Traditionally computers have been used in schools as mediums through which learning materials are disseminated to students. Since the earliest constructionist programs dating back to the 1970s more interacting and engaging programs have been introduced into classrooms. With the growing advancements in technology, educational media is common place in today's classrooms especially with the evolution of the internet and ideals of collaboration. The following sub-section provides an overview of the development of constructionist learning programs highlighting the advantages to be gained from their use in classroom contexts.

2.3.1. Constructionism: applying computational support to effective learning strategies

Constructionist learning programs have sought to place learning activities in meaningful contexts for students. These programs offer a virtual learning space in which students can explore concepts for themselves through active participation, knowledge sharing and collaborative construction of ideas (Bruckman, 1997). It is this form of educational media that seeks to provide students with empowerment, motivating them and making the learning experience more meaningful to them. Historical precedents of the constructionist approach are found in simulation worlds (Pask, 1975; Whalley, 1995). These 'worlds' are computer based simulation environments in which students construct their own reality to learn specific tasks. These environments are single or multi-user capable, and focus upon problem solving scenarios. Simulation worlds allow students to explore and experiment with elements characteristic of the real-world by enabling them to make tactical decisions to learn from simulated consequences in a virtual environment (Wilson, 1995). This lends support to multi-user environments and the benefits to be gained from collaborative learning.

The constructionist approach seeks to align educational media with the process of learning. Papert (1993) highlights problematic issues arsing in traditional class-based settings and using mathematics as an example he states: *"the trouble with learning mathematics at school is that it's not like mathematics in the real world"*. This is evident as the use of mathematics in the *'real world'* can be applied to areas such as science, engineering and accounting. Classroom-based mathematics learning often involves children sitting at desks calculating mathematical equations devoid of a real-world context. This highlights the need for teachers to be mindful, supportive and encouraging with regard to new methods of thinking and learning which are more synonymous with the natural learning process. Constructionist media acknowledges learning as an individual and social process focusing upon collaborative learning tasks. This holds significant educational value as students will be provided with the opportunity to attain input and feedback from their peers (Papert, 1990).

3. BACKGROUND MOTIVATION: CREATIVITY THEORY

3.1. Introduction to creativity theory

There have been a number of different approaches towards the study of creativity. Studies investigating the nature of the creative process have drawn influences from psychometrics, cognitive psychology, systems theory and social constructionism (Kearney, 1991). Early perceptions of creativity were characterised by the 'lone genius myth' (Sampson, 1993). Some scholars have advocated that creativity defies definition due to its multifaceted and complex nature (Hennessey & Amabile, 1999; Torrance, 1988). Others have argued that creativity resides within certain 'gifted' individuals (Ripple, 1989). However, it is now widely accepted that every individual possesses creative potential which is exhibited on different levels to differing degrees (Treffinger *et* al, 1997; Leytham, 1990; Runco & Bahleda, 1986; Sternberg, 1985; Amabile, 1983). It is also accepted that creativity is not a phenomenon which exists in isolation, rather ideas evolve from the relationship between the individual creator and their interactions with others (Piirto, 2005; Hennessey, 2004; Waugh, 2003; Fischer, 2000). Furthermore it is acknowledged that creativity is not mutually exclusive to any particular domain (Bonnardel, 2000).

Creativity is understood in terms of a product or idea which is new and valued (Csikszentmihalyi, 1996; Boden, 1995). This implies that for something to be considered creative it must be novel, appropriate and useful (Aldous, 2005; Mumford, 2003; Burleson & Selker, 2002; Lubart, 2001).

Stage model representations of the creative process

Creativity research originally focused upon stage models of the creative process starting with the work of Poincare (1913). Poincare described the creative process as commencing with conscious thought, followed by unconscious work, resulting in 'inspiration'. Based on Poincare's account of the creative process, Wallas (1926) formalised the four-stage model of creativity.

3.2.1. Wallas's four-stage model of creativity

Wallas defined creativity as a linear four-stage model, progressing through the stages of preparation, incubation, illumination and verification. Preparation concerns immersing one's self in a domain and developing a curiosity about a particular problem (Getzels, 1964). During this stage, knowledge is consciously accumulated and influences are drawn from previous experience. During the incubation stage, conscious thought pertaining to the problem is rested and left to the unconscious mind (Claxton, 1998). Illumination occurs when one experiences a sudden flash of insight (Wallas, 1926) or sudden inspiration (Poincare, 1913). Finally, verification concerns forming judgements upon the creative artefact produced.

Wallas noted that during the creative process an individual could return to earlier stages. This has been supported by subsequent research (i.e. Patrick 1937, 1938; Rossman, 1931; Hadamard, 1945). Patrick (1937, 1938) conducted experiments with artists and poets, observing their methods and relating them to Wallas's four-stage model. The results indicated that during the creative process an overlap frequently occurred between the preparation and incubation stages.

Shaw (1989) suggests that a number of feedback loops occur during each of the stages presented in Wallas's model. Shaw states that during the stages of preparation and incubation the *'Areti loop'* controls conscious and sub-conscious behaviour. The *'Vinacke loop'* controls conscious and sub-conscious activity during illumination, and that verification occurs when an explanation results in further illumination. The *'Communication loop'* is thought to predict feedback between verification and later validation of the creative artefact produced. Shaw also stipulates that multiple feedback loops involving both conscious and sub-conscious activity operate from the verification stage to all previous stages of the model. Shaw refers to these multiple loops collectively as the *'Rossman loop'*. Shaw's concept of 'feedback loops' acknowledges conscious and sub-conscious activity involved in the creative process. The role of the sub-conscious in creative thinking will be discussed later within this chapter.

Elements of Wallas's model are still employed today in studies of creativity (Csikszentmihalyi, 1996) and scholars interested in cognitive models of the creative process acknowledge Wallas's seminal contribution to creativity research (i.e. Nystrom, 1979). Many have continued to use the four-stage model as a basis of understanding the creative process (i.e. Ochse, 1990; Goswami, 1996), while others have extended upon it (i.e. Amabile, 1996; Runco & Dow, 1999) and others have updated the model to include a fifth *'elaboration'* stage (i.e. Csikszentmihalyi, 1996; Kao, 1989). The Elaboration stage is described as the point at which creative insight is actualised and transformed into the end product ready for presentation (Hills *et al.,* 1999). Despite the many revisions to Wallas's four-stage model, not all have accepted stage models as descriptors of creativity. Due to this, there have been many differing approaches. Some models of creativity have rejected the stage descriptions arguing that the process of creativity exists as an integrated and dynamic process, recursive in nature and differing from person to person (i.e. Weisberg, 1986; Ghiselin, 1963; Eindhoven & Vinacke, 1952). In line with this view, research has been conducted into sub-processes thought to comprise creativity (Sternberg & Lubart, 1999; Lubart, 2001).

3.3. Alternative approaches to stage models of creativity

Approaches which differ greatly from the traditional stage models of creativity sought to investigate sub-process involved in the creative process. These sub-process theories include: divergent thinking (i.e. De Bono, 1967; Guilford, 1967), bisociation (i.e. Koestler, 1964), janusian thinking (i.e. Rothenberg, 1996); articulation (i.e. Rothenberg, 1979); homospatial thinking (i.e. Rothenberg, 1986), analogy and metaphor (i.e. Weisberg, 1993), emotional resonance (i.e. Lubart & Gertz, 1997) and feature mapping (i.e. Boden, 1992). A number of these approaches state that sub-processes occurring within the creative process are comprised of sequences which recur many times over (Eindhoven & Vinacke, 1952; Mumford *et al.,* 1991; Runco (1994). Lubart (2001) offers support of this perspective over the traditional four-stage model as follows:

> "There is potentially an interaction between initial ideas and the developing work which is sometimes referred to as a dynamic evolving process rather than a static process in which one step follows another toward a problem solution".

With regard to the above statement, it appears Lubart has overlooked the essence of the four-stage model. In the proposition of the traditional model Wallas (1926) stated that iterative interactions between stages frequently occur, thus, the process of creativity is not perceived to be that of a static nature. It is argued here that rather than oppose each other the stage-model approaches and sub-process approaches actually compliment each other. Whereas stage models represent a generic overview of particular aspects involved in the creative process, sub-process theories focus upon attributes associated with these aspects. For example, sub-process theories focus upon attributes such as bisociation and analogy, which may occur in the incubation and illumination stages of Wallas's model. The use of approaches mentioned within sub-process theories may differ between individuals at differing instances, however, each individual will at some point, pass through Wallas's stages.

Although there have been many debates and redefinitions of the stages creativity progresses through, certain points gain widespread agreement (Osborn, 1953; Taylor, 1959). Firstly, there is a need for preparation for the creative act. Preparation can have a number of aspects, this can involve accumulating existing facts and resources and preparing mentally for the creative process. Secondly, time is required for the incubation of ideas. Thirdly, the verification of creative thoughts has both a personal and social element. The new work must satisfy the aims of the individual and stand up to evaluation by a wider community. With regard to this final point, Boden (1992) distinguishes between P (psychological creativity) and H (historical creativity). P-Creativity is novel with regard to the conceptual structures of the creator. H-Creativity is novel to the wider community concerned with the subject area. Similarly to research into learning theories, creativity research has focused upon creativity as an individual and social process. The view held depends upon the school of thought adhered to.

3.4. The importance of the external environment

Creativity is not a phenomenon which exists in isolation. Any creative idea or artefact evolves from the relationship between the individual creator and their interactions with others and their environment (Fischer, 2000). This is especially true regarding the phenomena of group creativity where group interaction and collaboration assists the creative process (Hennessey, 2004). Moran & John-Steiner (2004) argue that all creativity is collaborative in that it draws from ideas and products of past creators as raw materials. It is also suggested that the environment in which one is situated can invoke creativity by igniting an idea (Fasko, 2001; Sternberg & Lubart, 1991a; Torrance, 1981). In terms of education the creative development of students is largely dependent upon the environment in which they exist (Runco & Johnson, 2002). It is suggested that the overall educational experience can be enhanced for students by situating them in environments in which the follow up of creative ideas is encouraged, actively evaluated and rewarded (Fasko, 2001). Unfortunately there are a number of instances where education falls short of this such as: influencing students to work for an expected reward, setting up competitive situations and focusing students upon expected evaluations (Hennessey & Amabile, 2005; Hennessey & Zbikowski, 1993; Bull *et al*, 1995; Westby & Dawson, 1995; Cropley, 1992). The emphasis here is that it is important for teachers to understand the educational benefits arising from encouraging creative thinking within the classroom. Often creative attributes such as 'non-conformity' and 'autonomy' arc perceived as negative behaviour in the classroom context (Westby & Dawson, 1995). Expectations and perceptions held by educators situated in the student's environment may influence a student's creative ability (Rosenthal, 1991). Such perceptions may be implied when judgements are made concerning the student's work. This may take the form of unintentional standards against which students are assessed (Runco, Johnson & Bear, 1993). This may affect the student's creativity whether it is as a facilitator of inhibitor.

3.5. Facilitators of creativity: creative thinking in education

A number of researchers have offered models of the creative process, while others have focused upon techniques aimed at encouraging creative thinking within the individual (Davies, 1982; Sternberg & Williams, 1996), however, few have suggested that there exists an inherent relationship between learning and creativity (Karnes *et al*, 1961; Torrance, 1981). Guilford (1950) was among the first to highlight the relationship between the two concepts, stating:

> "A creative act in an instance of learning...[and] a comprehensive learning theory must take into account both insight and creative ability".

Expanding upon this, Guilford (1967) stipulates that in order to gauge an understanding of insight, conceptual transformation is the key. This is supported by the notion of problem restructuring (i.e. Jacobs & Dominowski, 1981; Martinsen, 1985). It is suggested that by placing students in learning scenarios in which an object is utilised in an 'unusual way' insight is more likely to occur with regard to solving problems.

Although there are differing schools of thought regarding the study of creativity they all share common themes. The most salient theme is that which focuses upon combining ideas in new and different ways (Koestler, 1964; Guilford, 1967). Creativity is often perceived as involving divergent thinking as opposed to convergent thinking, the latter concerning itself with predictable, logical cognitive operations (De Bono, 1967). The key aspect of creativity is change. It is owing to this reason that divergent thinking and the ability to view situations in a new and novel way are strongly associated with creativity. This change may occur through the formation of analogies, often referred to as 'creative leaps' (Holyoak & Thagard, 1995). Creative leaps are characterised in literature by flashes of insight incorporating sudden illuminations of new perceptions or framings of a situation. Analogy is an important contributor towards the emergence of creative ideas. This implies, at least in part, that creative ideas are inspired by previous situations and experiences (Koestler, 1964; Schank, 1999). It also appears that such association and emergence result from sub-conscious, pre-verbal processing, thus acts of creation appear intuitive. This indicates that creativity occurs via a complex interplay of internal and external contexts and influences (Bonnardel, 2000). Research within the domain supports the use of metaphorical and analogical representations as facilitators of creative thinking (Harrington, 1981). This is especially true with reference to ideation and alternative applications of understandings (Ainsworth-Land, 1982).

3.6. Towards an explanation of creativity: conceptual spaces and schema based approaches

Over the last decade there have been two fundamental approaches proposed towards understanding creativity, namely: conceptual spaces (i.e. Boden, 1990; 1994; 1995; 1996) and the schema approach (i.e. Gero, 1996). It has been identified that creative thinking concerns looking at a space in a way which one would not have usually perceived it (Ram *et al*, 1995). Boden refers to these spaces in terms of 'conceptual spaces'. These conceptual spaces are described as existing in one's mind (Boden, 1990; 1995; 1996; Aihara & Hori, 1998). The dimensions of the space are generally regarded as the organising principles which unify and add structure to the relevant domain (Boden, 1994).

Boden (1990) suggests that creative thinking concerns *"thinking what one hasn't thought before"*. This explanation appears impossible as, if one agrees with the notion of a conceptual space *'existing inside the mind"*, then how is it possible to change a space by thinking the unthinkable? According to Boden (1994) a conceptual space is defined by a set of constraints imposed by the creator or the culture in which one exists. These constraints guide the generation of ideas within a domain. Boden (1994) further investigates this through her discussion of two types of creativity, these are: improbablist and impossiblist creativity. Improbablist creativity concerns novel combinations of familiar ideas which can be achieved through analogical thinking. Impossiblist creativity concerns mapping, exploration and transformation of conceptual spaces. Boden (1994) refers to these as different types of creativity which she refers to as: combinational creativity, exploratory creativity and transformational creativity. Combinational creativity involves 'novel' combinations of familiar ideas where newly associated ideas share some inherent conceptual structure. Exploratory creativity is perceived as the exploration of structured conceptual spaces, resulting in the identification of ideas which are unexpected. Transformational creativity is perceived as involving the transformation of one or more dimensions of a space, thus implying that structures which did not previously exist can be generated. With regard to Boden's classifications of combinational, exploratory and transformational creativity, it is not clear how these categories are differentiated. In particular, there lacks any clear distinction between combination and exploration classifications (Ritchie, 2001). It appears that Boden's combinational and exploratory creativity are not necessarily different types of creativity, but can be perceived as stages of creativity. Firstly, a space needs to be explored to allow one to gauge an understanding of what exists within the space (environment). At this point combinations can be made to a 'space' or 'sub-space' to transform it. It further appears that 'combinational' and 'exploratory' stages are iterative and that they should continue for as long as necessary until the 'space' can be transformed in someway.

A similar but more fine-grained explanation of creativity arises from the work of Gero (1996a). Gero describes the use of 'schemas' as a mechanism through which a conceptual space can be viewed. According to Gero, schemas provide an opportunity to explore spaces, and the process of 'emergence' modifies the schemas. It is the modification of schemas which can be described as the *'creative process'* (Gero, 1996a). In essence, schemas are knowledge structures which provide frameworks containing expectations of what is to follow. Creativity is often perceived as involving the co-influence of schemas, resulting in an 'unexpected' result. By adopting this viewpoint, it is advocated that individuals view a domain or scenario (i.e. space) which exists in the world and form multiple perspectives of that space by adopting different schemas. These schemas can be thought of as a lens or series of windows through which the space is viewed. Gero (1996a) suggests this occurs via one of two ways. Firstly this can occur through a change in which a schema is extended in a homogenous manner, and the previous schema becomes wholly contained within the new schema (additive schemas), therefore, the previous schema can now only partially explain the current situation. Secondly, this can occur when a new schema is substituted for a previously existing schema when a new perspective of the existing situation arises (substitutive schemas). Gero (1996a) states that Emergence plays a vital role in the introduction of new schemas. Emergence occurs when a new schema is substituted for a previously existing one and is most likely to occur when one forms a new perspective of an existing situation. This allows new ideas to emerge as one views a given scenario or situation from different perspectives through alternate schemas. Thus, allowing one to form multiple perspectives of a situation. Creativity does not only concern searching a defined space, but also concerns the introduction of new schemas to allow for exploration of a space. Subsequently, a state 'space' can be altered by the adoption of different schemas. In short, schemas can be considered as the way in which we view our environment and situations, scenarios, domains and experiences within that environment. It is only by exploring and viewing these spaces and attributes of spaces in different and previously unfamiliar ways that creativity surfaces via moments of 'illumination'.

3.7. Similarities between learning and creativity

Theoretical underpinnings discussed within this chapter suggest that learning and creativity share a number of similarities. Firstly, learning is social in nature as people interact with and are influenced by others and their environment constantly (Vygotsky, 1978). Owing to this perspective learning has been described as the outcome of interactions between social agents and their environment (Vosniadou, 1996). Similarly, creativity is also social in nature and it is widely acknowledged that any creative idea or artefact arises from the relationship between the individual creator, others and the environment (Hennessey, 2004; Fasko, 2001; Sternberg & Lubart, 1991a; Torrance, 1981). Therefore, interactions with others and the surrounding environment are key to both learning and creativity.

Two other aspects of importance that both learning and creativity share are time and previous experience. Learning is not an instantaneous process as significant learning takes time. Time is required to allow students to revisit and reflect upon ideas. By allowing time for reflection students can form different perspectives on a scenario. Time is also important to creativity owing to subconscious processing during the incubation stage (Claxton, 1998). Creativity involves forming multiple perspectives on a situation (Runco, 1996; Guilford, 1967). This implies that creative ideas are inspired by previous situations and experiences. Similarly, learning takes place when the student is able to relate new concepts to previous situations and experiences (Schank, 1995; 1999).

3.7.1 Learning, creativity and constructionism

There exists a vast amount of evidence supporting the notion of learning by creating as an engaging method of learning. This is supported by constructionist learning approaches as discussed in chapter two (i.e. Papert, 2002; 1993; Rogers, 1969; Dewey, 1938). Papert (1993) suggests that learning is most effective when students construct an artefact which can be shared with others. Through such construction not only will students be more motivated to learn, but will gain a more in-depth understanding through learning in a contextualised setting. Similarly, creativity also involves creating an artefact which is meaningful to oneself and others (Csikszentmihalyi 1996; Boden, 1994; 1992). Research suggests that students can be encouraged to think deeply about concepts learned through exploring and creating artefacts, thus, learning by creating appears an effective way forward in terms of educational technology (Jarvinen, 1998).

4. A FRAMEWORK TO GUIDE THE DESIGN OF EDUCATIONAL SOFTWARE

4.1. A generative framework for creative learning

Drawing upon insights from the backgroun motivation, this chapter presents a framework which has been developed to support the design of e-learning environments. This framework represents a distillation of creativity theory focusing upon education. The framework is presented in the form of a generative framework, which exists as a design support tool to assist with the design of lesson support materials and the design of educational technologies. The framework assists the design of creative educational experiences for the classroom by providing scaffolding for supporting materials in terms of the six white component boxes of the framework (see figure 1). Wallas's four-stage model has been adapted as the fundamental basis for this generative framework, with the processes of preparation, generation and evaluation represented laterally across the framework. The vertical dimensions reflect individual (denoted here as personal) and social components of creativity. The social level refers to others, peers and society. Personal levels reflect explicit and tacit levels of thinking.

	Preparation	**Generation**	**Evaluation**
Social	Task Negotiation	Collaborative Design	Social Evaluation
Personal (explicit)	Personal Preparation	Individual Design	Personal Evaluation
Personal (tacit)	Tacit Preferences & Influences		

Figure 1: A generative framework for creative learning.

With regard to Figure 1, the lateral and vertical phases and sub-components of the generative framework are discussed within the following sub sections.

4.1.1 Lateral process: the preparation process

The processes of preparation, generation and evaluation are recognised herein as three integral concepts of the creative process, in that, every creative act will involve the preparation of ideas, whether this be in the form of tacit influences drawn from the environment, or conscious preparation for the task. Within this process, at the personal level, an individual will develop a curiosity or a desire to create. Once this desire or need has been established, information is consciously accumulated from the external environment and thoughts may be discussed with others on a 'social' level which the individual can reflect upon on a 'personal' level (Getzels, 1964). If working in a collaborative setting, group-wide negotiations of the task will also take place. Inevitably, the way in which an individual prepares for the task will be influenced by their past experiences which may be explicit or tacit (Schank, 1995).

4.1.2 Lateral process: the generation process

The generation process of the framework encompasses social and personal design. Within this process ideas are generated which can involve interactions and negotiations between the individual and peers in their environment. Additionally, idea generation is assisted partly by a continuous interaction occurring between levels of explicit and tacit thinking (Claxton, 1998). The terminology used in the creativity literature refers to these sub-conscious processes as incubation and illumination. These terms refer to the 'incubation' of ideas where conscious thought pertaining to the problem is rested, and 'illumination' is the point at which creative ideas are realised. A number of scholars suggest that influences from the environment at a 'social' level can trigger creative ideas to progress from tacit to more explicit thoughts at a 'personal' level (Claxton, 1998). Thus, the framework presented here acknowledges the importance of environmental factors upon the creative process, and the importance of allowing time for creative ideas to evolve.

This emphasises that although individuals may at times work alone to produce creative ideas and artefacts, interactions and collaboration with others and the external environment are crucial (Candy & Edmonds, 1999; Csikszentmihalyi & Sawer, 1995; Gardner, 1985; Gero & Maher, 1993). Previous studies concerning the advantages of collaborative learning further support the importance of the environment and interactions with others (Vygotsky, 1978; Brown et al, 1989; Fischer, 1991; Ertmer & Newby, 1993; Wilson & Myers, 2000). Therefore, it is acknowledged that creativity is not a phenomenon which exists in isolation, but rather any creative idea or artefact evolves from the relationship between the individual creator and their environment. This implies that individuals are constantly receiving information from the environment which may trigger elements of creative thought at the tacit level, which may arise to conscious explicit realisation. This implies that the environment in which one is situated can stimulate and evoke creativity by igniting a creative idea (Fasko, 2001). Additionally, as creativity involves the formation of multiple perspectives of a domain or scenario (Guilford, 1967, Runco, 1996), influences from the environment may also allow one to shift between differing perspectives leading to the generation of further ideas.

4.1.3 Lateral process: the evaluation process

The evaluation process concerns reviewing early creative ideas through to evaluating the final artefact. The evaluation process may be conducted by the individual at a personal level, and by the wider community, this fits with Boden's notion of P-creativity and H-creativity (Boden, 1992). Whilst the view here is that these are not distinct types of creativity, it is acknowledged that Boden's notion of P and H creativity represent two dimensions of evaluation. A wide body of literature also supports this (i.e. Mumford & Gustafson, 1988; Amabile, 1983; Csikszentmihalyi, 1988; 1999; Martindale, 1990). Although not all creative acts culminate in historically significant acts (Briskman, 1980), the creative individual may wish to verify their work with others residing within the community. This may lead to individual and or societal acceptance of the creative artefact, and in some instances, this may lead to the individual returning to earlier processes of the framework, for example for the refinement of an idea (Amabile, 1996). This is supported by previous studies which extend upon the work of Wallas (1926) indicating that a second incubation process may occur after initial illumination, depending on the creative idea or artefact produced (Sapp, 1992; Poincare, 1913; Leytham, 1990). Inevitably, what follows the evaluation process will differ between individuals and scenarios.

Additionally, evaluation may also concern the creator's emotional response to the artefact produced, in which implicit reactions occur. For example, an individual may feel 'uncomfortable' regarding work produced and return to earlier processes of the framework such as preparation or incubation (Schon, 1983). Similarly, an individual may feel 'satisfied' with their work and evaluate artefacts at the conscious level. It is suggested that in terms of personal evaluation, a natural dialogue takes place between explicit and tacit levels of thinking. It is also important to mention that the evaluation process does not necessarily refer to the reviewing of the end product, but rather as one progresses through the framework ideas may be reviewed and revised where necessary which may result in further preparation and or generation. It is only when this evaluation process has been reached, that it is possible to revisit earlier stages of the framework if further generation or preparation is required. This emphasises the cyclic nature of the framework, by which processes may be revisited iteratively until a positive evaluation has been attained and the individual is satisfied with their creative idea or artefact produced. Inevitably the number of iterations required will depend upon the scenario and the individuals involved.

4.1.4 Vertical dimensions: the roles of social, personal explicit and personal tacit levels of the framework

The vertical dimensions of the framework reflect the personal and social components of creativity. These dimensions encompass interactions and discourse with others and influences drawn from the environment. The personal levels, which are exclusive to the individual, encompass explicit and implicit levels of thinking. On the explicit level, an individual consciously prepares for the task, generates ideas and reviews them. Creativity literature supporting the generative framework states that at the tacit level, influences received from the environment and conscious thought may influence ideation to occur (Sanders, 2001). 'Ideation' refers to the formation of ideas, in which thoughts initially defy expression in language (Root-Bernstein & Root-Bernstein, 1999). Root-Bernstein & Root-Bernstein (1999) state that creative thinking occurs pre-verbally, manifesting itself via emotions, images and intuition. Furthermore, thoughts can only be translated into formal systems of communication such as language and become explicit, when they have sufficiently developed in tacit pre-logical forms (Kaha, 1983). Claxton (1998) states that time is required to allow for such processing to occur. It is further suggested that the sub-conscious mind can be understood by regarding preparatory materials and information as differing 'rays' impinging on a lens or prism. Given time, appropriate rays might be selected and brought to focus, thus forming a new pattern or characteristic (Leytham, 1990), which then brings new perspectives to the conscious mind. Therefore, thoughts may cross the boundary between implicit and explicit ways of knowing. Thus, illumination occurs and creative ideas can be evaluated.

Through all of the lateral processes, society plays a crucial role, in that an individual constantly receives information from the environment and the society in which they are immersed. For example in the domain of music, one is always influenced by the scales and concepts of tonality shaped by the culture in which they exist. In terms of preparation and generation stages, one continuously draws upon such influences at not only an explicit level, but also at a tacit level. The individual may collect information relating to the artefact they wish to create, whether it be in the form of literature, music and conversing with others. Finally, in terms evaluation, the individual may wish to discuss and evaluate their work with others by allowing those within the wider community to form judgments relating to their creative work. Throughout the component boxes represented on the framework, interaction occurs vertically between social aspects and the individual (see Figure 2).

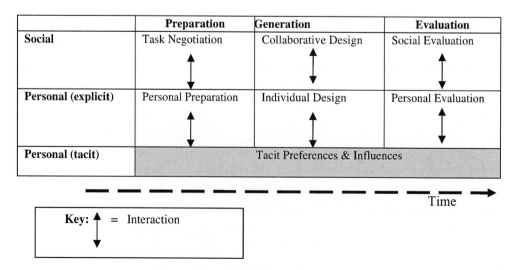

Figure 2: Vertical interactions occurring within the framework

Figure 2 illustrates interactions between social and personal levels, these interactions continuously occur as the individual is influenced by factors relating to the environment or culture in which they are immersed. Interaction also continuously occurs between explicit and tacit levels of thinking throughout the creative process.

4.1.5 Theoretical assumptions of the framework

The generative framework for creativity attempts to explain concepts and processes involved in creativity. As illustrated in the framework (see figure 1), the creative learning process begins with social and individual preparation, and finally ends with social and individual evaluation, and is characterised by three main processes. The framework also acknowledges social and individual elements within the creative process. The framework does not commit to a strict linear route, and it is emphasised here that the creative process is cyclic in nature, this is been supported by aspects reviewed within the theoretical background (i.e. Patrick, 1937; 1938; Rossman, 1931; Hadamard, 1945; Amabile, 1996). The review of creative ideas may result in a need to revise ideas which may result in further preparation, or evaluation or further generation and so on. The framework exists as a design support tool for facilitating creative learning and can be used to guide the design of lesson materials for the classroom and the design of e-learning environments. The framework can be utilised as a design support tool to facilitate creative thinking in the classroom by instantiating the framework. The framework assumes that creativity exists within all, albeit to differing degrees. This view is widely supported by contemporary literature within the domain of creativity (i.e. Runco & Bahleda, 1986; Sternberg, 1985; Edwards, 2001; Leytham, 1990, Hofstadter, 1979).

5. INSTANTIATING THE DESIGN FRAMEWORK: A MUSIC COMPOSITION EXAMPLE

The generative framework proposed here offers many advantages in terms of facilitating creative thinking and learning within the classroom context. Teachers and designers of educational technology can utilise the framework to assist with compiling lesson plans to ensure that all aspects of the creative process are considered. The framework has been designed so that it can be applied to any domain. Here it is instantiated through a music composition example in which students dare set the task of composing music in pairs. This instantiation is illustrated in Figure 3.

With regard to figure 3, over the long term, students will have acquired a great deal of knowledge about music and the kinds of musical styles dominant in their culture to which new ideas will be related to, allowing the student to construct their own meanings based on previously acquired knowledge and influences. In the short-term, preparation will also concern students working in pairs negotiating how to carry out the task. Each member of the pair will also bring unique experiences to the task in terms of any musical instrument training and personal musical preferences. Students may then reach a point at which ideas are acted upon in the generation phase leading to the evaluation of ideas. This may result in students returning to earlier phases to refine ideas. Evaluation occurs at the personal level in which the individual student reflects upon the composed work. At the social level, evaluation will involve students evaluating the composition within the pair. This may also lead to students seeking evaluation from the wider community in terms of the larger student group or discussions with their teacher in which others are encouraged to comment on the compositional piece.

	Preparation	Generation	Evaluation
Social	Short term – discussion with fellow student about task. Long term – social enculturation of music	Pair-wise problem solving and discussion	Feedback from peers and teacher, and pair-wise reflection and judgement of composition
Personal (explicit)	Individual experience (music training etc.) Musical preferences (heavy metal, eminem etc.). Personal ideas about how to carry out the task	Personal construction of ideas	Personal reflection and judgement of the composition
Personal (tacit)	Tacit preferences and influences		

Time →

Figure 3: Instantiation of the framework - a music composition example

6. CHAPTER CONCLUSIONS

Developing effective creative learning environments mediated through technology involves forming an appreciation of aspects integral to the processes of learning and creativity at the design stage. This thesis has identified the similarities between the processes of learning and creativity, drawing upon insights from literature related to these processes in the form of the generative framework for creative learning. This framework exists as a design support tool for designers of educational technology and for planning lesson materials in the classroom

In terms of implications for theory, the generative framework for creative learning proposed in this thesis offers an extension of Wallas's original four stage model of creativity encompassing aspects of social learning theory and creativity theory. In terms of implications for practice, the framework has been developed to assist the design of educational technologies and lesson planning materials through instantiating the framework. The framework is not domain specific and can be applied to different curriculum areas.

REFERENCES

Aihara, K & Hori, K (1998) Enhancing creativity through reorganising mental space concealed in a research notes stack. *Knowledge Based Systems*. 11. p 469 – 478.

Ainsworth-Land, V (1982) Imagining and creativity: an integrating perspective. *Journal of Creative Behaviour*. 16. p 5 – 28.

Aldous, C. R (2005) Creativity in problem solving: uncovering the origin of ideas. *International Education Journal*, ERC2004 Special Issue. 5, 5. p 43 – 56.

Amabile, T.M (1996) *Creativity in Context*. Boulder, CO; Westview.

Amabile, T.M (1983) The psychology of creativity: a componential conceptualization. *Journal of Personality and Social Psychology*. 45. 357 – 376

Argyris, C & Schon, D (1978) *Organisational learning: a theory in action perspective*. New York. Addison-Wesley.

Baccarini, D (2004) The implementation of authentic activities for learning: A case study. Proceedings of the 13th Annual Teaching Learning Forum. 9-10 February. Perth: Murdoch University, Australia.

Bandura, A (1986) *Social Foundations of Thought and Action: A Social Cognitive Theory*. Englewood Cliffs; NJ Prentice Hall.

Boden, M. A (1996) *Dimensions of Creativity*. London: MIT Press.

Boden, M. A (1995) Modelling creativity: reply to reviewers. *Artificial Intelligence*. 79. p 161 – 182.

Boden, M. A (1994) Precise of the creative mind: myths and mechanisms. *Behavioural and Brain Sciences*. 17, 3. p 619 – 570.

Boden, M (1992) Creativity. *Journal of Creativity Behaviour*. 26,3. p 213- 217.

Boden, M.A (1990) The Creative Mind: Myths and Mechanisms. London. Cardinal.

Bonnardel, N (2000) Towards understanding and supporting creativity in design: analogies in a constrained cognitive environment. *Knowledge Based Systems*. 13. p 505-513.

Briskman, L (1980) Creative product and creative process in science and art. *Inquiry*. 23. p 83 – 106.

Brown, Collins & Duguid (1989) Situated Cognition and the Culture of Learning. *Educational Researcher*. January – February. 32-43

Bruckman, A (1997) MOOSE Crossing: construction, community and learning in a networked virtual world for kids. [online]. Available from: http://www.cc.gatech.du/~asb/thesis (Accessed January 2002).

Bruckman, A (1998) Community support for constructionist learning. *Computer Supported Co-operative work*. No 7. pp 47 – 86.

Bull, K. S, Montgomery, D & Baloche, L (1995) Teaching creativity at the college level: A synthesis of curricular components perceived as important by instructors. *Creativity Research Journal*. 8. p 83 – 90.

Burleson, W & Selker, T (2002) Creativity and interface: introduction. Communications of the ACM. 45, 10. p 88 – 90.

Claxton (1998) *Hare Brain Tortoise Mind: Why Intelligence Increases When you Think Less*. London. Fourth Estate Limited.

Crawford, K (1996) Vygotskian approaches to human development in the information era. *Educational Studies in Mathematics*. 31. pp 43 – 62.

Cropley, A.J (1992) *More Ways than One: Fostering Creativity*. Norwood, NJ; Albex.

Csikszentmihalyi, M (1999) Implications of a systems perspective for the study of creativity. In Sternberg, R.J (Ed) *Handbook of Creativity*. Cambridge; Cambridge University Press. P 313-335.

Csikszentmihalyi, M (1996) *Creativity: Flow and the Psychology of Discovery and Invention*. New York. Harper-Collins.

Csikszentmihalyi, M (1988) Society, culture and person: a systems view of creativity. In Sternberg, R.J (Ed), *The Nature of Creativity*. Cambridge; Cambridge University Press. P 325 – 339.

Csikszentmihalyi, M & Sawer, K (1995) Creative insight: The social dimension of a solitary movement. Sternberg, R.J & Davidson, J.E (Eds.) *The Nature of Insight*. MIT Press. Cambridge, MA.

Davies, G. A (1982) A model for teacher for creative development. *Roeper Review*. Vol 5, No. 2. P 27 – 29.

De Bono, E (1967) *New Think: the Use of Lateral Thinking in the Generation of New Ideas*. New York; Basic Books.

Derry, S.J (1999) A fish called peer learning: searching for common themes. In A. M O'Donnell & A. King (Eds.) *Cognitive Perspectives on Peer Learning*. Mahwah; NJ. Lawrence Erlbaum Associates.

Dewey, J (1938) *Experience and Education*. New York. Macmillan.

Dewey, J (1916) *Democracy and Education*. New York. Macmillan.

Dreyfus, H.L & Dreyfus, S.E (1986) *Mind over machine: the power of human intuition and expertise in the era of the computer*. Oxford; Basil Blackwell.

Driscoll, M. P (1994) *Psychology for Learning Instruction*. Needham; MA. Allyn & Bacon.

Edwards, S.M (2001) The technology paradox: efficiency versus creativity. *Creativity Research Journal*. 13, 2. p 221 – 228.

Eindhoven, J.E & Vinacke, W.E (1952) Creative processes in painting. *Journal of General Psychology*. 47. p 165 – 179.

Ertmer, P.A & Newby, T.J (1993) Behaviourism, Cognitivism, Constructivism: comparing critical features from an instructional design perspective. *Performance Improvement Quarterly*. 6, 4. pp 50 – 72.

Fasko (2001) Education and Creativity. *Creativity Research Journal*. Vol 13. Nos. 3 & 4. p 317 – 327

Fischer, G (2000) Symmetry of ignorance, social creativity and meta-design. *Knowledge Based Systems*. 13. p 527 – 537.

Fischer, G (1991) Supporting learning on demand with design environments. In Birnbaum, L (Ed), *International Conference on the Learning Science*. Evanston;IL. P. 165 – 175.

Forrester, D & Jantzie, N (2001) Learning Theories. [online]. Available from: http://www.ucalgary.ca/~gnjantzi/learning_theories.htm (Accessed January 2002)

Frank, C (2005) Teaching and learning theory: who needs it? *College Quarterly*. No. 2, Vol 8.

Gardner, H (1985) *The Mind's New Science: A History of the Cognitive Revolution*. New York; Basic Books.

Gero, J.S (1996a) Creativity, emergence and evolution in design. *Knowledge Based Systems*. 9. p 435 – 448.

Gero, J & Maher, M (1993) *Creativity and Knowledge Based Creative Design*. Lawrence Erlbaum. Hillsdale, NJ.

Getzels, J.W (1964) Creative Thinking, Problem-Solving, and Instruction. In E.R. Hilgard (Ed), *Theories of Learning and Instruction*. Chicago; University of Chicago Press.

Ghiselin, B (1963) Ultimate criteria for two levels of creativity. In Taylor, C.W & Barron, F (Eds.) *Scientific Creativity: Its Recognition and Development*. P 30 – 43. New York. Wiley.

Goswami, A (1996) Creativity and the quantum: A unified theory of creativity. *Creativity Research Journal*. 9. p 47 – 61.

Guilford, J. P (1967) Creativity: yesterday, today and tomorrow. *Journal of Creative Behaviour*. 1. p 3 – 14.

Guilford, J. P (1950) Creativity. *American Psychologist*. 5. p 444 – 454.

Hadamard, J (1945) *An Essay of Invention in the Mathematics Field*. Princeton, NJ; Princeton University Press.

Harel, I (1991) *Children Designer's: Interdisciplinary Constructions for Learning and Knowing mathematics in a Computer Rich School.* Norwood; NJ. Ablex Publishing.

Harrington, D.M (1981) creativity, analogical thinking and muscular metaphors. Journal of Mental Imagery. 6. 121 – 126.

Hausfather, S. J (1996) Vygotsky and schooling: creating a social context for learning. *Action in Teacher Education*. 18. pp 1 – 10.

Hein, G (1991) Constructivist Learning Theory. [online]. Available from: http://www.exploratorium.edu/IFI/resources/constructivistlearning.html.(Accessed December 2001).

Hennessey, B.A. (2004). Creativity, classrooms, culture, and communication. *Review of the Educational Psychology of Creativity* by John Houtz (Ed.). Contemporary Psychology: APA Review of Books. 49.761-763.

Hennessey, B.A & Amabile, T.M (2005) Extrinsic and intrinsic motivation. In Nicholson, Audia & Pillutla (Eds.). *Blackwell Encylopedia of Management*. 2nd Edition, Organisational Behaviour. Pp 121 – 122. Malden, MA: Blackwell Publishing.

Hennessey, B.A & Amabile, T.M (1999) Consensual assessment technique. In M. Runco & S. Pritzker (Eds.). *Encyclopaedia of Creativity*. (pp 347 – 359). New York: Academic Press.

Hennessey, B.A., & Zbikowski, S.M. (1993). Immunizing children against the negative effects of reward: A further examination of intrinsic motivation training techniques. *Creativity Research Journal*, 6, 2

Hills, G.E, Shrader, R.C & Lumpkin, G.T (1999) Opportunity recognition as a Creative Process. [online]. Available from: http://www.babson.edu/entrep/fer/papers99.htm (Accessed July 2007).

Hofstadter, D. R (1979) Godel, Escher, *Bach: An Eternal Golden Braid*. New York; Basic Books.

Holyoak, K. J & Thagard, P (1995) *Mental Leaps: Analogy in Creative Thought*. Cambridge, MA. MIT Press.

Honebein, P.C, Duffy, T. M & Fishman, B. J (1996) Constructivism and the design of learning environments: Context and authentic activities for learning. In Duffy, T. M, Lowyck, J & Jonassen, D.H (Eds.) *Designing environments for constructive learning*. Berlin; Springer-Verlag.

Jacobs, M.K & Dominoswki, R.L (1981) Learning to solve insight problems. *Bulletin of the Psychonomic Society*. 17. p 171 – 174.

Jarvinen, E.M (1998) The LEGO/LOGO learning environment in technology education: an experiment in a Finnish context. *Journal of Technology Education.* 9, 2. p 47 – 59.

Jaworski, B (1996) Constructivism and teaching – the social-cultural context. [online]. Available from: http://www.grout.demon.co.uk/barbara/chreods.htm. (Accessed June 2003).

Johnson, J & Dyer, J (2005) User-defined content in a constructivist learning environment. Proceedings of M-ECITE 2005: Recent research developments in learning technologies.

Kaha, N (1983) The creative mind: form and process. *Journal of Creative Behaviour.* 17. pp 84 – 94.

Kao, J.J (1989) *Entrepreneurship, Creativity & Organisation.* Englewood Cliffs, NJ; Prentice Hall.

Karnes, M. B, McCoy, G.F, Zehrbach, R.R, Wollersheim, J.P, Clarizio, H.F, Costin, L & Stanley, L.S (1961) *Factors Associated with Overachievement of Intellectually Gifted Children.* Champaign, IL.

Kearney, R (1991) *Poetics of Imaging: From Husserl to Lyotard.* London; Harper Collins.

Koestler, A (1964) *The Act of Creation.* New York; MacMillan.

Lave, J (1998) *Cognition in Practice: Mind, Mathematics and Culture in Everyday Life.* Cambridge. Cambridge University Press.

Lave, J & Wenger, E (1991) Situated learning: Legitimate Peripheral Participation. Cambridge. Cambridge University Press.

Leytham, G (1990) *Managing Creativity.* Norfolk; Peter Francis Publisher

Lubart, T (2001) Models of the creative process: past, present and future. *Creativity Research Journal.* 13, 3 and 4. p 295 – 308.

Lubart, T. I & Gertz, I (1997) Emotion, metaphor and the creative process. *Creativity Research Journal.* 10. p 285 – 301.

Martinsen, O (1985) Cognitive styles and experience in solving insight problems: Replication and extension. *Creativity Research Journal.* 8. p 291 – 298.

McMahon, M (1997) Social constructivism and the world wide web: A paradigm for learning. Proceedings of the ASCILITE Conference. Perth, Australia. December.

Moran, S & John-Steiner, V (2004) How collaboration in creative work impacts identity and motivation. In Meil, D & Littleton, K (Eds.) *Collaborative Creativity: Contemporary Perspectives.* London; Free Association Books. Pp 11 - 25

Mumford, M. D (2003) Where have we been, where are we going? Taking stock in creativity research. *Creativity Research Journal.* 15, 2 and 3. p 107 – 120.

Mumford, M.D & Gustafson, S.B (1988) Creativity syndrome: integration, application and innovation. *Psychological Bulletin.* 103, 1. p 27 – 43.

Mumford, M.D, Mobley, M.I, Uhlman, C.E, Reiter-Palmon, R & Doares, L.M (1991) Process analytic models of the creative capabilities. *Creativity Research Journal.* 4. p 91 – 122.

Nymstrom, H (1979) Creativity and Innovation. New York; John Wiley & Sons.

Ochse, R (1990) *Before the Gates of Excellence: The Determinants of Creative Genius.* New York; Cambridge University Press.

Osborn, A.F. (1953). *Applied Imagination* (Revised Ed.). New York; Scribners.

Papert, S (2002) Constructionism Vs Instructionism. [online]. Available from: http://www.papert.org/articles/SituatingConstructionism.html. (Accessed January 2003).

Papert, S (1999) The Century's Greatest Minds: Papert on Piaget. *Time* Magazine. P 105. 29th March 1999.

Papert, S (1993) *The Children's Machine: Rethinking School in the Age of the Computer.* New York; Basic Books.

Papert, S (1990) A Critique of Technocentrism in Thinking about the school of the Future. [online].Available from:http://www.papert.com/articles/ACritqueofTechnocentrism.html. (Accessed November 2001).

Pask, G (1975) *Conversation, Cognition and Learning: A Cybernetic Theory and Methodology.* Amsterdam. Elsevier Scientific Publishing Company.

Patrick, C (1938) Scientific Thought. *Journal of Psychology.* 5. p 55-83.

Patrick, C (1937) Creative Thought in Artists. *Journal of Psychology.* 4. p 35-73.

Piaget, J (1972) *The Principles of Genetic Epistemology.* London. Routledge & Kegan Paul.

Phillips, J. L (1981) *Piaget's Theory: A Primer.* San Francisco. W.H Freeman and Company

Piaget, J (1926) *The Language and Thought of the Child.* New York. Harcourt.

Piirto, J (2005) The creative process in poets. In J. Kaufman & J, Baer (Eds.) *Creativity in Domains: Faces of the Muse.* (pp 1 – 20). Parsippany, NJ: Lawrence Erlbaum.

Poincare (1913) in Leytham, G (1990) *Managing Creativity.* Norfolk. Peter Francis Publishers.

Ram, A, Willis, L, Neressian, N & Kolodner, J (1995) Understanding the creative mind: a review of Margaret Boden's the creative mind. *Artificial Intelligence.* 79. p 111 – 128.

Raskin, J. D (2005) Constructivism in psychology: personal construct psychology, radical constructivism and social constructivism. *American Communication Journal.* 3 , 5.

Resnick, M, Sargent, R & Silverman, B (1996) Programmable bricks: Toys to think with. *IBM Systems Journal.* 35, 3 – 4. pp 443 – 452.

Reynolds, B (1965) *Learning and teaching in the practice of social work* (2nd ed.). New York; Russell & Russell.

Ripple, R.E (1989) Ordinary creativity. *Contemporary Educational Psychology.* 14. p 189 – 202.

Ritchie, G (2001) Assessing creativity. Proceedings of the AISB01 Symposium on Artificial Intelligence and Creativity. P 3 – 11.

Rogers, C. R (1969) *Freedom to Learn.* Ohio, U.S .Charles E. Merrill Publishing Company.

Root-Berstein, R & Root-Berstein, M (1999) *Sparks of Genius: The 13 Thinking Tools of the World's Most Creative People.* New York; Houghton-Mifflin.

Rossman, J (1931) *The Psychology of the Inventor.* Washington DC; Inventors Publishing.

Rothenberg, A. (1996) The Janusian process in scientific creativity. *Creativity Research Journal.* 9. p 207 – 231.

Rothenberg, A. (1986) Artistic creation as stimulated by super-imposed versus combined-composite visual images. *Journal of Personality and Social Psychology.* 50. p 370 – 381.

Runco (1996) Creativity from Childhood through Adulthood. *New Directions for Child Development* no. 72.Summer 1996.

Runco, M.A (1994) *Problem Finding, Problem Solving and creativity.* Norwood, NJ; Ablex.

Runco, M.A & Bahleda, M.D (1986) Implicit theories of artistic, scientific and everyday creativity. *Journal of Creative Behaviour.* 20. p 93-98.

Runco, M.A & Dow, G (1999) Problem Finding. In Runco, M.A & Pritzker, S.R (Eds) *Encyclopedia of Creativity.* (Vol. 2). P 433 – 435. San Diego, CA; Academic Press.

Runco, M.A, Johnson, D.J & Bear, P.K (1993) Parent's and teacher's implicit theories of children's creativity. *Child Study Journal.* 23, 91 – 113.

Sampson, E (1993) *Celebrating the Other: A Dialogic Account of Human Nature. Boulder*; Westview Press.

Sanders, E.B (2001) Collective creativity. LOOP: AIGA *Journal of Interaction Design Education*. No 4.

Sapp, D.D (1992) The point of creative frustration and the creative process. A new look at an old model. *Journal of Creative Behaviour*. 26. p 21 – 28.

Schank, R (2002) *Designing World Class E-Learning*. New York. McGraw-Hill.

Schank, R (1999) *Dynamic Memory Revisited*. Cambridge; MA. Cambridge University Press.

Schank, R (1995) *What we Learn when we Learn by Doing*. Technical Report No. 60. Institute of Learning Sciences, Northwestern University, Illinois.

Schon, D.A (1983) *The Reflective Practitioner: How Professionals Think In Action*. London. Temple Smith.

Shaw M.P (1989) The eureka process: A structure for the creative experience in science and engineering. *Creativity Research Journal*. 2, pp 286 – 298.

Sternberg, R.J (1985) Implicit theories of intelligence, creativity and wisdom. *Journal of Personality and Social Psychology*. 49. p 607 – 627.

Sternberg, R. J & Lubart, T. I (1999) *The concept of creativity: prospects and paradigms*. In Sternberg, R. J (Ed) Handbook of Creativity. Cambridge; Cambridge University Press.

Sternberg, R & Lubart, T (1991a) An investment theory of creativity and its development. *Human Development*. 34. p 1 – 31.

Sternberg, R. J & Williams, W.M (1996) *How to Develop Student Creativity*. Alexandria, VA.

Tam, M (2000) Constructivism, instructional design and technology: implications for transforming distance learning. *Educational Technology & Society*. 3, 2. pp 50-60.

Tavangarian, D, Laypold, M, Nolting, K, Roser, M & Voigt, D (2004) Is e-learning the solution for individual learning? *Electronic Journal of E-Learning*. 2, 2. December 2004.

Taylor, A (1959) *The nature of creative process*. In P.Smith (Ed), Creativity. New York. Hastings House.

Torrance, E.P (1988) The nature of creativity as manifest in its testing. In Sternberg, R (Ed) *The Nature of Creativity*. p 43 – 75. Cambridge; Cambridge University Press.

Torrance, E.P (1981) *Creative teaching makes a difference*. In Gowan, J.C, Khatena, J & Torrance, E.P (Eds.) Creativity: Its Educational Implications. Dubuque, IA; Kendall/Hunt

Treffinger, D. J, Isaksen, S.G & Dorval, K.B (1997) *Creative Problem Solving: An Introduction* (Revised Edition). Sarasota, Florida: Centre for Creative Learning, Inc.

Voigt (1989) Social functions of routines and consequences for subject matter learning. *International Journal of Educational Research*. 13, 6. pp 647 – 656.

Von Glaserfeld, E (1995) A constructivist approach to teaching. In L.P Steffe & J. Gale (Eds.), *Constructivism in Education*. Pp 3 – 15.

Von Glaserfeld, E & Steffe, L (1991) Conceptual models in educational research and practice. *The Journal of Educational Thought*. 25, 2. pp 91 – 103.

Vosniadou, S (1996) Towards a Revised Cognitive Psychology for New Advances in Learning and Instruction. *Learning and Instruction*. Vol. 6. No. 2. 95 – 109

Vygotsky, L. S (1978) *Mind in Society: The Development of Higher Psychological Processes*. Cambridge: Massachusetts. Harvard University Press.

Wallas (1926) *The Art of Thought*. London; Johnathan Cape [republished in 1931].

Waugh, A (2003) Thinking and Creating. [online]. Available from: http://www.nesta.org.uk/ignite/downloads/ignite_seminar.pdf. (Accessed August 2004).

Weisberg, R.W (1993) *Creativity: Beyond the Myth of Genius*. New York; Freeman.

Westby, E.L & Dawson, V.L (1995) Creativity: Asset or Burden in the Classroom? *Creativity Research Journal*. 8. p 1 – 10.

Whalley, P (1995) Imagining with Multimedia. *British Journal of Educational Technology*. 26, 3. p 190 – 204.

Wilson, B (1995) Metaphors for instruction: why we talk about learning environments. *Educational Technology*. 35, 5. p 25 – 30.

Wilson, B. G., & Myers, K. M. (2000). *Situated cognition in theoretical and practical context*. In D. H. Jonassen & S. M. Land (Eds.) Theoretical foundations of learning environments. Mahwah; NJ. Erlbaum. pp. 57-88.

Wozniak, R & Fisher, K (1993) *Development in Context: Acting and Thinking in Specific Environments*. Hillsdale; NJ. Lawrence Erlbaum Associates.

In: E-Learning: 21st Century Issues and Challenges
Editor: A.R. Lipshitz and S. P. Parsons

ISBN : 978-1-60456-156-2
©2008 Nova Science Publishers, Inc.

Chapter 8

WHEN COLLABORATIVE PBL MEETS E-LEARNING: HOW DOES IT IMPROVE THE PROFESSIONAL DEVELOPMENT OF CRITICAL-THINKING INSTRUCTION?

Yu-chu Yeh

Institute of Teacher Education and Research Center for Mind, Brain & Learning
National Chengchu University, Taiwan

ABSTRACT

This study investigated whether collaborative PBL in conjunction with blended learning would improve preservice teachers' critical-thinking skills. Employing the before-and-after design, the researcher conducted an 18-week experimental instruction program with 34 preservice teachers enrolled in an undergraduate class of "Critical-thinking Instruction." The program incorporated collaborative PBL with blended learning, where face-to-face instruction was combined with e-learning. It was found that: (a) all participants held positive views about the instructional design of this study, claiming that it provided them with opportunities to put theory into practice, increased their motivation to participate, encouraged authentic thinking, and provoked multiple-perspective thinking; (b) the experimental instruction considerably improved the preservice teachers' critical-thinking skills; and (c) the precise mechanisms that facilitated such positive effects were evidently the problem-based learning, guided practice, discussions and sharing, observational learning, and the self-reflection activity.

Key words: blended learning, collaborative PBL, critical-thinking skills, E-Learning.

Critical thinking is a thought mode for generating knowledge (Schroyens, 2005), an effective learning strategy (Browne & Meuti, 1999; Gadzella & Masten, 1998; Halpern, 1998; McCarthy-Tucker, 2000), and a prerequisite for success in business (Harris & Eleser, 1997). A particularly recent surge of interest in teaching critical thinking and advances in online education have been driving forces behind the development of methods for professional development in critical-thinking instruction via e-learning.

To be an effective instructor of critical thinking, solid critical-thinking skills are required. To date, many researchers (e.g., Carmen & Kurubacak, 2002; Ellis, 2001; Mackinnon, 2006; Nelson & Oliver, 2004) have conducted research focusing on the use of e-learning to develop learners' critical-thinking skills and have found positive effects. In related research, two important teaching approaches have aroused a great deal of interest. First, problem-based learning (PBL) is a constructivist educational approach that organizes curricula and instruction around a carefully-crafted "ill-structured" problem. This is expected to help students develop their critical-thinking skills, problem-solving abilities, and collaborative skills as they identify problems, formulate hypotheses, conduct data searches, formulate solutions, and determine the best "fit" solution to a given problem (Ram, Ram, & Sprague, 2004). Some research (e.g., Albion & Gibson, 2000; Ochoa et al., 2001) have reported that PBL is an effective teaching approach used in professional executive training. Recently, the concept 'collaborative PBL' has sparked considerable interest and gained increasing popularity. Collaborative PBL stands apart from traditional PBL since learners experience personal and social cognitive conflicts within the context of a discussion and their goal is to collectively disentangle these conflicts by explaining the reasoning behind their thinking with one another in the group (Lee & Kim, 2005). The second important teaching approach involves blended learning which combines face-to-face instruction and e-learning. It has in fact been found to be a more effective approach than a pure e-learning approach (Osguthorpe & Graham, 2003). With these two promising approaches in mind, this study integrated collaborative PBL with blended learning in order to investigate whether it could improve preservice teachers' critical-thinking skills. This study also explored the mechanisms that could contribute to such an improvement.

CRITICAL-THINKING SKILLS

Critical-thinking skills are often referred to as higher-order thinking. Higher-order thinking, which is reflective, sensitive to the context, and self-monitored, requires synthesis, analysis, and judgment (Halpern, 1998). Numerous definitions of critical thinking have been proposed (e.g., Bailin, Coombs, Browne & Meuti, 1999; Giancarlo & Facione, 2001; Halpern, 1998, 2003; McCarthy-Tucker, 2000; Paul & Elder, 2001). Halpern (1998), for example, defined it as purposeful, reasoned, and goal-directed, further arguing that it is the kind of thinking that involves solving problems, making inferences, calculating likelihoods, and making decisions. Paul and Elder (2001) state that critical thinking is a mode of thinking in which the thinker improves the quality of his or her thinking by skillfully taking charge of the structures inherent in thinking and imposing intellectual standards upon them. To sum up, critical thinking is self-disciplined, self-monitored, self-directed, and self-corrective thinking, and it typically involves effective communication and problem-solving skills. Paul and Elder characterize a well-cultivated thinker as someone who:

- Raises vital questions, identifies problems, and formulates these clearly and precisely;
- Gathers and assesses relevant information, and can effectively interpret it;
- Comes to well-reasoned conclusions and solutions, and can test them against relevant criteria and standards;
- Thinks openmindedly within alternative systems of thought, and can recognize and assess assumptions, implications, and practical consequences in those alternative systems; and
- Communicates effectively with others in devising solutions to complex problems.

In terms of the cognitive processes involved in critical thinking, Marzano claimed that it comprises 8 stages: concept formation, principle formation, comprehension, problem-solving, decision-making, research, composition, and oral discourse (as cited in Bailin et al., 1999). But, Daniel Eckber contended, stating that critical thinking involves 6 steps: defining dilemma, evaluating electives, considering consequences, determining importance, deciding on direction, and assessing ends (as cited in Bailin et al., 1999). In light of the above, there can be little doubt that critical thinking is closely related to problem-solving.

PBL AND COLLABORATIVE PBL

PBL provides great possibilities for improving learning (Mayo, Donnelly, Nash, & Schwartz, 1993). Since first developed in medical schools as a means to prepare interns students for their future profession (Savery & Duffy, 1995), PBL has been employed in various domains to improve learning.

Delisle (1997) defined PBL as a teaching technique that requires students to solve problems in a certain situation. Students are assigned to teams that are responsible for framing a problem and deciding how best to use their knowledge to solve it (Engel, 1997). Moreover, the goals of PBL are to familiarize students with the types of problems that they may face in the future, equip them with relevant knowledge, facilitate their application of problem-solving skills, and finally help them refine their problem-solving skills (Gerber, English, & Singer, 1999; Savery & Duffy, 1995).

According to Savery and Duffy (1995), there are four major features in PBL:

- Students develop a new cognition with each goal;
- All problems proposed by the teacher are related to students' real-life;
- Both the problem and the teacher play a part in increasing learners' learning motivation; and
- The teacher is a facilitator during the learning process.

Egg and Kauchak (2001) claim that PBL strategies typically have the following characteristics:

◆ Lessons begin with a problem or question, and solving the problem is the focus of the lesson;

◆ Students are responsible for investigating the problem, designing strategies, and finding solutions; and

◆ The teacher guides students' efforts through questioning and other forms of instructional scaffolding.

As for the learning process, Boud (1985) reported that PBL begins with the presentation of a problem. Students then work in small groups to analyze the problem and decide what information is required for a solution. Once they identify the required learning, students begin individual work and conduct research before returning to the group to share their thoughts and findings concerning the problem. In the final phase, in groups, students are asked to summarize and integrate what they have learned. In the same vein, Jordan and Porath (2006) claim that PBL involves working in cooperative groups and thinking about real-world problems. These descriptions of PBL indicate that, in essence, it must be conducted in a collaborative way. As a result, collaborative PBL has now become a more widely-used term.

According to Lee and Kim (2005), collaborative PBL is a learning method in which learners have a common goal, in which they perform given tasks at the same level, and in which they interact with one another while problem-solving. Accordingly, collaborative PBL emphasizes the importance of interactive discussions; this is based on the principals of social constructivism which emphasizes that learning is achieved via negotiating thoughts and building mutual understanding with others. In other words, collaborative PBL is the product of social interactions through negotiations and mutual understanding (Littleton & Hakkinen, 1999).

Apart from this, in collaborative PBL, learners are expected to construct a problem representation and to manipulate the problem space, transferring their internal representations into external ones (Lee & Kim, 2005). Representation tools mediate collaborative learning interactions by providing learners with the means to express their newly-created knowledge in a stable medium, where the new knowledge then becomes part of the shared context. In this sense, concept maps provide an effective presentation tool (Lee & Kim, 2005). A concept map is a drawn picture that reflects a learner's understanding and interpretation of various aspects of a given topic (Raymond, 1997). In that PBL requires learners to summarize and systemize relevant information when searching for a solution to a problem, concept maps not only provide learners with summarized information that contributes to learning, but also provide learners with a framework that helps them when they systematize materials in a particular knowledge domain (Alvermann, 1986; Moore & Readence, 1984; Novak, 1984; Novak & Gowin, 1984; Stewart, 1984). Concept mapping, therefore, can be an ideal vehicle for visualizing relevant arguments for use in problem-solving.

In addition to this, PBL generally includes case studies which have been recognized as valuable instructional tools (Carter & Unklesbay, 1989; Merseth & Lacey, 1993). When PBL includes this approach, students are presented with a problem embedded within the resource-rich context of a case study, and assuming the role of primary researchers, they proceed to analyze the problems, come up with and weigh all possible solutions, develop a plan and evaluate all possible outcomes (Simons, Klein, and Brush, 2004). Such a rich context as a case study, therefore, encourages, if not necessitates, the employment of critical-thinking skills.

COLLABORATIVE PBL AND BLENDED LEARNING

E-learning has five particularly salient features (Rich, 2001). First, it is available via the Internet at any time and place. Second, its multi-faceted format allows for relatively high levels of interactivity. Third, the contents can be adapted on the basis of individual needs and advancement opportunities. Fourth, learning experiences range from very basic exercises to highly interactive forms of communication, and from textbook learning to performance simulation. Finally, a web-based learning management system has the capacity to track attendance, record test scores, and even correlate training effectiveness with business results.

In addition, e-learning encompasses various communication modes in both synchronous and asynchronous modes. Synchronous discussions take place in real time, which means participants communicate with each other at the same time. Asynchronous discussions, on the other hand, do not take place in real time and allow for delays in receiving and responding to communications; these are often referred to as threaded discussions, asynchronous conferencing, electronic discussion boards, or text-based computer conferencing (Beaudin, 1999). Among these media, the asynchronous discussion board is by and large the most frequently used; it not only encourages thoughtful reflection and more complex responses, but also enhances collaboration and provides greater flexibility and convenience for group discussions (Rossman, 1999).

Given the advantages of PBL and e-learning, integrating them should make it possible to maximize the acquisition of critical-thinking skills. One example of the successful integration of PBL and e-learning is cited in the study of Garrison, Anderson, and Archer (2001) who employed computer-mediated communication in PBL to improve students' critical-thinking skills; more specifically, based on the concepts of problem-solving, they employed a four-stage process: (1) triggering: posing the problem; (2) exploration: searching for information; (3) integration: constructing possible solutions; and (4) resolution: critically assessing different solutions. Lee and Kim (2005), however, suggest that although a web-based collaborative PBL environment has great potential for cultivating the ability to solve problems in practical situations, compared to traditional classrooms, it offers learners relatively few opportunities to solve problems through face-to face interactions. In a case study involving of the ITESM-CCM, the most competitive private higher education institution in Mexico, Mortera-Gutiérrez (2006) finds that the worst teaching approach takes place when instructors make their e-learning platform the main engine of their courses and totally overlook face-to-face instruction. Blended learning, which combines face-to-face instruction with e-learning, can maximize the benefits of both face-to-face and online methods (Osguthorpe & Graham, 2003). Therefore, with the complementary use of e-learning, especially that with asynchronous discussion boards, it is expected that collaborative PBL is considerably more effective in the classroom than a pure approach which only employs either face-to-face instruction or e-learning, not both.

COLLABORATIVE PBL, E-LEARNING, AND CRITICAL THINKING

Very little research has investigated the relationship between collaborative PBL in a blended learning context and teachers' professional development in teaching critical thinking Owing to the paucity of research in this line of study, the following literature review mainly centers on the relationships between PBL or collaborative PBL and critical thinking as well as the relationship between e-learning and critical thinking.

There is no question that many researchers (e.g. DaRosa, D. A., ÓSullivan, P. S., Younger, M., & Deterding, R., 2001; Kamin, C., ÓSullivan, P., Deterding, R., & Younger, M., 2003; Semerci, N., 2006; Tiwari, A., Lai, P., So, M., & Yuen, K., 2006) take the position that PBL can significantly improve critical-thinking skills. Tiwari, Lai, So, and Yuen (2006), for example, compared the effect of PBL with that of lecturing approaches on the development of students' critical thinking and found that those who took PBL courses made considerably greater improvements in their critical-thinking dispositions than their counterparts who merely took lecture courses. In the same vein, in his study comparing the beneficial effects of PBL with those of traditional teaching methods on students' critical thinking, Semerci (2006) finds that the former far surpassed those of the latter,.

As for the relationship between e-learning and critical thinking, previous findings (e.g., Carmen & Kurubacak, 2002; Ellis, 2001; Kumta, Tasng, Hung, & Cheng, 2003; Mackinnon, 2006; Nelson & Oliver, 2004) suggest that e-learning provides a natural framework for the strengthening of critical-thinking skills. For example, based on their study designed to stimulate the abilities of analysis, application, and evaluation, Kumta et al. (2003) find that a web-based tutorial program can foster medical students' critical-thinking skills. Along similar lines, Ellis (2001) finds that computer-based multimedia tutorials do help students develop their critical-thinking skills. And, integrating electronic discussions with electronic concept mapping, Mackinnon (2006) concludes that preservice teachers were able to significantly improve their ability to both formulate arguments and lead effective discussions. These findings suggest that the e-learning interface enables participants to express their opinions using sound reasoning, to develop arguments supported by logic and solid evidence, and to reflect on and share ideas with others by making thinking transparent.

Hughes and Daykin (2002) suggest that with the move to online delivery, greater attention must be paid to the design and development of facilitator skills than previously thought. From a constructivist viewpoint, a critical component of online interaction is the interpersonal/social component. Social interaction can contribute to learner satisfaction and increase frequency of interaction in an online learning environment. Blended learning emphasizes social interaction and it places a high priority on the objective of using technological resources in critical and reflective ways in the classroom; moreover, blended learning provides opportunities for sharing information in a faster way, while creating a positive educational environment for feedback (Mortera-Gutiérrez, 2006). Therefore, as long as a teaching program is well designed, the integration of PBL and blended learning should benefit preservice teachers by helping them to improve their critical-thinking skills. This study therefore hypothesized that integrating collaborative PBL and blended learning should effectively improve preservice teachers' critical-thinking skills.

METHOD

Participants

The participants were 34 preservice teachers (6 males and 28 females) enrolled in the Critical-thinking Instruction class in a teachers' training program for secondary school teachers. Among them, 16 (47.1%) were undergraduates and 18 were graduates (92.9%). Their mean age was 23.00 (*SD* = 2.54).

Instruments

The instruments employed in this study were the e-learning website developed by National Chengchi University, the *Critical Thinking Test, Level II* (CTT-II), the *Situation-based Critical Thinking Test* (SB-CTT), and a reflection questionnaire.

The structure of the e-learning interface consists of curricular content, curricular information, curricular interaction, an individual area, and a system area (see Figure 1). The instructional design in this study required participants to complete a project based on PBL which required a great deal of online discussions; as a result, the "discussion board" under "curricular interaction" was the most commonly used interface.

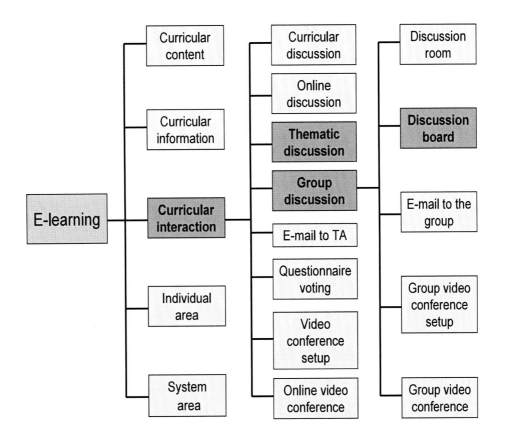

Figure 1. Structure of the e-learning interface.

The CTT-II, based on the *Cornell Critical Thinking Test* (Ennis, Millman, Tomko, 1985) and the *Watson-Glasser Critical Thinking Test* (Watson & Glasser, 1980), was developed by Yu-Chu Yeh (2005). It consists of 30 multiple-choice items evenly divided into five subtests: assumption identification, induction, deduction, interpretation, and argument evaluation. Each item consists of one statement and four multiple-choice answers. With a 25-minute time limit, the CTT-II has a total possible score of 30 points. In this study, a correct answer was given a score of 1 point and a wrong answer 0. The average discrimination index of the CTT-II is .35 (with a range of .21 - .53) and the average difficulty index is .58 (with a range of .24-.84). The test can effectively discriminate between the high-ability group (upper 27%) and the low-ability group (lower 27%) on the ability to think critically. Moreover, the subtest scores and total score are significantly correlated, rs (492) = .352 - .665, ps < .001 (Yeh, 2005).

The SB-CTT, developed by Yu-Chu Yeh (2005), is based on Paul and Elder's (2001) concepts of 10 intellectual standards and 8 reasoning elements. This test consists of a paragraph entitled *The Life of Albert* and 7 open-ended questions. With the theme "being happy", the paragraph describes Albert's beliefs and thoughts about life. It also consists of several assumptions and a few personal feelings or characteristics, such as being happy, selfish, pessimistic, and being irresponsible, as well as believing in fate. After reading the paragraph, the participants were required to analyze the paragraph from seven perspectives: (1) purpose and information; (2) issues; (3) assumptions; (4) points of view; (5) inferences; (6) implications; and (7) evaluation (Yeh, 2005). In this study, a consensual assessment by two trained graduate students was employed to score the responses in this test.

Finally, a reflection questionnaire, consisting of 9 open-ended questions, was developed by the researcher based on the research needs and contents of the experimental instruction. Each of the 10 questions and a summary of the responses are given in the Results section.

Procedures

This study employed the before-and-after design. An 18-week experimental instruction program integrating collaborative PBL and blended learning was implemented. The pretests were administered in the first week, and the posttests in the 18th week. The pretests comprised the CTT-II and the SB-CTT, while the posttests comprised all of the pretests as well as the reflection questionnaire. In the second week, the participants were put into their self-assigned groups of 5-6 for a total of 6 groups and started to prepare for their project in which PBL was implemented

During the instruction period, throughout the first seven weeks, the researcher introduced the concepts of critical thinking and related strategies. Meanwhile, the participants were asked to find a suitable case on which to develop arguments based on PBL. From the 8th week on, the participants were provided scaffolding to complete the PBL assignment. During this period of learning, the researcher also asked that the participants construct a group contract consisting of learning goals and conflict resolutions, a concept map depicting the arguments they prepared for problem-solving, and a role play to act out the process of solving the authentic problem they had chosen. At the end of the 18-week course, the participants were asked to reflect on their PBL experiences by compiling a learning portfolio in which they described the developmental steps in their learning under PBL. Added to this, the participants were encouraged to read other groups' homework online and to use the e-learning interface, especially the discussion board, to complete their project. More specifically, the case study approach along with the strategies of concept mapping, role play, observational learning, guided practice, cooperative learning, and self-reflection were adopted to scaffold the participants to complete their PBL assignments in this study.

Data analysis

To evaluate the participants' performance on the CTT-II and the SB-CTT, several one-way (within group: pretest vs. posttest) Repeated Measure Analyses of Variance were performed.

RESULTS

Improvements in critical-thinking skills

This study employed the CTT-II and the SB-CTT to determine whether the participants' critical-thinking skills had improved since the onset of the experimental instruction. Table 1 and Figure 2 depict the means and standard deviations as well as the patterns of change in the participants' performance on the subtests of the CTT-II. The Repeated Measure Analysis of Variance indicates that Test (pretest vs. posttest) had a significant effect on the CTT-II scores, $F(1, 26) = 9.194$, $p = .005$, $\eta^2 = .261$ (See Table 2). A comparison of the means makes it clear that the participants performed better on the posttest than on the pretest.

Table 1. Participants' Mean Scores and Standard Deviations on the Subtests of the CTT-II

Test	Pretest			Posttest		
	N	M	SD	N	M	SD
Assumption	27	3.11	1.40	27	2.70	.95
Induction	27	4.41	.89	27	4.78	.80
Deduction	27	3.44	1.31	27	4.07	1.44
Explanation	27	2.93	1.38	27	3.26	1.29
Evaluation	27	2.30	1.10	27	3.07	1.00

Table 2. Test Results of Within-Subjects Contrasts on the Total Score of the CTT-II

Source	M	SD	Type III SS	df	MS	F	Sig.	η^2
Pretest	16.19	2.54	39.185	1	39.185	9.194	.005	.261
Posttest	17.89	2.82						

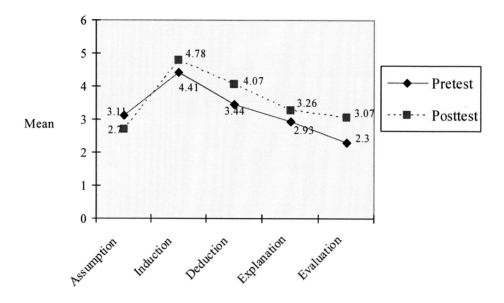

Figure 2. Changes in the patterns of participants' performance on the subtests of the CTT-II.

Table 3 and Figure 3 depict the means and standard deviations as well as the changes in the patterns of the participant' performance on the subtests of the SB-CTT. The Repeated Measure Analysis of Variance indicates that Test (pretest vs. posttest) had a significant effect on the CTT-II, $F(1, 31) = 42.136$, $p = .000$, $\eta^2 = .584$ (See Table 4).. A comparison of the means again confirms that the participants performed better on the posttest than on the pretest

Table 3. Participants' Mean Scores and Standard Deviations on the Subtests of the SB-CTT

Test	Pretest			Posttest		
	N	M	SD	N	M	SD
Q1	32	3.75	.508	32	3.97	.315
Q2	32	3.25	.672	32	3.55	.810
Q3	32	3.31	.535	32	3.39	.667
Q4	32	3.88	.871	32	3.87	.670
Q5	32	3.53	.671	32	4.23	.425
Q6	32	3.16	.448	32	3.29	.461
Q7	32	2.81	.471	32	4.06	.250

Table 4. Test Results of Within-Subjects Contrasts on the Total Score of the SB-CTT

Source	M	SD	Type III SS	df	MS	F	Sig.	η^2
Pretest	23.61	2.14	116.532	1	116.532	42.136	.000	.584
Posttest	26.35	2.17						

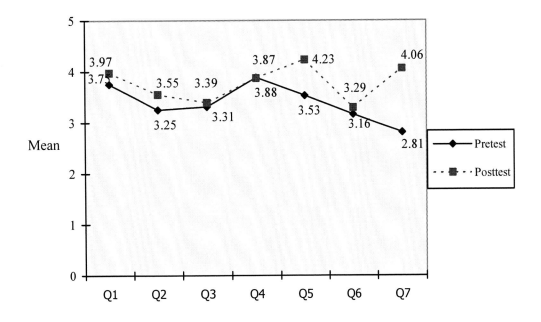

Figure 3. Changes in the patterns of participants' performance on the subtests of the SB-CTT.

Mechanisms for improving critical-thinking skills

This study analyzed the different mechanisms intended to improve critical-thinking skills. A summary of the results based on the participants' answers on the reflection questionnaires is presented in the following.

> ⚓ Have you read the other groups' work online and how do you feel about having the opportunity to read their work? Why?

All the participants claimed to have read the other groups' work online and to have benefited from it. The primary benefits were that it helped them to better self-reflect by observing the work of others (26%); it gave them a chance to practice their own critical-thinking skills (23%); the other groups' work served as examples (19%); the other groups' work gave them inspiration and stimulated new ideas (16%); and it helped them to understand the contents of the curriculum (10%).

> ⚓ This class integrated PBL and blended learning. Did such an instructional design contribute to the improvement in your critical-thinking skills? How?

Ninety-seven percent of the participants reported that this instructional design contributed to the improvement in their own critical-thinking skills. The principal ways in which it helped them were that it increased their opportunities for online discussions (19%); online discussions increased their opportunities to practice critical-thinking skills (19%); observing the performance of others helped them solve problems on their own (11%); the integration of PBL and blended learning improved their thinking skills and knowledge (10%); it helped them better retain class learning and gave them motivation to participate more actively (10%); and it provided them with opportunities to exchange information and clarify relevant concepts (10%).

🔸 Did the instructional design encourage you to reflect on your critical-thinking skills, attitude, and teaching? Why?

All the participants responded to this question in the affirmative. The main reasons were that the discussion and interaction encouraged self-reflection (55%); the online learning was convenient for extensive learning and discussions (35%); and it helped them with their teaching (10%).

🔸 What were the benefits of the blended learning—that is, e-learning integrated with classroom learning? Why?

All the participants had a positive attitude about the blended learning and were very willing to share their ideas. The main benefits they cited were that it was very convenient for group discussions and for completing assignments (48%); it increased their opportunities to review and practice critical-thinking skills outside the classroom (23%); it increased their opportunities to share reports (13%); and it saved time and resources (10%).

🔸 Did the learning contract enhance the spirit of cooperation among you and your group members and help you with the completion of group tasks? Why?

Sixty-eight percent of the participants agreed with this statement and the main reasons included the fact that it kept everyone on track and helped them resolve conflicts among group members (52%); it helped them establish rules and therefore improved their sense of belonging to the group (13%). On the other hand, some participants challenged the notion, contending that the contract did not have much influence as all group members had already been working hard from the start (20%).

🔸 Did the use of the real-world cases in PBL contribute to your learning of critical thinking? Why?

All the participants held positive attitudes toward this question. The main reasons were that the case studies helped them integrate theory into practice (25%); the case studies were authentic and therefore made sense to them (23%); and they provoked multi-perspective thinking and critical thinking (10%).

🔸 Did the use of role plays to act out your arguments contribute to your learning of critical thinking? Why?

Most participants (94%) had positive feelings about the role plays. This seemingly stemmed from their highly interactive and interesting nature. They responded that the role plays provoked empathy and multiple-perspective thinking (48%), helped audiences to understand their arguments (30%), and increased their friendships with other group members (10%). A few participants, however, claimed that the role plays did not contribute to their learning of critical thinking (3%) and that the role plays gave group members unnecessary stress (3%).

> ✦ Did the representation of arguments via concept mapping contribute to your improvement in critical thinking? Why?

All the participants agreed that concept mapping was valuable and the reasons cited were that it helped them with the presentation and systemization of complex thinking (29%); it helped them with the drawing of conclusions from complex data, which further became good arguments (26%); it helped them understand the relationships among concepts since it visually compared and contrasted them (23%); and it helped them refocus on problems (19%).

> ✦ What are your feelings about, or what have you gained from this class? Why?

All of the participants had positive attitudes toward the class. The primary reasons were that their critical-thinking skills and abilities had greatly improved (48%); they had benefited substantially from group discussions (17%); and they had become better able to think rationally when faced with problems (10%). However, a few participants responded that there were too many assignments and that the discussions were too long (10%).

DISCUSSION

Effects of integrating collaborative BPL and blended learning

In conducting this research, it was somewhat difficult to get the control group to finish all of the same tests that the experimental group was administered. Therefore, the participants' improvements in critical-thinking skills were evaluated by comparing their scores on the pretest with those on the posttest. Although a pretest-posttest control group design is generally considered superior to a before-and-after design, the before-and-after design is still commonly deemed acceptable, particularly when a control group is difficult to get. To compensate for the shortcoming of the before-and-after design, this study employed 2 complementary instruments: the SB-CTT and the reflection questionnaire. The results of the Repeated Measure Analyses of Variance as well as the content analysis of the participants' responses in the reflection questionnaire fully supported the two hypotheses put forth in this study. In other words, all of the evidence indicates that integrating collaborative PBL and blended learning enhanced the preservice teachers' professional development in critical-thinking instruction.

This study employed two tests (the CTT-II and the SB-CTT) to evaluate whether or not the participants improved their critical-thinking skills during the 18-week period of experimental instruction. The analytical results indicate that the participants scored significantly higher on the posttest than on the pretest of both the CTT-II and the SB-CTT. These findings determined that the experimental instruction in this study was effective in improving the preservice teachers' critical-thinking skills. Important to note, 97% of the participants reported that the instructional design improved their critical-thinking skills and the most important reason for this was that the instructional design increased the number of opportunities they had for online discussions. Commonly cited too was the fact that the online discussions increased their opportunities to practice their critical-thinking skills. It is also worth noting that the participants were completely supportive of the use of collaborative PBL and stated that the approach helped them connect theory and practice, while serving as a stimulus to multi-perspective thinking. In their own words, such learning "made sense" to them. The participants also strongly supported the use of learning contracts, concept mapping, and the role plays during the problem-solving process.

The instructional design in this study—collaborative PBL in a blended learning environment—incorporated the case study approach as well as the strategies of cooperative learning, discussion, concept mapping, role play, observational learning, guided practice, and self-reflection. The findings are in line with earlier findings and suggestions (e.g. DaRosa, et al., 2001; Halpern, 1998; Kamin et al., 2003; Mackinnon, 2006; Semerci, 2006; Tiwari et al., 2006) that PBL is an effective approach for improving critical thinking. Halpern (1998) explained that problems and arguments can indeed enhance the transcontextual transfer of critical-thinking skills. And, DeRoche (2006) recently suggests that PBL provides students with loosely structured real-life problems and that as students go about trying to solve a problem, they are guided by the problem itself and must continually seek, find, organize, and evaluate information.

With regard to the learning processes involved in collaborative PBL, Lee and Kim (2005) point out that students are required to: (1) explore and represent a problem; (2) identify what they already know about the problem; (3) make clear what they do not know; (4) identify their goals and make an action plan; (5) collect relevant information; (6) discuss the information collected; (7) apply their prerequisite knowledge to the problem; and (8) review the above steps. However, they point out that the sequences can differ more or less in accordance with students' newly-formed ideas. Generally, this study closely followed these procedures. To help the participants define their goals and make an action plan, they were asked to construct a group contract; to facilitate their discussion and problem-solving skills, they were asked to make a concept map; and to encourage them to review the learning process, they were asked to make a group portfolio. The extent to which PBL served to facilitate the preservice teachers' critical-thinking skills may very well, at least partially, be attributed to these supplementary strategies.

The findings in this study also lend support to the argument that case studies are invaluable in teacher education (Carter & Unklesbay, 1989). In addition, the results support the position that concept mapping contributes to self-reflection, knowledge construction, and the identification of causal relationships, all of which are essential for good critical thinking. Based on Ausubel's assimilation theory of cognitive learning, concept mapping requires that cognitive structures be organized hierarchically, with new concepts being subsumed under more inclusive ones. When learners arrange newly-acquired knowledge in such a ranked fashion and explore the possible linkages among various notions, meaningful learning occurs (as cited in Novak & Gowin, 1984). Moreover, in constructing a concept map, learners' self-reflection and cognitive reasoning skills are sharpened since they are organizing the concepts meaningfully, making connections among them and deciding on their causal relationships.

E-learning is moving towards providing an environment that facilitates broad-based content creation, sharing, reuse, and distribution, rather than just focusing on replacing information that is traditionally learned in a common classroom setting. Soft skills are emerging as the current and immediate future direction of e-learning (Tastle, White, & Shackleton, 2005). Skills in problem-solving and critical-thinking are certainly among these soft skills. According to multichannel communication theory, humans have several channels through which data are communicated. If information is presented by way of two or more of these channels, then there is additional reinforcement and greater retention, thereby improving learning (Bagui, 1998). Accordingly, this study employed multiple methods to develop preservice teachers' critical-thinking skills. First, the experimental instruction was conducted via the integration of PBL, e-learning, and classroom teaching. Second, PBL was employed by combining the case study approach and several different strategies, such as a learning contract, concept maps, role plays, and self-reflection.

As Mortera-Gutiérrez (2006) puts it, the combination of face-to-face instruction and communication technology in a blended learning environment creates a myriad of educational possibilities that reflect a certain pedagogical richness. To have technological media supporting course activities and assignments in a blended learning course allows students to have greater control of their goals. However, the aim of using blended learning approaches is to find a harmonious balance between online access to knowledge and face-to-face human interaction (Osguthorpe & Graham, 2003). The findings in this study indicate that such a harmonious balance was reached in this study.

Mechanisms that contribute to instructional effectiveness

Problem-based learning

In this study, the participants were unanimous in their opinion that the PBL in this study, with authentic case studies and concept mapping, contributed to their personal improvement in critical thinking. In addition, 94% held a positive attitude toward the use of role plays and 68% toward learning contracts. An analysis of the reasons for their positive attitudes suggests that the PBL applied in this study triggered preservice teachers' motivation and encouraged discussion, interaction, practice, and multiple-perspective thinking, in turn improving their critical-thinking skills.

As a general rule, PBL immerses learners into an authentic context with ill-structured problems (Simons et al., 2004), and they are assigned to groups to solve these problems; each participant therefore learns how to apply his/her related knowledge and strategies to solve problems (Ochoa & Gottschall, 2004). And, as critical thinking is usually used in problem-solving, PBL can be effective in improving critical-thinking skills.

Guided practices

Participants in this study were given opportunities for guided practices when they were asked to decide on a case for PBL, to form a learning community via group discussions and by making group contracts, to visualize their arguments via concept mapping, to act out their arguments via role plays, and to self-reflect via creating a group portfolio of the PBL process. What the findings suggest is that the preservice teachers' improvements in critical-thinking skills are rooted in adequate opportunities to practice critical-thinking skills. Thus, it can be concluded that guided practices contribute to mastering critical-thinking skills.

Discussion and sharing

During the process of developing their critical-thinking skills, learners must be active participants on the grounds that their success is contingent on the quality of interactions, discussions, and cooperation. As Eggen and Kauchak (2001) suggest, for students to develop their critical-thinking skills, a classroom environment that values different perspectives and a great deal of discussion is essential. This was reflected in the reflection questions in which many participants stated that discussions, especially those online, were a great contributor to the improvement in their critical-thinking skills.

Bastiaens and Martens (2000) note that web-based learning provides users with opportunities to express their ideas and that this stimulates thinking through interpersonal interactions. It is pertinent here that Eastmond (1995) also argued that learners should be provided opportunities to interact and reflect and that such learning occurs when an instructor merges online discussions and learning methods in computer-mediated communications. This study confirms the importance of discussion and sharing in e-learning.

Observational learning

To provide the participants with opportunities for peer modeling and observational learning in this study, the groups were asked to hand in all assignments to the e-learning interface, and these assignments were always available for all participants to read; moreover, a group presentation on instructional design and a teaching demonstration were required of all groups. The findings in this study indicate that reading other groups' assignments online contributed to self-reflection, provided extra practice with critical-thinking skills, and encouraged the generation of novel ideas. Such skills are central characteristics of good critical thinking (Paul & Elder, 2001), and observational learning clearly contributes to the cultivation of these skills.

Self-reflection

All of the participants in this study agreed that the inclusion of blended learning increased the extent of their reflection about their attitudes toward their skill in and teaching of critical thinking; it is noteworthy that such effects are generally derived from discussions, especially those online. This finding supports Maher and Jacob's (2006) claim that the use of computer-mediated communications facilitates peer interactions and the reflective consideration of instructional practices.

A reflective mind is the hallmark of critical thinking (Schroyens, 2005). Titone, Sherman, and Palmer (1998) maintained that providing feedback is an effective method of increasing mindful learning, which further contributes to nurturing reflective practices. The instructional design of this study simultaneously incorporated the use of "peer feedback" and "teacher feedback". Whereas peer feedback was mainly provided through online discussions, teacher feedback was provided through classroom interactions. This study provided additional feedback through the test results, all in an effort to increase participants' self-awareness and self-reflection.

CONCLUSIONS AND SUGGESTIONS

Cultivating critical thinkers has been one of the most important educational goals of secondary school education throughout the past decade. The need for secondary school teachers' professional development in teaching critical thinking cannot be overstated. In that collaborative PBL provides a natural framework for professional development and blended learning allows participants to develop more critical and reflective attitudes toward learning goals, this study integrated collaborative PBL with blended learning, and based on this framework, provided preservice teachers with experimental instruction. The findings from this study are convincing: preservice teachers' critical-thinking skills improved considerably in this training program. The mechanisms that facilitated such effects were mainly problem-based learning, guided practice, discussion and sharing, observational learning, and self-reflection.

Due to the difficulty in getting a control group, this study employed a before-and-after design. Future studies should try to use a pretest-posttest control group design to confirm the instructional benefits found in this study. Moreover, to maximize the effects of blended learning, teachers need to determine how to reach a perfect balance between online learning and in-class learning and learn how to employ different kinds of online learning strategies.

ACKNOWLEDGMENT

The author would like to thank the National Science Council of the Republic of China, Taiwan, for financially supporting this research under Project No. NSC94-2520-S-004-001.

REFERENCES

Albion, P., & Gibson, I. (2000). Problem-based learning as a multimedia design framework in teacher education. *Journal of Technology and Teacher Education, 8*(4), 315-326.

Alvermann, D. E. (1986). Graphic organizers: Cueing devices for comprehending and remembering main ideas. In J. F. Baumann (Ed.), *Teaching main idea comprehension* (pp. 210-226). Newark, DE: International Reading Association.

Bagui, S. (1998). Reasons for increased learning using multimedia. *Journal of Educational Multimedia and Hypermedia, 7*(1), 3-18.

Bailin, S., Case, R., Coombs, J. R., & Daniels, L. B. (1999). Common misconceptions of critical thinking. *Journal of Curriculum Studies, 31*(3), 269-283.

Bastiaens, T. J., & Martens, R. L. (2000).Conditions for web-based learning with real events. In B. Abbey (Ed.), *Instructional and cognitive impacts of web-based education* (pp.1-31). London: Idea Group Publishing.

Beaudin, B. P. (1999). *Keeping on-line asynchronous discussion on topic.* Retrieved April 2, 2007 from WWW: http://www.aln.org/publications/jaln/v3n2/v3n2_beaudin.asp

Boud, D. (1985). Problem-based learning in perspective. In D. Boud (Ed.), *Problem-based learning in education for the professions* (pp. 13-18). Sydney: Higher Education Research Society of Australasia.

Browne, M. N., & Meuti, M. D. (1999). Teaching how to teach critical thinking. *College Student Journal, 33*(2), 162–170.

Carmen, C., & Kurubacak, G. (2002). The use of the internet to teach critical thinking. *Society for Information Technology and Teacher Education International Conference, 2002*(1), 2504-2505.

Carter, K., & Unklesbay, R. (1989). Cases in teaching and law. *Journal of Curriculum Studies, 21*(6), 527-536.

DaRosa, D. A., ÓSullivan, P. S., Younger, M., & Deterding, R. (2001). Measuring critical thinking in problem-based learning discourse. *Teaching and Learning in Medicine, 13,* 27-35.

Delisle, R. (1997). *How to use problem-based learning in the classroom.* Alexlandria, VA: Association for Supervision and Curriculum Development.

DeRoche, S. J. K. (2006). An adventure in problem-based learning. *Phi Delta Kappan, 87*(9), 705-708

Eastmond, D. V. (1995). *Alone but together: Adult distance study through computer conferencing.* Cresskill, NJ: Hampton Press.

Eggen, P. D., & Kauchhak, D.P. (2001). *Educational Psychology: Windows on the classroom* (5th ed.). Upper Saddle River, N.J: Merrill Prentice Hall.

Ellis, T. J. (2001). Multimedia enhanced educational products as a tool to promote critical thinking in adult students. *Journal of Educational Multimedia and Hypermedia, 10*(2), 107-124.

Engel, C.E. (1997). Not just a method but a way of learning. In D. Boud and G.E. Feletti (Eds.), *The challenge of problem-based learning* (pp. 17-27). London: Kogan Page Limited.

Ennis, R. H., Millman, J., & Tomko, T. N. (1985). *Cornell Critical Thinking Tests, Level X & Level Z--Manual.* CA: Midwest Publications.

Gadzella, B. M., & Masten, W. G. (1998). Critical thinking and learning processes for students in two major fields. *Journal of Instructional Psychology, 25*(4), 256-261.

Garrison, D. R., Anderson, T., & Archer, W. (2001). Critical thinking, cognitive presence, and computer conferencing in distance education. *American Journal of Distance Education, 15*(1), 7-23.

Gerber, M.M., English, J., & Singer, G.S. (1999). Bridging between craft and academic knowledge: A computer-supported, problem-based learning model for professional preparation in special education. *Teacher Education and Special Education, 22*, 100-113.

Giancarlo, C. A., & Facione, P. A (2001). A look across four years at the disposition toward critical thinking among undergraduate students. *Journal of General Education, 50*(1), 29-55.

Halpern, D. F. (1998). Teaching critical thinking for transfer across domains, dispositions, skills, structure training, and metacognitive monitoring. *American Psychologist, 53*(4), 449-455.

Halpern, D. F. (2003). *Knowledge and thought: An introduction to critical thinking* (4th ed.). Hillsdale, NJ: Lawrence Erlbaum.

Harris, J. C., & Eleser, C. (1997). Developmental critical thinking: Melding two imperatives. *Journal of Developmental Education, 21*(1), 12-19.

Hughes, M., & Daykin, N. (2002). Towards constructivism: Investigating students' perceptions and learning as a result of using an online environment. *Innovations in Education and Teaching International*, 39(3), 217-224.

Jorden, E. A., & Porath, M.J. (2006). *Educational psychology: A problem-based approach.* Boston, MA: Allyn and Bacon.

Kamin, C., ÓSullivan, P., Deterding, R., & Younger, M. (2003). A comparison of critical thinking in groups of third-year medical students in text, video, and virtual PBL case modalities. *Academic Medicine, 78,* 204-211.

Kumta, S. M., Tasng, P. L., Hung, L. K., & Cheng, J. C. Y. (2003). Fostering critical-thinking skills through a web-based tutorial progamme for final year medical students—a randomized controlled study. *Journal of Educational Multimedia and Hypermedia, 12*(3), 267-273.

Lee, M., & Kim, D. (2005). The effects of the collaborative representation supporting tool on problem-solving processes and outcomes in web-based collaborative problem-based learning environments. *Journal of Interactive Learning Research, 16*(3), 273-293.

Littleton, K., & Hakkinen, P. (1999). Learning together: Understanding the process of computer based collaborative learning. In P. Dillenbourg (Ed.), *Collaborative learning: Cognitive and computational approaches.* New York, NY: Pergamon.

Mackinnon, G. R. (2006). Contentious issues in science education: Building critical-thinking patterns through two-dimensional concept mapping. *Journal of Educational Multimedia and Hypermedia, 15*(4), 433-445.

Maher, M., & Jacob, E. (2006). Peer computer conferencing to support teachers' reflection during action research. *Journal of Technology and Teacher Education, 14* (1), 127-150.

Mayo, P., Donnelly, M. B., Nash, P. P., & Schwartz, R. W. (1993). Student perceptions of tutor effectiveness in problem based surgery clerkship. *Teaching and Learning in Medicine, 5*(4), 227-233.

McCarthy-Tucker, S. N. (2000). Teaching style, philosophical orientation and the transmission of critical thinking skills in the U.S. public schools. *Korean Journal of Thinking and Problem Solving, 10*(1), 69-77.

Merseth, K. K., & Lacey, C. A. (1993). Weaving stronger fabric: The pedagogical promise of hypermedia and case methods in teacher education. *Teaching and Teacher Education, 9*(3), 283-299.

Moore, D. W., & Readence, J. E. (1984). A quantitative and qualitative review of graphic organizer research. *Journal of Educational Research, 78*(1), 11-17.

Mortera-Gutiérrez, F. (2006). Faculty best practices using blended learning in e-learning and face-to-face instruction. *International Journal on E-learning, 5*(3), 313-337.

Nelson, T., & Oliver, W. (2004). Maximizing critical thinking skills with technology. In P. Kommers and G. Richards (Eds.), *Proceedings of World Conference on Educational Multimedia, Hypermedia and Telecommunications, 2004,* 3982-3986.

Novak, J. D. (1984). Application of advances in learning theory and philosophy of science to the improvement of chemistry teaching. *The Journal of Chemical Education, 61*(7), 607-612.

Novak, J. D., & Gowim, D. B. (1984). *Learning how to learn.* Cambridge, England: Cambridge University Press.

Ochoa, T. A., & Gottschall, H. (2004). Group Participation and Satisfaction: Results from a PBL Computer-Supported Module. *Journal of Educational Multimedia and Hypermedia, 13*(1), 73-91.

Ochoa, T. A., Gerber, M. M., Leafstedt, J. M., Hough, S., Kyle, S., Rogers-Adkinson, D., & Kumar, P. (2001). Web technology as a teaching tool: A multicultural special education case. *Journal of International Forum of Educational Technology & Society, 4*(1), 50-60.

Osguthorpe, R. T., & Graham, C. R. (2003). Blended learning environments: Definitions and directions. *The Quarterly Review of Distance Education, 4*(3), 227-233

Paul, R., & Elder, L. (2001). *Critical thinking: Tools for taking charge of your learning and your life.* Upper Saddle River, NJ: Prentice Hall.

Ram, P., Ram, A. & Sprague, C. (2004). A web-based system to bring PBL into your classroom. *Proceedings of Society for Information Technology and Teacher Education International Conference, 2004,* 3007-3012.

Raymond, A. M. (1997). The use of concept mapping in qualitative research: A multiple case study in mathematic education. *Focuses of Learning Problems in Mathematics, 19*(3), 1-28.

Rich, D (2001). E-learning: A new way to develop employees. *Electronic Business, 27*(8), 20.

Rossman, M. H. (1999). *Successful online teaching using an asynchronous learner discussion forum.* Retrieved June 6, 2007, from http://www.aln.org/publications/jaln/v3n2/v3n2_rossman.asp

Savery, J. R., & Duffy, T. M. (1995). Problem-based learning: An instructional model and its constructivist framework. *Educational Technology, 35*(5), 31-38.

Schroyens, W, (2005). Knowledge and thought: An introduction to critical thinking. *Experimental Psychology, 52*(2), 163-164.

Semerci, N. (2006). The effect of problem-based learning on the critical thinking of students in the intellectual and ethical development unit. *Social Behavior and Personality, 34,* 1127-1136.

Simons, K., Klein, J., & Brush, T. (2004). *Instructional strategies utilized during the implementation of a hypermedia, problem-based learning environment: A case study. Journal of Interactive Learning Research, 15*(3), 213-233.

Stewart, J. H. (1984). The representation of knowledge: Curricular and instructional implications for science teaching. In C. D. Holley and D. F. Dansereau (Eds.), *Spatial learning strategies: Techniques, applications, and related issues* (pp. 235-253). San Diego, CA: Academic Press.

Tastle, W. J., White, B. A., & Shackleton, P. (2005). E-learning in higher education: The challenge, effort, and return in investment. *International Journal on E-learning, 4*(2), 241-251.

Titone, C., Sherman, S., & Palmer, R. (1998). Cultivating student teachers' dispositions and ability to construct knowledge. *Action in Teacher Education, 19* (4), 76-87.

Tiwari, A., Lai, P., So, M., & Yuen, K. (2006). A comparison of the effects of problem-based learning and lecturing on the development of students' critical thinking. *Medical Education, 40, 547-554.*

Watson, G., & Glaser, E. M. (1980). *Watson-Glaser Critical Thinking Appraisal.* San Antonio, TX: Psychological Corp.

Yeh, Y. (2005). *Integrating e-learning into a teacher education curriculum: Its effects on improving preservice teachers' ability to teach critical thinking.* Taipei: National Council of Science. (NSC93-2520-S-004-002)

In: E-Learning: 21st Century Issues and Challenges
Editor: A.R. Lipshitz and S. P. Parsons

SBN : 978-1-60456-156-2
©2008 Nova Science Publishers, Inc.

Chapter 9

TEACHER TRAINING IN E-LEARNING: HOW TO SUPPORT THE FOLLOW-UP ANALYSIS

Guglielmo Trentin and Elisabetta Vallarino

Institute for Educational Technology, National Research Council, Italy

ABSTRACT

Despite the numerous initiatives undertaken towards in-service teacher training, there are just a few cases where their actual effect on classroom teaching has been analyzed. We probably need to get to the root of the cause since serious evaluations into learning acquired by teachers attending any educational/training course have very rarely been carried out. As will be shown in this chapter, learning evaluation is a necessary requisite for a reliable follow-up analysis in education. It is indeed a fairly onerous evaluation process generally dealt with by a special monitoring team, which is rarely allocated specific resources within an educational programme. The question arising in this chapter is therefore to understand whether a follow-up analysis can be carried out all the same with the aid of survey tools capable of 'replacing' the task of a special monitoring team. Therefore, a methodological approach tailored to the design, development and evaluation of a questionnaire to support the follow-up analysis will be illustrated. Although this approach has been developed for a specific educational programme, useful elements will emerge from discussion showing its generalizability even to contexts other than what it was originally designed for.

INTRODUCTION

Follow-up analysis in education has not been given much prominence in specialized literature. Having in fact undertaken research into documents and publications on the topic [Willen, 1981; Dillon et al., 1991; Johnston and Barker, 2002; Formica et al., 2003; Welle-Strand and Thune, 2003; Grant, 2004], there is clear evidence of a lack of documented cases as well as experimented tools for the purpose. The few studies found generally refer to teacher training in the use of information and communication technologies (ICT). However, they are limited to a follow-up analysis in terms of level of ability acquired in the 'technical' use of the technological tool and of ways of using it for personal productivity. What is much more complex though is analyzing the type of effect that the acquisition of these competences can have on classroom teaching.

Consequently, having noted the lack of experience and operational tools, the Institute for Educational Technology (ITD) of the Italian National Research Council (CNR) undertook research between 2003 and 2004 into the development and experimentation of an approach to planning and evaluating tools for the follow-up analysis of in-service teacher training.

RESEARCH CONTEXT

The research has been fostered by the participation of ITD-CNR in the Procopius project on networked collaborative learning, intended for a group of 44 teachers of different school levels from Alto Adige Region and conducted in collaboration with the School Superintendency of Bolzano and 'Carducci' high school (specializing in classical studies) of Merano. This project envisages a two-stage development:

1. a first year of blended training on the methodologies and technologies of collaborative learning;
2. a second year of 'assisted' experimentation of that learned i.e. a sort of 'accompaniment' of teachers when they first try to use their recently acquired knowledge to use the tools (technological and methodological).

TRAINING PROGRAMME EVALUATION AND FOLLOW-UP ANALYSIS

In Procopius the follow-up was considered as the effect in classroom teaching of what was learned in view of the training course. The key points that had to be tackled regarded *when* to place the follow-up analysis temporally and *how* to conduct it in terms of methods and tools to be used.

The reference model for the training programme evaluation

For the overall evaluation of Procopius, Kirkpatrick's model [1998] was followed. It concerns an approach devised for an organization but, with appropriate changes and rephrasing, it can be exported effectively to teacher training too [Trentin, 2000]. In brief, here is the reformulation of the four points of Kirkpatrick's model for the purpose of Procopius:

1. *Reaction* – It consists in the survey of the participants' degree of satisfaction and of how they intend to apply what they have learned during the training course. In Procopius this survey was conducted by administering a short approval questionnaire at the end of every course module.

2. *Learning* – Here the focus is what the participants have learned during the training process; to this end it is possible to use tests, practical activities, role-plays, simulations and generally all those strategies that can help in the process of evaluating the learning. In Procopius, the progression level in reaching the course objectives was measured by both exercises on technologies for networked collaboration and qualitative analysis of trainees' online and face-to-face interactions.

3. *Behaviour* – This point refers to the 'know what to do', i.e. to the trainees' ability to use what they have learned during the training stage. In Procopius, this ability was measured by observing the participants as they apply their technological and methodological course knowledge to developing their project work.

4. *Result* – To measure the impact of the training programme on the classroom teaching, it was envisaged to adopt both the class of each teacher involved in Procopius and the network of classes on which the use of methodologies and technologies for collaborative learning was experimented in the second year of the project.

In Procopius, the follow-up analysis was made to coincide with this fourth point. It is an obvious temporal placement since the follow-up analysis cannot prescind from a careful evaluation of the first three above-listed points of the model, in order to be sure that the results obtained are really the actual consequence of the training programme and therefore, ultimately, represent its actual follow-up.

Tools and methods used in the follow-up analysis

The follow-up analysis made use of both direct interaction with the teachers (monthly) and observation of their way of acting and interacting in the realization stage of the project devised during the first year of training.

Understandably, such a structured qualitative analysis requires considerable resources, especially in terms of the undertaking of those involved in the monitoring and survey work. An undertaking of human resources that may only be possible within an experimental study when there is the need to thoroughly research a model or a process implemented for the first time. In a standard situation, the same type of approach is hard to propose and so, for the purpose, survey tools might be useful which are perhaps qualitatively not as good but are more 'practical'.

For this reason, by benefiting from their involvement in the Procopius project, the ITD-CNR research team wanted to experiment with a specific survey questionnaire for the follow-up analysis. This tool has therefore been administered to the participants of Procopius and its effectiveness has been evaluated by way of a cross-check comparison with data from the main estimative channel envisaged by the project, that is, the direct monitoring in the classroom use of the methods and technologies studied on the teacher training course.

RESEARCH METHODOLOGY

The research-work that has lead to the realization, experimentation and evaluation of a questionnaire for the follow-up analysis has been framed as follows:

- definition of the objectives to be met with the help of the tool;
- identification of the survey indicators to devise the survey tool;
- implementation of the survey tool and then its administration to the teachers involved in the research;
- evaluation the tool's effectiveness.

OBJECTIVES DEFINITION

To identify the survey tool's elements i.e. those elements which can be traced back to the measurable dimensions of the phenomenon to be analysed [Lazarsfeld, 1958], a detailed definition of the objectives to be met using the tool was drawn up. Essentially, two principal sets of objectives were singled out related to the survey:

- changes in the methodological teaching approach adopted by the teacher in the class and associated results (students' motivation, learning, collaboration among colleagues/students, etc.);
- effectiveness of training carried out over the first year of Procopius for the purpose of experimentation envisaged for the second year.

IDENTIFICATION OF THE SURVEY INDICATORS

The survey indicators coincide with the variables to be used in the empirical representation of the item to be studied [Goode and Hatt, 1952; Gellner, 1964; Gerstlé, 1989]. They are actually the result of an abstraction process intended to isolate the representative elements of the study, strictly necessary for the very study to be carried out.

In Procopius, the detailed definition of the survey objectives represented the starting point for the process of identifying the indicators (see column 1 of Table A in Appendix) which were the grounds for the subsequent development of the survey tool.

In defining them, a distinction was also made between *indicators of cause* and *indicators of effect.* Each of the two sets, in fact, has specific characteristics and a mistake in placing the indicators in one or the other may compromise the validity of the survey model adopted [Bollen & Lenox, 1991]. By way of example, in Table A, the indicators referring to the level of 'achievement of stated disciplinary and cross-disciplinary objectives' depend upon the effect of the project on the curricular activity (effect indicators). On the other hand, the 'respect (or not) of the expected deadlines' influences the evolution of the project in progress (cause indicators).

IMPLEMENTATION AND ADMINISTRATION OF THE SURVEY TOOL

Every survey tool should be a support to the evaluation process, calibrated according to the specific requirements of the context in which it is applied [Rossi et al., 2004]. In Procopius, the choice and development of the survey tool are founded on the following considerations:

- since the whole project is based on networked communication among all the players in the process, the survey tool should have also been readily transmittable via the same communication channel;
- having to simulate a standard situation where there is no possibility of directly observing the protagonists in action, the tool should have been open and flexible enough to allow the interviewees to express their opinions in a not too structured way;
- having to facilitate the follow-up analysis, the questions addressed to the teachers had to spur them to explain and motivate their own attitudes as well as others without feeling they are 'being judged'.

Paying close attention to these considerations, it was decided to opt for a questionnaire as the survey tool, that was to be administered online. The stages in its realization outlined as follows:

- definition of the questionnaire format;
- matching every single indicator to the most effective question type to use for the survey of the corresponding piece of data;
- validation of a first version of the questionnaire.

Definition of the questionnaire format

According to the definition of the general objectives previously described, the questionnaire was divided into two sections dedicated to the survey, respectively, of the changes brought about in classroom teaching by the introduction of collaborative methodologies/technologies and of the effectiveness it had on the training course offered to teachers during the first year course of Procopius.

On the other hand, starting from the definition of the indicators (Table A, column 1), the items correlated to them were then defined (Table A, column 2).

Selecting the most effective question type to match with each indicator

Defining the questions was the conclusive step in devising the questionnaire. In formulating them every attempt was made to eliminate any ambiguity, the primary source of misunderstanding during the administration stages and therefore of little effectiveness in surveying data associated with the different indicators [Belson, 1981].

How was the project initiative received by the class group?
• All the pupils expressed enthusiasm
• Only some pupils expressed enthusiasm
• There was a certain indifference
• Some pupils were not in agreement
What do you think this attitude depends on?

Figure 1. Example of a mixed-question format.

In selecting the most suitable question type to associate with every single item, reference was made to what is suggested in specialized literature [Schuman and Presser, 1991; Schwarz and Hippler, 1991; Frary, 1996], particularly regarding the reliability of open or closed question formats.

In this respect, it was decided to leave more room for closed questions to trigger those memory processes which help gather information, reduce distortions due to not understanding the question correctly, and simplify the processing stage of the data generated from the answers [Kahn and Cannel, 1957; Schwarz and Oyserman, 2001].

In some cases, though, when there was the need to find out information of greater complexity than that detectable with the proposed pre-defined closed-question format alone, a mixed-question format was used. For example, this was the case for the indicator relating to the 'reactions of class involved'. Here, it was seemingly not enough to ask the interviewee to select among a closed list of possible class reactions. It was therefore considered helpful to also give an unstructured question so as to stimulate deeper reflection on the likely reasons for the attitude adopted by the class (Figure 1).

In other cases, where it was considered suitable to offer structured questions – but without giving up an in-depth survey on the subject in question - the choice fell on the use of grids. This solution actually makes it possible to:

- highlight important aspects of the phenomenon under examination, thereby favouring its reconstruction;
- avoid long, disorganized answers full of insignificant information;
- facilitate the data processing stage.

This is exemplified by the grid used in relation to the indicator 'organization of extracurricular activities/excursions useful for the purpose of the project' (Figure 2):

List the extracurricular activities done specifying their aim in the different stages of the project			
place	*with whom*	*type of activity/excursion*	*relative stage*
1)			
2)			
3)			

Figure 2. Example of a question type with a grid format.

In formulating the questions one tried to find solutions that would help the teacher to recall important information from memory [Schwarz and Oyserman, 2001]. For example, aware that the structure of autobiographical memory is organized in a hierarchical network [Belli, 1998], 'recall cues' [Baddley, 1990] - a time reference - were required to help recall memories of specific events. This concerns the question related to the indicator on 'students' motivation'.

What was, on average, the motivation of pupils *during the material research stage*?

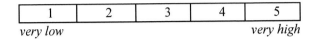

What has just been described are just some of the criteria followed to formulate the questions but it is thought that they can still give an idea of the general approach used. On the one hand, the approach is intended to avoid ambiguous formulations or their possible influence on the answers, and on the other hand help to recall from memory information and data referring to events even a long time before compiling the questionnaire [Schwarz and Oyserman, 2001]. It is worth remembering though that a questionnaire has two functions and acts as a neutral tool to gather information as well as a guide for the compiler to facilitate the meaning and understanding of the set questions [Schwarz, 1996].

The complete version of the questionnaire may be consulted on the web page: http://polaris.itd.cnr.it/questionario_procopius_2.pdf.

Validation of the evaluation tool

Before administering the questionnaire to all the teachers involved in the experience, its validation was carried out by bringing it to the attention of three teachers (of different school levels) to provide both indications of its general pertinence with regard to the purpose intended for the tool, and suggestions on how to improve and/or complete it.

To the same end, the questionnaire was also examined by two of the course tutors, who both have a long experience in the use of ICT as a support for collaborative learning

The two feedback channels were then used to ultimately devise the questionnaire that was later administered online to all the teachers involved in the experimentation towards the end of the school year.

EVALUATION OF THE TOOL'S EFFECTIVENESS

Having administered the questionnaire and collected the data, it was decided to evaluate the tool's effectiveness by integrating two different approaches:

- the first (quantitative) based on the *alpha reliability coefficient* [Cronbach, 1951], which is helpful to determine the degree of homogeneity and internal coherence of items with respect to what one sets out to measure [Harrison et al., 1991];

- the second (qualitative) based on comparing questionnaire-based data with what was found through the direct interaction among the researchers and teachers and by observing the way these teachers act and interact throughout the whole experimentation.

As shown, the two approaches aim to assess the tool's different qualitative aspects and so, as we will see, they complement each other.

EVALUATION OF THE TOOL'S RELIABILITY

Cronbach's coefficient α calculus refers to the correlation consistency among a set of items with a closed-form answer associated with a given indicator. Therefore an α value ranging between 0.5 and 1 indicates a strong correlation among the items, implying homogeneity for measuring their reference indicators. The formula for Cronbach's coefficient calculus is given below:

Table 1. Matrix for Cronbach's coefficient calculus in the case of 8 items and 5 respondents using a 7-point Likert scale

Respondent	Item 1	Item 2	Item 3	...	Item 8	Total	$(X_i - \bar{X})^2$
01	7	5	6	...	6	46	0,16
02	6	5	6	...	7	48	2,56
03	7	6	7	...	6	50	12,96
04	5	4	5	...	7	40	40,96
05	6	5	5	...	7	48	2,56
s_j^2	0,7	0,5	0,7	...	0,3	$\bar{X}=46,4$	59,2

Education towards Collaboration	0-5
Level of collaboration among class-group members	
Regularity of class-group communication with students from other schools involved in the project	
Level of collaboration of class-group members in organizing networked tasks	
Level of reciprocal trust among class-group members	
Level of class-group collaboration with students from other schools involved in the project	
Level of collaboration between the interviewed teacher and the other teachers from the same school involved in the project	
Level of collaboration between the interviewed teacher and the teachers from the other schools involved in the project	
Level of reciprocal trust between the interviewed teacher and the other teachers from the same school involved in the project	
Level of reciprocal trust between the interviewed teacher and the teachers from the other schools involved in the project	

Figure 3. Example of complex question structured into more items.

$$\alpha = k / (k-1) (1 - \Sigma\ s_j^2 / s_x^2)$$

where *k* is the number of items; s_j^2 represents the variance of values found by the item j-th; s_x^2 is the variance referring to the total of values found:

$$s_x^2 = \frac{\sum(X_i - \overline{X})^2}{(n-1)}$$

Here is an example of Cronbach's coefficient calculus:

$$s_x^2 = 59,2 / (5-1) = 14,8$$

$$\sum s_j^2 = 4,9$$

$$\alpha = \frac{8}{7} \cdot 1 - \frac{4,9}{14,8} = 1,14 \cdot (1-0,33) = 1,14 \cdot 0,67 = 0,76$$

In the case of the questionnaire experimented in Procopius, Cronbach's coefficient was calculated for complex questions and structured into more items (which represent as many aspects related to the investigated dimension), with a closed-form and that require an answer on the Likert scale (see example in Figure 3).

For example, in the specific case of the question reported in Figure 3, coefficient α has a value equal to 0.78, indicative of a good internal coherence among the 9 items used to study 'education towards collaboration' within each collaborative project.

QUALITATIVE EVALUATION

On the one hand, the coefficient α calculus is useful to determine the reliability level of the questionnaire in surveying the attitude in question. On the other hand, the quantitative data alone does not enable definite conclusions to be drawn on the truthfulness of the answers given by the interviewees which are often compromised by the phenomenon of *social desirability* [DeMaio, 1984] or by the difficulty in understanding the question. Hence emerged the idea of a crosscheck by comparing questionnaire-based information with that acquired more qualitatively by:

analyzing the messages circulated in the forums dedicated to each collaborative project;
analyzing, during the closing meeting of Procopius, how the various projects were experienced, described directly by the teachers and their students;
analyzing what emerged from the focus group arranged for the conclusive meeting among just teachers and researchers;
analyzing the forum and face-to-face interactions among the project staff (tutors and researchers) and experimenter teachers during the project's realization.

The third column of Table A, corresponding to each item, reports which of the four observation methods was used to compare with the questionnaire-based data.

Analysis of forum interactions among experimenter teachers

The analysis of forum interactions among experimenter teachers was conducted by classifying the messages by *communication type* (messages regarding teaching methodology, coordination, co-decision) and by *significance level* (actual contribution to the collaborative work), so as to:

- identify specific content areas that are easily comparable with the questionnaire indicators;
- estimate the degree of participation and role adopted by each trainee in devising and developing the project, so as to be able to confirm or contradict what is declared in the questionnaire concerning the individual involvement in the project-work.

The graph in Figure 4, for example, compares the data relating to the indicator on the 'Difficulties met in the various stages of the project', identified by means of the two information sources, namely the questionnaire and forum messages. In this case, as is evident, there is a good correspondence between the two different observations.

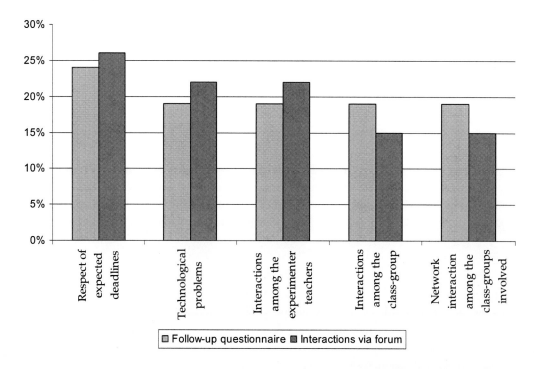

Figure 4. Comparison of the difficulties emerged in the follow-up questionnaire and those found in interactions via forum.

Analysis of accounts of experiences

The analysis of the content of the teachers' and students' accounts at the conclusion of the experimentation as regards their personal and group experience, has enabled some dimensions of the follow-up to be isolated that are easily comparable with the corresponding items of the questionnaire. In particular, it is possible to confirm the answers given with regard to:

- *objectives* of the project: their attainment and criteria used to evaluate it;
- *methodological and organizational aspects:* organizational arrangement (class subdivision, roles, etc.) and cooperation-type implemented; project timing, students' motivation; etc.;
- *technologies* used to produce materials and communicate at a distance;
- *critical aspects* in the project's development.

To show this, we can draw on what a trainee says about her class students' regaining their motivation and the results of their collaborative work:

> "The most interesting result, educationally speaking, was the individual and group maturity that they all noticed, especially the awareness of reciprocal respect and the need to collaborate making their personal skills available to the group and paying attention to their companions' needs. In this regard, it was nice to see how some of them were aware that knowledge consists in querying 'certainties' by comparing them with the opinions of others to build together a way to discover reality"

Her observation is confirmed by the answer to the question in the follow-up questionnaire 'How was ability to relate to one another measured?'

> "From the dynamics established in the groups during the preparation stage, the speed in determining the outline of themes, in arranging themselves into groups and in distributing specific competences within the groups, discussions were always held in an atmosphere of healthy argument, where disputes generated ideas more than contrasts. They showed a very good willingness to illustrate to their companions the topics that they examined, […]. The negative contrasts were confined to just a few cases, but they were resolved spontaneously by the students anyway. They showed a good willingness to collaborate with the teachers, which was demonstrated by the care they took in carrying out their tasks assigned to them and by the creativity with which they did the assignments"

Analysis of the focus group

The focus group is what specialized literature nowadays recognizes as a reliable evaluation technique [Morgan, 1988, 1993; Templeton, 1994]. Precisely because it is a tool based on interaction, it has been possible to realistically reproduce the process that has lead to opinions being formed regarding the impact of the course on the activity in class.

The specific objective of the focus-group was to analyze what occurred in the classroom, discussing the results obtained in a structured manner and isolating a set of useful key elements for an overall evaluation of the experience.

A large number of concepts emerging during the focus-group have also been found in the answers to the questionnaire questions.

As an exemplification, we have transcribed how a teacher answered the question 'What were the greatest difficulties met during the different stages of the project?'.

> "Poor propensity to collaborate effectively with group companions: one person performs, while the others watch. There is a considerable gap between what is declared and what is actually carried out as regards their skills in using new technologies"

A succinct account that is explained and justified in detail when the same teacher expresses herself to the focus group with these words:

> "[...] this experience has taught me a great deal: 1) to check everything before-during-after in minute detail; 2) to deglamorize some skills which seem to be common knowledge.
>
> A severe lack that I noticed for our project is that, as far as I'm concerned, I believed too much in the students' prerequisites – according to what they and colleagues told me – for 'actions speak louder than words'.
>
> [...] they claimed they were very good and that they were actually guiding the teachers in doing research even online. But it's not so!
>
> [...]... it seemed from what they said that they did group-work in all their subjects.
>
> For the students, group-work meant that one of them works and the others do something else. A long time was needed to combat these deep-rooted habits but then, eventually, the students discovered that it's is in fact true that what they were doing before wasn't group-work. After a three-month discussion, they are now starting to appreciate group-work and to accept it as a method of study."

Analysis of interactions of teachers with the project staff

To give a follow-up evaluation of Procopius the trainees' interactions with the project staff and in particular with the tutors were taken into consideration too. The tutors, who had helped and supervised in developing every project idea until it was completely carried out, were able to make a precious contribution to the follow-up analysis since it was based on:

- *direct observation* of group dynamics, of each trainee's approach to the course and experimental stages, of the interactions within the forum and so on. The tutor could therefore say what the teachers were doing while they were carrying out the experimentation;
- *indirect observation* from the trainees' blog on the project's progress in the class. The tutor could therefore notice the intentions and expectations of the teachers while they were carrying out the experimentation.

During the experimental stage, the tutors were also asked to outline key aspects of the ongoing process through periodical reports. For example, with regard to the difficulties met in the planning stage of the experience, they noted: minimum interaction and collaboration among the members of some project groups; hindrances integrating the project with everyday teaching activities; constrictions outside the class which conditioned the project; the limitations related to the project's feasibility.

In this case too, the same type of critical issues were identified by analyzing the answers given by the trainees using the questionnaire. Here is an example:

> "The project I'm following didn't acquire adequate backing from the class-teachers' meeting. Furthermore, this year I'm very busy in other things too. I'm considering at this point of proposing a variation to the project by simplifying the original idea"

DISCUSSION OF THE RESULTS

The overall comparison of questionnaire-based data with that acquired using other more direct channels for the follow-up analysis showed a strong bearing between the two survey typologies. This enables us to affirm that the questionnaire met its objective, which was that of providing an alternative tool to direct action by those responsible for the on-site survey of the data required for the follow-up analysis. However, it should be pointed out that the use of fewer resources in the administering and analysis of the questionnaire has 'paid the price' though in terms of the quality of the survey, which is to a certain extent lower than the direct action of an assigned monitoring team.

Therefore if, on the whole, the tool has demonstrated its effectiveness, a closer evaluation reveals some critical areas all the same which would be advisable to reassess in view of any future uses. Two aspects in particular are worth being discussed:

- the timing in administering the questionnaire;
- identifying a more complete set of indicators capable of representing every significant aspect of what is to be analyzed.

As already mentioned, the questionnaire was administered at the end of the experimental stage and this determined the teachers' difficulties of recalling information about one's behavior memory to compile the questionnaire. Personal memory decreases over time (Cannel et al., 1965) and memories therefore tend to fade. Respondents, in their attempt to fill in the missing memory gaps to give the fullest answer possible tend to apply a variety of inference strategies to arrive at a plausible estimate of past events [Conrad and Brown, 1996].

These are the reasons which suggest the questionnaire should be distributed to teachers at the start of the experimentation so that it can be used as a sort of survey grid on which to note down the information on the on-going experience as they go along. This solution would have facilitated answers to questions on the frequency a certain activity was carried out or a given attitude was shown.

Instead, with regard to the completeness of the set of indicators, there was a lack in relation to the analysis of the link between project development and institutional and organizational context (class-teachers' meeting, parents, director, timetable, etc.) outside the working group made up teachers, students and researchers.

The reaction of the environment, as defined by Lan [2001], becomes decisive in facilitating or hindering the 'continuation' of what is learnt on the training course. Indeed, the teachers involved in Procopius often declared that the class-teachers' meetings resulted in consequences on the progress of the experimentation. This therefore suggests that a specific space should be made on the follow-up questionnaire for this problem area.

One last observation concerns the reliability of the questionnaire analyzed on the basis of Cronbach's coefficient. Almost all the assessable indicators reached high values. The reliability coefficient calculated on the items representative of the 'ability to relate to one another' was the only one which did not reach a high value ($\alpha = 0,60$). This fact has called for the need to re-examine the adequacy of each item in relation to the area to be measured. To identify these items, the Bravais-Pearson *product-moment correlation* coefficient [Pearson, 1938] was used, that is to say, the correlation between the values found through each item and the total of values found through the set of items referring to a specific indicator. This is the calculus formula:

$$r_{XY} = \frac{\sum_{i=1}^{N}(X_i - \bar{X}) \cdot (Y_i - \bar{Y})}{\sqrt{\sum_{i=1}^{N}(X_i - \bar{X})^2 \cdot \sum_{i=1}^{N}(Y_i - \bar{Y})^2}}$$

where:

- X_i = score given by the i-th respondent (the respondents go from 1 to N) to the item in question
- $\bar{X}$ = average value observed for that item
- Y_i = sum of score given by the i-th respondent
- $\bar{Y}$ = total average score observed

Here is an example of the Bravais-Pearson correlation calculus:

Table 2. Matrix for the Bravais-Pearson correlation calculus in the case of 9 items and 15 respondents using a 7-point Likert scale.

Respondent	Item 1	Item 2	Item 3	...	Item 9	Y_i
01	3	5	3	...	5	39
02	5	4	3	...	4	42
03	4	4	4	...	4	39
...	...	...	...	...	...	...
15	3	3	4	...	4	40
$\bar{X}$	3,86	3,86	4,00		4,20	
r_{XY}	0,21	0,66	0,08	...	0,69	

This calculus shows which items need to be reformulated or eliminated if they should indicate very low correlations (around 0,20).

CONCLUSION

The results of the qualitative and quantitative analyses - with which the evaluation was carried out on the questionnaire used to obtain data on the Procopius follow-up - showed a substantial reliability of the indicators selected to represent the respondents' direction and behavior. Furthermore, the opinion of individuals (tutors and sample of teachers) consulted during the evaluation stage also confirmed the tool's validity, in that the items were adequate as indicators of the area intended to be measured.

As far as its reusability, it is noteworthy though that since the questionnaire is tailored on the specific themes tackled in Procopius, its use (short of slight changes) may not be envisaged outside an educational context on contents connected to networked collaboration.

It should be pointed out that the purpose of this article was not to propose a specific questionnaire on the follow-up but rather to discuss, analyze and generalize the methodological approach used for the planning, development and evaluation of similar tools to support the follow-up analysis of an educational programme.

APPENDIX A:
INDICATOR, ITEM AND SOURCE CORRELATIONS USED TO COMPARE THAT SURVEYED VIA QUESTIONNAIRE

Dynamics, tools and effects of experimental activity		
Indicator	Item	Source used for comparison
Organizational and methodological aspects in starting the experimentation		
Ways the project took shape	Role of the teacher and/or their colleagues during the planning stage of the project	A - D
	Class organization-type when searching for material	B
Class organization when searching for material	Criteria for arranging the subgroups	B
	Possible changes in subgroup arrangement during the working activity and motivation	B
Assigning roles within the class	Evidence or not of defined roles among the class	B
	Criteria for possible subdivision of roles	B
Commitment required by the teacher to coordinate the experimentation	Estimated percentage of time spent coordinating the experimentation in relation to the overall involvement in the project	A - C
Class attitudes towards the proposed approach		
Reactions of class involved	Type of class reaction	A - B
	Comment to the reaction shown by the class	A
Working climate in the class	Evidence or not of critical situations among the students during collaborative work	A - C

APPENDIX A. CONTINUED

Dynamics, tools and effects of experimental activity		
Indicator	Item	Source used for comparison
	Level of class understanding during the working stages	A - C
Students' motivation	Level of students' motivation during the working stages	A - B
Ongoing development of the project		
Ongoing changes to the original version of the project	Percentage estimate to changes made to the original version of the project	A - B - D
	List of possible changes made	C
Respect of expected deadlines	Reasons for possible delays or postponements of deadlines	A - B
Difficulties met in the various stages of the project	List of difficulties met for each stage of the project	B - D
Effect of the project on curricular activity		
Integration of the project in the curricular activity and in each discipline	Opinion on the actual integration of the project in the curricular activity	A - B - C - D
	List of connections between the project and the disciplines involved	B
Achievement of stated disciplinary and cross-disciplinary objectives	Achievement level of stated objectives	A - B - C
	List of objectives met for each discipline involved	B
	Way achievement of disciplinary objectives was measured	A - B
Achievement of objectives related to technological education	Achievement level of objectives	B - C
	Way achievement was measured	C
Achievements of objectives related to education towards collaboration	Achievement level of objectives	A - B
	Way achievement was measured	C
Achievements of objectives related to mediation/negotiation education	Achievement level of objectives	A - B
	Way achievement was measured	C
Achievements of objectives linked to the ability to relate to one another	Achievement level of objectives	A - B
	Way achievement was measured	B - C
Achievement of objectives related to the ability to understand, produce, analyse, evaluate	Achievement level of objectives	C
	Way achievement was measured	C
Time dedicated to the project	Estimated average time dedicated weekly to the project for class activity	B
	Estimated average time dedicated to the project for possible extra-curricular activities	B

APPENDIX A. CONTINUED

Dynamics, tools and effects of experimental activity		
Indicator	Item	Source used for comparison
Organization of extra-curricular activities/excursions useful for the purpose of the project	Staff involved in possible extra-curricular activities/excursions	A
	Description of possible extra-curricular activities/excursions in terms of their aims in the different stages of the	A - B
Commitment required by the teacher to coordinate the collaborative activity	Estimated percentage of time spent coordinating the collaborative activity in relation to the overall involvement in the project	D
	Problems found in coordinating the collaborative work	A - D
	Main problems emerged in class during collaborative work	A - B - C
Use of communication tools		
Use of asynchronous communication	Frequency using electronic messaging by different players in the process (students, teachers, researchers and so on) specifying the main interlocutors	A - B - D
Use of synchronous communication	Frequency using chat by different players in the process specifying the main interlocutors	A - B - D
Use of production software	Indications on application software used for collaborative production	B
Types of technologies used by students in collaborative work	List of technologies used and opinion on their aptitude regarding the parts of the work in which they were employed	B
Propaedeutic evaluation of Procopius I		
Usefulness of themes tackled in Procopius I for the purpose of collaborative educational activities developed in Procopius II	Estimated percentage of usefulness of each topic studied on the course in Procopius I for the purpose of collaborative teaching in Procopius II	A - C
	Free opinion regarding the most useful topic	C
	Free opinion regarding one or more topics that would be useful to tackle in Procopius I	C
Suggestions on possible improvements to be made	Suggestions to improve the Procopius I course	C
	Suggestions to improve the Procopius II experimental activity	B - C
	Free comment for a real critical evaluation of the entire Procopius project	C

A: Asynchronous interaction (via forum) among trainees.

B: Trainees' accounts.

C: Focus group discussion.

D: Asynchronous interaction (via forum) among project staff.

REFERENCES

Baddeley, A. (1990). *Human memory: Theory and practice*. Hillsdale, NJ: Erlbaum.

Belli, R. (1998). The structure of autobiographical memory and the event history calendar: Potential improvements in the quality of retrospective reports in surveys. *Memory* 6, 383-406.

Belson, W.A. (1981). *The design and understanding of survey questions*. Aldershot, Hampshire: Gower Publishing Limited.

Bollen, K.A., & Lenox, R. (1991). Conventional wisdom on measurement: A structural equation perspective. *Psychological Bulletin* 110, 305-14.

Cannel, C.F., Fisher, G., & Bakker, T. (1965). Reporting on hospitalization in the Health Interview Survey. *Vital and Health Statistics*, PHS Publication No. 1000, Series 2, No. 6. Washington D.C.: US Government Printing Office.

Conrad, F.G., & Brown, N.R. (1996). Estimating frequency: A multiple strategy perspective. In M. Herrmann, C. Johnson, C. McEvoy, C. Hertzog, & P. Hertel, (Eds.), *Basic and applied memory: Research on practical aspects of memory*, 167-178. Hillsdale, NJ: Erlbaum.

Cronbach, L.J. (1951). Coefficient Alpha and the internal structure of tests. *Psychometrik* XVI, 297-334.

DeMaio, T. J. (1984). Social desirability and survey measurement: a review. In C.F. Turnern, & E. Martin (Eds.), *Surveying subjective phenomena*, 257–281. New York: Russell Sage.

Dillon, C.L., Hengst, H.R., & Zoller, D. (1991). Instructional strategies and student involvement in Distance Education: A study of the Oklahoma Televised Instruction System. *Journal of Distance Education/Revue de l'enseignement à distance* 6(1), 28-41.

Formica, S.W., Harding, W.M., & Giguere, P.J. (2003). *Evaluating Results from Distance Learning Courses for U.S. Department of Education Middle School Coordinators*. Retrieved from: http://hhd.org/documents/MSC_document_4.pdf

Frary, R.B. (1996). *Brief guide to questionnaire development*. ERIC Clearinghouse on Assessment and Evaluation, Washington, DC.

Gellner, E.A. (1964). Concept. In J. Gould, & W.L. Kolb (Eds.), *A Dictionary of the Social Sciences*. NY: The Free Press of Glencoe.

Gerstlé, J. (1989). Concepts, théories et programmes de recherche. *Revue Internationale des Sciences Sociales* 122, 673-681.

Goode, W.J., & Hatt, P.K. (1952). *Methods in Social Research*. NY: McGraw-Hill.

Grant, M.M. (2004). Learning to teach with the web: factors influencing teacher education faculty. *The Internet and Higher Education* 7, 329-341.

Harrison, P.J, Seeman, B.J., Behm, R., Saba, F., Molise, G., & Williams, M.D. (1991). Development of a Distance Education Assessment Instrument. *Educational Technology Research and Development* 39(4), 65-77.

Kahn, R.L., & Cannel, C. (1957). *The dynamics of interviewing*. NY: Wiley.

Kirkpatrick, D.L. (1998). *Evaluating training programs*. San Francisco, CA: Berret-Koehler Publishers.

Johnston, J., & Barker, L.T. (2002). *Assessing the impact of technology in teaching and learning: a sourcebook for evaluators*. Retrieved from: http://www.rcgd.isr.umich.edu/tlt/TechSbk.pdf

Lan, J. (2001). Web-based instruction for education faculty: A needs assessment. *Journal of Research on Computing in Education* 33(4), 385-399.

Lazarsfeld, P.F. (1958). Evidence and Inference in Social Research. *Daedalus* LXXXVII(3), 99-130.

Morgan, D.L. (1988). *Focus group as Qualitative Research*. Newbury Park. CA: Sage Publications.

Morgan, D.L. (1993). *Successfull focus group*. London: Sage Publications.

Pearson, E. S. (1938). *Mathematical Statistics and Data Analysis* (2nd ed.). Belmont, CA: Duxbury.

Rossi, P.H., Freeman, H.E., & Lipsey, M.W. (2004). *Evaluation: A Systematic Approach*, 7th edition. Newbury Park, CA: Sage Publications.

Schuman, H., & Presser, S. (1981). *Questions and answers in attitude survey*. New York: Academic Press.

Schwarz, N. (1996). *Cognition and communication: Judgmental biases, research methods, and the logic of conversation*. Hillsdale, NJ: Erlbaum.

Schwarz, N., & Hipper, H.J. (1991). Response alternatives: the impact of their choice and ordering. In P. Biemer, R. Groves, N. Mathiowetz, & S. Sudman (Eds.), *Measurement error in surveys*, pp. 41-56. Chichester: Wiley.

Schwarz, N., & Oyserman, D. (2001). Asking questions about behavior: cognition, communication, and questionnaire construction. *American Journal of Evaluation* 22, 127-132.

Templeton, J.F. (1994). *The focus group*. Chicago: Probus Publishing Company.

Trentin G. (2000). The quality-interactivity relationship in Distance Education. *Educational Technology* 40 (1), 17-27.

Welle-Strand, A., & Thune, T. (2003). E-learning policies, practices and challenges in two Norwegian organizations. *Evaluation and program planning* 26, 185-192.

Willen, B. (1981). *Distance education at Swedish universities: An evaluation of the experimental programme and a follow-up study*. Uppsala Studies in Education, Uppsala University, Stockholm, Sverige.

In: E-Learning: 21st Century Issues and Challenges
Editor: A.R. Lipshitz and S. P. Parsons

ISBN : 978-1-60456-156-2
©2008 Nova Science Publishers, Inc.

Chapter 10

EXPERIENCE IN E-LEARNING FROM BEPI, AN INTERNET COURSE IN BASIC EPIDEMIOLOGY FOR MEDICAL STUDENTS AND PUBLIC HEALTH TRAINING

Christiane Meier and Ursula Ackermann-Liebrich

Institute of Social- and Preventive Medicine of the University of Basel,
Switzerland

ABSTRACT

BEPI – from Basic Epidemiology – is an E-Learning course in Epidemiology for medical students and for public health training. The course is supported by the Swiss Virtual Campus and by the medical faculties of the Swiss universities. The leadership as well as the coordination are situated at the Institute for Social- and Preventive Medicine in Basel.

This E-Learning course offers realistic scenarios through which the student learns the epidemiological methods and becomes familiar with the important medical and public health data sources in Switzerland.

Our course is targeted for medical students at different levels in different universities as well as for people in public health training. In order to comply with different requirements of the learning environment we created an independent tool suitable for people without E-Learning experience.

Epidemiology offers ideal examples with illustrating material for learning the methods and testing the knowledge that is crucial to profit from the possibilities of E-Learning. Getting involved in these realistic scenarios requires a certain motivation and time, but then a deeper understanding of the content can be achieved.

However, the authors have to become familiar with E-Learning and know the different didactic scenarios to take advantage of the possibilities E-Learning offers.

E-Learning can be seen as another learning- and teaching-aid, as an alternative to a textbook or to a lecture offering many didactical advantages: it adapts to individual pace, the question-answer-options (multiple choice, complete a text, calculations, put in order, form pairs) can be tailored to the subject, exercises can be prepared for different levels of understanding, elaborative feedback facilitates the learning process, and references and links to authentic data sources create a methodological and up-to-date background for practical and understandable exercises.

Although E-Learning will never replace lectures with a more personal contact or books providing the theoretical background in a compact form, it can be seen a. a supplement.

INTRODUCTION

E-Learning is seen as a modern and flexible way of learning with different advantages:

- Each student can choose his own pace; can learn in groups or alone.
- Film and graphic material can be used for illustration and increase the interest.
- Real data sources guarantee the actuality and application of the theoretical background.
- Several answer-possibilities demand a thorough reflection about the questions.
- Specific feedback can be given for a solution chosen.
- The different types of question-answer-options (multiple choice, complete a text, calculations, put in order, form pairs) prevent automatically "clicking through".
- A separate forum opens the possibility to solve problems in groups under supervision of a tutor.

Within the interuniversity project "Swiss Virtual Campus" we got the opportunity to create an E-Learning course (in German and French) in epidemiology for Swiss medical students and for public health training. In this chapter we want to share some of our experiences during the realisation of BEPI, our course in *Basic EPI*demiology.

EPIDEMIOLOGY

There are many reasons why E-Learning is particularly useful for teaching and learning epidemiology, which "...is the study of how disease, physiological variables, and social consequences of disease are distributed in populations as well as the factors that influence or determine this distribution."[1]

For example:

In 1981 many mainly working poor persons in Madrid were observed with a sudden fever with pulmonary affection; some of them even died. Often all members of a family where affected, but neither a bacterium nor a virus could be isolated and also those who recovered from the disease would get sick again when back home. This authentic story leads to a case-example of our course, where the student has to find out – as an epidemiologist – what caused this sudden outbreak of a disease with many hospitalizations (see Figure 1).

---

[1] Definition of Epidemiology from the World Health Organisation.

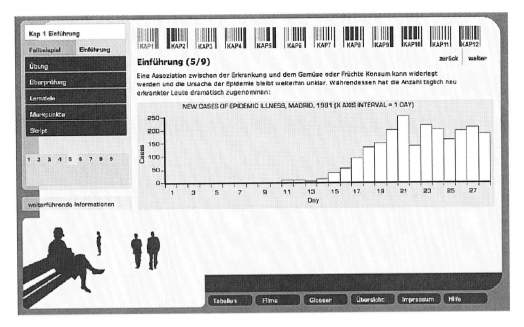

Figure 1. BEPI – Case-example, toxic oil syndrome in Madrid.

In the course, information about the disease and the distribution in the population are given as they were available at the time. So students learn that mainly people living in a certain part of town got sick, but no children under the age of six months. There was a hypothesis that the disease was caused by the consumption of fruits and vegetables, another that the disease was transmitted by birds – both of which were proven untrue. Finally, the students found out, that the poisoning of olive-oil bought on the street was the reason for the "Spanish Toxic Oil Syndrome".

An "epidemiological case" consists of many pieces, which must be collected from various sources and put in the right order to find a possible cause.

Epidemiology means also observing, for instance the number of cancer cases and looking for a possible relation to eating, drinking and smoking habits as well as to the working and living environment and even considering genetic background. Sometimes also a change in the way diseases are defined or detected can increase or decrease numbers in the population, as happens for instance when a screening program is introduced.

In one exercise, the students have to describe the trend in the incidence of melanoma in Switzerland between 1985 and 2003 (see figure 2). They are also asked for an interpretation of the change in numbers of cases they observe and they can find explanations in the next screen.

The epidemiological work can be compared with the one of a detective asking the following questions: "Who is sick? When did people get sick? Do sick people have similarities as compared to those who did not get sick? Why are they sick? Are there possible alternative explanations?"

There are many historical and contemporary examples with valuable data sources for learning epidemiological practice. Through a realistic scenario with the use of authentic material the students can get involved and step by step, learn the methods and manage a case-example.

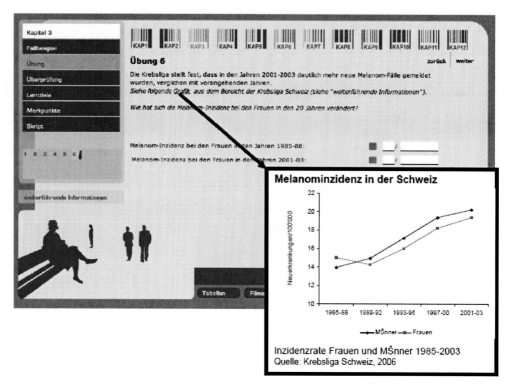

Figure 2. BEPI – exercise, incidence of melanoma in Switzerland.

During this work the students also become familiar with national (Swiss) data sources and learn how to use them.

OUR EXPERIENCE

As our aim was to create the course for medical students as well as for public health training, we could neither rely on common background knowledge nor on compulsory lectures from where the course could start. BEPI, our course in epidemiology, should be applicable in different didactic scenarios or different circumstances: individual learning or learning in groups or as part of lectures with individual exercises to mention only three options. We think, supported by the literatures and online sources [Gray, Bersin], that blended learning - a combination of lectures and E-Learning - should be favoured.

A script is provided with basic knowledge of epidemiology that explains the theoretical basis, split into the chapters of BEPI. This script is also a chapter of a new public health textbook [Gutzwiller]. With this knowledge it should be possible to solve the case-examples and most of the exercises. Yet a pilot evaluation showed that the students – depending on their previous knowledge – experience some difficulties at the start of the course and in following the structure. Students with more experience didn't need too much introduction, whereas beginners asked for more guidance.

It's a challenge to find a start which is not discouraging for beginners but does not bore the more experienced.

Once started, the questions appear to be clear and the students can solve case-examples or exercises without greater difficulties.

With this course we want to give the possibility to either deepen the theoretical understanding of epidemiology or to refresh one's epidemiological knowledge. Therefore, BEPI offers *case-examples* telling a longer story which should be followed from A to Z as well as *exercises* which can be solved separately and are restricted to one or two screens. In both the case-examples and the exercises, elaborative feedbacks (see below) are given. In contrast, the *check-exercises* simulate an exam-situation without feedback but instead a rating at the end of each chapter.

The course consists of *learning sentences* which outline the most important content of each chapter, *learning goals* for medical students and a *glossary* explaining the most common epidemiological expressions, these elements can be used independently from the rest of the course.

To understand the epidemiological methods it's important to work with different data sources containing information about the health of the population. These data have to be evaluated for their reliability and validity and they have to be put in relation to other information and the related question.

E-Learning offers an ideal possibility to learn and practice epidemiological procedures. Using authentic epidemiological cases allows illustrating the exercise with real publications, figures or tables. This also increases the awareness of the students and prepares them ideally for later work.

The students have to use tables containing data about a specific health aspect for calculations or have to interpret them in combination with information they find on the Internet through links provided. This work needs motivation, commitment, and time, which sometimes contrast with the expectation that E-Learning is a quick and easy way to learn.

One big advantage of E-Learning as compared to a textbook or a lecture is the individual pace and the immediate feedback that can be given for different answer possibilities. This *elaborative feedback* is very welcome and some students read all of them, not only the one appearing after they have chosen a specific answer.

From the learning perspective one should get a stimulation to think about a solution and then get a feedback matching the previous thoughts. These feedbacks consist ideally of an explanation of why the chosen answer is wrong or right and give – if necessary – a hint to the right answer without just giving it. Through comparing thoughts with the right answer a high learning-success can be achieved. [Krause].

A further option to stimulate the learning process is the use of different question-answer options. E-Learning offers many possibilities like multiple choice questions, complete a text, calculations, put in order, or form pairs. These alternatives increase the concentration by preventing "clicking through" and make the learning-process more playful.

Personal contacts between students and between students and teachers are an important element of learning – a certain limitation of E-Learning. In a verbal exchange more and specific questions can be asked. The possibility of electronical exchange by chat and forums exists but not all student-groups make use of this media. The installation of such structures requires the supervision of a tutor – one has to think about this in a long-term perspective.

As BEPI will be offered to learning institutions as an independent course, we leave it up to them if they want to link it with a learning management system like OLAT[2], for example.

Last but not least, we have to mention that the realisation of our course took more time than planned. Others have had the same experience. The implementation of one hour E-Learning requires at least 40 to 50 working hours, excluded the writing of the content and the development of flash activities. The opportunities of E-Learning go far beyond putting text on a screen. The appropriate use of the electronic possibilities but also its limitations must be known. As some of our content was written by people not directly involved in E-Learning, the adaptation of the content suitable to E-Learning was very time consuming. Most teachers are familiar with text books or exercises in a paper format and this is not automatically useful for E-Learning.

CONCLUSION

E-Learning must be seen as a new didactical opportunity that has big advantages, but also some limitations. People often think of E-Learning as a cheap solution for teaching or / and as an easier way to learn.

Still, one has to learn, but for some people it's a more pleasant or playful way, although it needs time and concentration to get involved. It may require even more commitment to work with E-Learning than listening to a lecture or reading a book. It's important to understand each step when going through the case-examples and exercises on one's own. However, it can be expected that through this involvement a better understanding and remembrance will be achieved.

E-Learning is not just putting text and Power Point presentations on a homepage ready for downloading. E-Learning means using the interactive possibilities to enhance the interest of the students. Consequently, it needs a lot of work and commitment in different fields to create such a course.

Our experience shows that not every epidemiological case qualifies for an E-Learning example or exercise. It shouldn't be too complex, the sources for illustration must be available for public use, and it should be solvable with the knowledge at the stage of the course. Being aware of these points, very challenging case-examples and exercises can be elaborated referring to authentic data sources and creating a realistic ambience.

The user-group should be well known so that the content can be focused. To get an E-Learning course that fits "any person", not knowing what previous knowledge they have, is demanding. Beginners should easily find enough explanatory notes, and at the same time it shouldn't be boring for the more experienced users.

To fulfill these requirements is time-consuming and the budget to create interesting and long-lasting E-Learning tools shouldn't be calculated too narrowly. Furthermore, a course on the Web needs to be updated from time to time, especially regarding links to other websites.

---

[2] OLAT: Online Learning And Training; an open source Learning Management System (LMS) developed at the University of Zurich, Switzerland.

We think also in the future students will attend personal lectures, amongst other reasons because they want to meet their fellow students [Lovell]. No matter whether it is a lecture, a book or E-Learning, the learning process will improve when the didactical scenario is adequate and the content interesting.

Finally, a good lecture is always better than a bad E-Learning course, and vice versa!

REFERENCES

Gray, C. (2006). *Blended Learning: Why Everything Old Is New Again – But Better*. www.learningcircuits.org/2006/March/gray.htm

Bersin, J. (2003). *What Works in Blended Learning*. www.learningcircuits.org/2003/jul2003/bersin.htm

Gutzwiller, F.; Paccaud F. (editors) *Sozial- und Präventivmedizin - Public Health*; third edition; Hans Huber Verlag: Bern CH, 2007.

Krause, U.-M.; Stark, R.; Mandl, H. *Förderung des computerbasierten Wissenserwerbs im Bereich empirischer Forschungsmethoden durch kooperatives Lernen und eine Feedbackmaßnahme*. Forschungsbericht (research report), Ludwig Maximilians Universität München. 2003.

Lovell, K.; Plantegenest, G.; Stephenson, R.; Mindock-Wilkins, C.; Waggott, D.; Thakore, D.; Ford, J. *Digital version of classroom lectures: evaluation and impact on student learning*. Workshop-presentation at the 18th International Meeting for Medical Multimedia Developers and Educators. Slice of Life 2006.

In: E-Learning: 21st Century Issues and Challenges
Editor: A.R. Lipshitz and S. P. Parsons

ISBN : 978-1-60456-156-2
©2008 Nova Science Publishers, Inc.

Chapter 11

THE RELEVANCE OF RESEARCH IN COGNITIVE NEUROSCIENCE RELATED TO E-LEARNING

Norbert Jaušovec[*,1] *and Ivan Gerlič*[+2]

*Professor of Educational Psychology, Pedagoška fakulteta, Slovenia
+Associate Professor for Physics Education, University of Maribor, Slovenia

ABSTRACT

The aim of the present chapter is to answer the question: Has neuropsychology anything to say about e-learning? Our review is organized as follows: The first section deals with some key-issues of multimedia and computer-supported instructions which set them apart from a 'classical' teaching approach. In the second section, we briefly examine some of the methods that are used to infer brain-cognition relations (e.g., reaction time, EEG and different imaging techniques, like MRI, fMRI, and PET). Reviewed are also some animal and lesions studies. Next, we describe what these methods have revealed about the brain with a special focus on findings that have direct relevance to the field of educational psychology and e-learning. Findings related to attention and memory are discussed, as well as individual differences related to ability (giftedness, and creativity), and gender are reviewed. Finally, we discuss neuropsychological studies of e-learning, and we suggest new avenues of research.

1. INTRODUCTION

Over the past years, the benefits of incorporating findings from cognitive neuroscience into the field of educational psychology have been vigorously discussed. The outcome is ambivalent – from total rejection to enthusiastic acceptance. In Bruer's (1997) opinion neuropsychology has little to offer to educators: "Educational applications of brain science

---

[1] Correspondence should be send to Norbert Jaušovec, Professor of Educational Psychology, Pedagoška fakulteta, Koroška 160, 2000 Maribor, Slovenia, jausovec.norbert@uni-mb.si

[2] Ivan Gerlič, Associate Professor for Physics Education, University of Maribor

may come eventually, but as of now neuroscience has little to offer teachers in terms of informing classroom practice" (Bruer, 1977, pp. 4). More optimistic is the position of Hunt (1998), suggesting that new technologies such as magnetic resonance imaging (MRI) and positron emission tomography (PET) have led to recent discoveries about how the brain works, and how we learn. It is further suggested that this knowledge can help to design instructional strategies which will better match how we teach with how we know students learn. A possible reason for this ambivalence is the fact that the field of education has a troubled history as a scientific discipline (Condliffe Lagemann, 2000). Evidence for international disparities in educational achievement among nations with comparable economic success have once again brought to the forefront discussions about the science of education (Gonzales, et al. 2004). Therefore some researchers suggest that cognitive neuroscience can provide a bridge to a new science of education and learning (Blakemore, and Frith 2005; Goswami, 2006; Posner, and Rothbart, 2005), but also warn before so called "brain based learning packages". Some of these contain alarming amounts of misinformation, and oversimplified, misrepresented 'neuromyths', yet such packages are being used in many schools. One of the potentially most potent mechanisms to overcome such uncritical use of "brain-based programs" involves increasing scientific and cognitive neuroscience literacy amongst educators.

A more realistic expectation, which is in agreement with our viewpoint, has been put forward by Goldman-Rakic (1996): "Research [findings in neuroscience] must surely have some implications for how we approach education" (p.3). As stressed by Ansari and Coch (2006) it is not currently useful to focus solely on product or content; instead, it is suggested that more engagement, concerted thinking and discussion about the mechanisms that will enable success and sustainable productivity in the emerging field of mind, brain and education are necessary.

2. COMPUTER-BASED MULTIMEDIA INSTRUCTION AND E-LEARNING VERSUS CLASSROOM LECTURES: WHAT MAKES THE DIFFERENCE?

Multimedia is the use of text, pictures, video, and sound to present information. Similar is the definition for E-learning – any kind of learning process that takes place mainly in a virtual environment, or Internet-enabled learning (Bouras and Tsiatsos, 2006). Online learning allows for flexibility of access, from anywhere and usually at anytime, however, the learning materials must be designed properly to engage the learner and promote learning. According to Rossett (2002), online learning has many promises, but it takes commitment and resources, and it must be done right. "Doing it right" means that online learning materials must be designed properly, with the learners and learning in focus, and that adequate support must be provided. Ring and Mathieux (2002) suggest that online learning should have high authenticity (i.e., students should learn in the context of the workplace), high interactivity, and high collaboration.

As stressed by Salomon (1998), at first glance it appears that the multimedia give everything that a constructivistic approach to learning would wish to have. But does a flood of information aid the construction of knowledge? Reiman (1999) argued that multiple representations also have their costs: not only does the encoding effort increase, but relating two or more representations to each other can also be quite demanding, which can turn against the learner. On the other hand, Hunt (1998) suggested that the combination of text, pictures, video, and sound enables the creation of multi-sensory experiences which are more likely to be remembered because they stimulate the growth of additional neural connections.

Najjar (1996) has pointed out that computer based instruction may force the instructional designer to better organize and structure the learning material compared to the traditional classroom lecture. By contrast Salomon (1998) finds hypermedia programs anything but logical, and deliberately based on causal association and on visual fascination. Kaput (1992) has stressed that a potential educational payoff of computer supported multimedia instruction is that the medium of computers allows routine computations to be off-loaded, thus enabling learning to be more compact and enriched. In that way computers can also take away learning opportunities. Reducing the amount of low-level cognitive activities required during learning may make it too difficult for the learner to carry out high-level cognitive activities and in that way hinder the understanding of the material learned (Salomon, Perkins and Globerson, 1991).

Najjar (1996) has further argued that multimedia education is interactive, allowing the learner to personally set the pace of learning, and may be more novel and stimulating. These are arguments which are rather vague. Multimedia instruction is extremely low on social interaction, which is according to Vigotsky (1978) a key issue of successful learning. It is rather difficult to conclude anything about the motivational aspects of multimedia because this issue is seldom addressed by the studies dealing with multimedia instruction (Reimann, 1999).

The main problem with multimedia education lies in the fact that we are far from understanding how humans integrate multiple representations (Van Someren et al., 1998). Answers to such questions are difficult because the cognitive processes are hidden from our observation. The dilemma is to find a methodology that would make invisible thinking processes observable. Methods used in cognitive neuropsychology could provide a deeper insight into thinking and learning processes

3. How Can We Make Invisible Thinking Processes Observable?

We briefly describe the nature of five methods that have been used to infer brain-cognition relations in educationally-relevant areas. Our goal is to give the gist of these methods rather than all of the technical details.

3.1. Reaction time

There are reliable individual differences in the speed with which subjects can make simple and complex responses (Jensen, 1992). Faster responses have been found to correlate in the .3-.4 range with IQ, as does the speed with which neurons conduct impulses (Vernon and Mori, 1992). As stressed by Byrnes and Fox (1998) the major benefits of the method are that it is easy, inexpensive, and noninvasive. The major shortcoming is that it gives no information about the cognitive processes.

3.2. The electroencephalogram (EEG)

A simple method for recording the electrical activity of the brain is electroencephalography (EEG). To record EEG a small metal disk is attached to the scalp to detect the electrical activity of neurons in the underlying brain area. This activity is than amplified and displayed on a computer, or on a chart recorder. The main issues currently confronting EEG researchers are the choice of the number and placement of electrodes and the choice of parameters used to describe EEG recording. Most often 16 to 20 electrodes are used. They are placed according to the Jasper (1958) Ten-twenty Electrode Placement System of the International Federation. However, some newer sophisticated imaging systems are capable of simultaneously recording up to 256 channels.

EEG measurement requires collection of a huge amount of data which are unusable in raw form. Therefore they are subjected to data reduction methods (Etevenon, 1986). These reduction methods could be roughly classified into two groups: first, methods that are partly or completely based on the magnitude of EEG (e.g., absolute power measures); and second methods that measure the inter-relations of EEG activity between different scalp locations (e.g., coherence measures). Most often a Fast Fourier Transformation (FFT) is performed on artifact-free chunks of data to derive estimates of absolute power values, or relative percentage power values in different frequency bands: $\delta = 1.5 - 3.5$ Hz; $\vartheta = 3.6 - 6.5$ Hz; $\alpha_1 = 6.6 - 8.5$ Hz; $\alpha_2 = 8.6 - 10.5$ Hz; $\alpha_3 = 10.6 - 12.9$ Hz; $\beta_1 = 13.0 - 17.5$ Hz; $\beta_2 = 17.6 - 23.5$ Hz; $\beta_3 = 23.6 - 31.5$ Hz . The decision to select these 8 bands is mainly based on recent findings relating some of the bands to different mental processes. In several studies using the event-related desynchronization (ERD)-method, Klimesch and his colleagues found that theta synchronization, and desynchronization in the lower alpha band were associated with episodic memory tasks and attentional demands of the tasks (Klimesch et al., 1997a, 1997b). On the other hand, semantic memory tasks showed significant alpha desynchronization only in the upper alpha band (Klimesch et al., 1993). The conclusion drawn from these experiments was that the lower alpha band was primarily associated with attentional processes, whereas the upper alpha band was primarily associated with semantic memory processes. Some recent studies (Traub, et al., 1999; Stein and Petsche, 1995) have further associated neuronal oscillations within the EEG beta and gamma bands (15 - 80 Hz) with intense mental activity and perception – the so-called "binding phenomenon" (the selection and binding together of pertinent aspects of a sensory stimulus into a perceived whole). The majority of analyses reported focus on measures in the alpha band (7.5-13 Hz). Evidence indicates that alpha power is inversely related to mental effort (e.g., Donchin, Kutas, and McCarthy, 1977, Glass, 1964, Butler and Glass, 1976, Gutierrez and Cabrera, 1988, Nunez, 1995).

According to Petsche (1996, 1997), a more suitable indicator of brain functioning, than measures based on the magnitude of EEG, is coherence, the normalized cross-correlation that provides information about the cooperation between various brain areas. Looking for functional relations between brain regions rather than for localized power measures is useful because of the basic structure of the cortex. An essential function of such an interconnected system must be the maximal possible convergence or divergence of signals. Therefore when studying the brain, more information can be provided by measures which determine electrical relations between different areas, rather than just the level of activity in different areas.

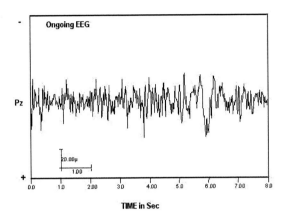

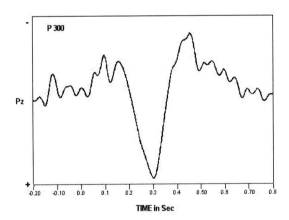

Figure 1. Relationship between the ongoing EEG and the averaged ERP for an oddball task.

Yet another measure using a similar recording technique as the ongoing EEG are average evoked potentials (AEP) also called event-related potentials (ERP). ERPs consist of a brief change in EEG signal in response to a sensory stimulus. The changes are small and hard to see in the background of EEG activity. Therefore sensory stimuli are given repeatedly and the brain activity is averaged. Major interest was devoted to, so called late components in ERPs, that occur after 100 ms after the stimulus onset (Detterman, 1994). Figure 1 shows the relationship between the ongoing EEG (upper part) and the averaged ERP for an oddball task (lower part) – the respondent was asked to count the more rarely occurring 1100 Hz tones (15%) and to ignore the frequently occurring 1000 Hz tones (85%).

The major benefits of using EEG and ERPs are that the approach is noninvasive, it can be used on alert subjects, and it provides the best temporal resolution between behavior and brain activity. The central problem with EEG, however, is that it "is a composite signal from volume conduction in many different parts of the brain, and it is far from clear what a signal means in terms of how neurons in the relevant networks are behaving" (Sejnowski and Churchland, 1989, p. 332).

3.3. Imaging techniques

Functional magnetic resonance imaging (fMRI) and PET can reveal active brain areas. PET takes advantage of the unique characteristic of positron-emitting radio topes (Metter and Hanson, 1994). During the uptake period given by the half-life of the isotope the subject works on a task given by-the experimenter. Then the subject is placed in a ring of sensors that measure the by products of the decay of the radioactive isotopes. The idea is that areas of the brain that are active will use more glucose and hence become more radioactive, than less active brain areas. The data are accumulated for the entire brain by sections or slices. MRI produces a picture of any structure showing differences in tissue density. It is based on the principle that hydrogen atoms behave like spinning bar magnets in the presence of a magnetic field. When the magnetic field is turned off and a pulse of radiation is beamed across the atoms, they emit detectable radio waves that are characteristic of their density and their chemical environment. MRI can be used to assess changes in blood oxygenation, which is a fMRI (Binder and Rao, 1994).

In recent years fMRI has become the method of choice because it has excellent spatial and temporal resolution and subjects are not exposed to radiation (Cohen, 1996). However, a major problem derives from the so-called subtraction technique to determine areas of high activity for a particular task. Numerous t-tests are performed to identify significant differences in the pixels of a pair of images. If the significance levels, are not adjusted to compensate for the number of tests performed, errors of statistical inference could be made. Another problem is that fMRI and especially PET are rather expensive techniques which restrict the sample size to less than ten per group, thus questioning the reliability of statistical inferences made.

3.4. Animal studies

Several experiments have been performed with animals that could not be done on humans (e.g., removing portions of the brains, transplanting brain tissues, etc.) (Goldman-Rakic, 1986). Although much has been learned from these experiments, there are also limitations as to what can be inferred about human brain functioning. As stressed by Vigotsky (1978) behaviors in animals are far less flexible than behaviors in humans.

3.5. Lesions

Cognitive neuropsychologists have tried to link specific brain lesions with cognitive functions. These analyses have revealed a lot about the nature of cognitive processes such as reading and memory. However there are several limitations to this approach. There is considerable individual variability in the locations that cause a specific deficit in people.

Further, specific components of a larger skill are related to rather small regions of the brain. In general occurring lesions affect multiple small regions at once (Kosslyn and Koenig, 1992).

4. WHAT ARE THE EDUCATIONAL IMPLICATIONS OF COGNITIVE NEUROSCIENCE?

The 1990s have been designated by several federal agencies as the "Decade of the Brain". This has also had a significant influence on trends in educational practice as indicated by the growing number of articles published on this topic (e.g., Brynes and Fox, 1998; O'Boyle and Gill, 1998; Dunn, et. al, 1992; Anderson, 1997; Beringer and Abbott, 1992; Hansen and Monk, 2002; Schaverien and Cosgrove, 1999; Schaverien and Cosgrove, 2000). Further, there have been several attempts which have endeavored to give an overview of neuropsychological findings related to different cognitive processes like memory, selective attention, imagery, language comprehension, etc. (e.g., Rugg and Coles, 1995; Cabeza and Nyberg, 2000). As stressed in the introduction this hunger in schools for information about the brain, can have also a negative effect, especially when it is based on neuromyths. In addition to the left brain/right brain learning myth, neuromyths that relate to critical periods for learning (suggesting that the brain will not work properly if it does not receive the right amount of stimulation in the right time), and to synaptogenesis (teaching will be more effective if it coincides with increases in synaptic density) can be identified. The next section will give a brief review of recent findings in neuroscience that could be relevant to education

4.1. Attention

Attention is a cognitive system that is particularly important for acquiring many forms of learning and for regulating one's own emotion and behavior. ERP studies have shown that attention can indeed modulate early sensory and perceptual processing (Mangun and Hilyard, 1995). Transferred to education this means that what students learn and experience is very much a function of what they attend to. Individuals who lack the ability of selective and sustained attention have notable problems in school (Hinshaw, 1994). The short attention spans of some children pose continual problems for their teachers. Children with attention deficit/hyperactivity disorder (ADHD) are particularly challenging to educate, as they are inattentive and impulsive, cruising the classroom instead of focusing on their work. Young children experience some difficulties in sustaining attention and inhibiting impulses. Therefore attentional training might benefit all scholars.

A PET study has shown that selective attention to one sensory modality is correlated with suppressed activity in regions associated with other modalities (Haxby et al., 1994). It was further found that as long as the attentional load is low, task-irrelevant stimuli are perceived and they elicit neural activity. However, when the attentional load is increased, irrelevant perception and its associated activity is strongly reduced (Rees et al., 1997). Posner and Rothbart (2005) have examined the development of attentional networks involved in self regulation from infancy through childhood. Executive attention shows a strong period of development between 2 and 7 years of age. Changes in this network can be observed from tasks that involve conflict between sensory dimensions. The developmental and genetic findings related to attention raise the issue of whether this network could be influenced during its development. The idea would be to improve attention and determine whether the changes generalize to the many domains influenced by attention. A recent brain imaging study (Rueda et all., 2005) claimed that 5 days of attention training significantly improved performance on tests of intelligence in 4- and 6-year-old children.. Even though, attention training did not improve performance in attention, but only improved IQ test performance an electro physiological effect was found for the trained 6 year olds at the target electrode (Cz).

These findings have some implications for the presentation of information in e-learning. According to Mayer and Moreno (2002) one of the principles of multimedia presentation is the redundancy principle – present animation and narration rather than animation, narration, and onscreen text.

4.2. Memory and learning

The best currently accepted idea about how information is stored in the nervous system is based on the concept of the "cell assembly," and what is now called "Hebb synapse" (Hebb, 1949; Martinez and Kesner, 1998). Hebb synapse is a model synapse with a rule that simultaneous pre- and postsynaptic activity increases synaptic efficacy. The cell assembly is a sort of irregular three-dimensional net connected to each other in a closed loop that reactivates itself repeatedly. This recurrent connectivity and reverbatory activity keeps the cell assembly active, allowing a newly formed assembly to retain information. Cell-assemblies are therefore acquired, depend on learning and developmental experience, and are stored in a distributive way in the cerebral cortex, and are built from neural building-blocks processes described in Hebbs neurophysiological postulate. Hebbian synapses generate cell-assemblies. At a superordinate level, in Hebb's hierarchical scheme, cell-assemblies can be linked together associatively to form phase sequences. These constitute the neural bases of higher-order percepts and concepts — the brain's realization of thoughts. Changes in the synapses resulting from the simultaneous (or near-simultaneous) activation of the neurons that form them is generally thought to be the basis of all changes in behavior due to experiences, including those that involve learning. Hebb's (1949) notion of the cell assembly was based on evidence suggesting that memory is a time-dependent process, thus it can be influenced in different stages. Priming refers to the facilitative effect of performing one task on the subsequent performance of the same or similar tasks; whereas consolidation refers to the post-training period during which the hypothesized process of synaptic change occurs and transforms from a labile state into a more permanent one. There is also evidence that certain post training treatments can modulate memory storage in a way that enhances retention.

In a recent study in our lab the influence Mozart's music has on brain activity in the process of learning – priming and memory consolidation – was investigated (Jaušovec, et all., 2006). It was shown that music had a beneficial influence on both learning stages, however physiological differences in EEG patterns were only observed in groups who have been exposed to Mozart's music prior and after learning. The displayed pattern of brain activity (lower alpha and gamma approximated entropy - a measure of low deterministic chaos, more alpha and gamma band event related synchronization) of the respondents who prior to and after learning listened to Mozart's music is similar to findings reported in studies investigating neurophysiological differences in brain activity related to verbal and performance components of intelligence (Jaušovec, 1996; 1998; Anokhin et al., 1999; Jaušovec and Jaušovec, 2000a,b; Neubauer, et al., 1995, 1999, 2002; Neubauer and Fink, 2003), creativity (Mölle et al., 1999), emotional intelligence (Jaušovec and Jaušovec, 2005), as well as research comparing brain activity between musicians and non-musicians while performing different tasks (e.g., listening to music or text, and mental rotation). Musicians while listening to music and during spatial imagination displayed higher levels of gamma band synchronicity than did non-musicians (Bhattacharya, et al., 2001a; 2001b).

Cognitive neuroscience has also revealed that human memory is multifaceted and distributed across multiple brain regions (Klimesch, 1999; Cabeza and Nyberg, 2000). PET studies have shown that even simple stimuli are often represented in a number of different codes: e.g., visual, phonological, articulatory and semantic (Posner et al. 1988). The multifaceted quality of memory emerges also in the distinction among five different memory types: (a) working memory, (b) semantic memory, (c) episodic memory, (d) procedural memory, and (e) perceptual priming (Tulving, 1983). Procedural memory allows us to retain simple behaviors. Perceptual priming is expressed in enhanced identification of objects after repeated exposures. Working memory consists of three main components: a phonological loop for the maintenance of verbal information, a visuospatial sketchpad for the maintenance of visuospatial information, and a central executive for attentional control (Baddeley, 1986). Semantic memory refers to knowledge we share with other members of our culture, such as knowledge about the meaning of words. Episodic memory involves the recording of events within an individual's personal history.

These findings do have some impact on educational practice. For example, on the presentation of information: Should information be presented just in one modality (verbal) or in different modalities (verbal and graphical)? Another question is, what kind of stimuli should be presented prior to- and after learning?

4.3. Individual differences in brain networks

Although there is strong evidence of common networks underlying cognitive processes, there are also individual differences in their details that influence the efficiency of the network.

Intelligence represents the individual's overall level of intellectual ability. It serves as a general concept that includes several groups of mental abilities. One of the most influential divisions of intelligence splits it into verbal, performance and social intelligence (Thorndike, 1920). In recent years the term social intelligence has been replaced by emotional intelligence – the ability to recognize emotion, reason with emotion and emotion-related information, and process emotional information as part of general problem-solving (Mayer, et al., 2000). Neurophysiological research has been mainly interested in the verbal and performance components of intelligence (Anokhin, et al., 1999; O'Boyle, et al., 1995; Haier, and Benbow, 1995; Haier, et al., 1988; Haier, et al., 1992; Jaušovec, 1996, 1998, 2000; Jaušovec and Jaušovec 2000 a, 2000 b, 2001; Lutzenberger, et al., 1992; Neubauer, et al., 1995; Neubauer, et al., 1999; Neubauer, et al., 2002; Neubauer and Fink, 2003) and has, only recently paid some attention to emotional intelligence (Jaušovec, et al. 2001; Jaušovec and Jaušovec, 2004;

2005). Most of these studies have demonstrated a negative correlation between brain activity under cognitive load and intelligence. The explanation of these findings was an efficiency theory. This efficiency may derive from the non-use of many brain areas irrelevant for good task performance as well as the more focused use of specific task-relevant areas in high intelligent individuals. It was even suggested that high and low intelligent individuals preferentially activate different neural circuits even though no reasoning or problem solving was required (Haier, White and Alkire, 2003; Jaušovec and Jaušovec, 2003). Some studies have shown a specific topographic pattern of differences related to the level of intelligence. High-ability subjects made relatively greater use of parietal regions, whereas low-ability subjects relied more exclusively on frontal regions. (Gevins and Smith, 2000; Jaušovecand Jaušovec, 2004a). More generally these results suggest that higher-ability subjects tend to better identify strategies needed for the solution of the task at hand. It was further reported that high intelligent subjects displayed more brain activity in the early stages of task performance, while average individuals showed a reverse pattern. This temporal distribution of brain activity suggests that cognitive processes in high intelligent individuals are faster than in average intelligent individuals (Jaušovecand Jaušovec, 2004b).

Experiments conducted by O'Boyle et al. (1995) have revealed that there is a unique cortical substrate that mediates superior intellectual abilities. Specifically, it appears that enhanced involvement of the right cerebral hemisphere during basic information processing may be a physiological correlate of intellectual giftedness. Logically, what might work best in terms of teaching the gifted student would be the utilization of classroom techniques that capitalize on the manner in which their brain operates. As suggested by O'Boyle and Gill (1998) the best approach would be directed toward the specialized contributions of both hemispheres during the acquisition of any cognitive skill.

Recent work by neuroscientists has shown that sex differences in the functional organization of the brain may underlie some of the cognitive performance differences found between males and females on a variety of tasks, particular by those involving verbal skills (Shaywitz et al., 1995), and the formation of mental images (Gill and O'Boyle, 1997). There is some consensus that the male brain is more lateralized than the female brain, which is more bilateral in its functional organization. Some recent EEG studies relating intelligence with brain activity under cognitive load have shown that males while solving numerical and figural tasks are more likely to produce cortical activation patterns which are in line with the neural efficiency hypothesis (i.e. less activation in brighter individuals), whereas in females for the same tasks no significant differences could be observed (Neubauer et al., 2002; Neubauer and Fink, 2003). Sex related differences were also observed in EEG coherence and global field power studies. The results of Corsi-Cabera et al., (1997); and Rescher and Rappelsberger (1999) indicate different intra- and interhemispheric correlations of EEG activity in males and females, a finding commonly related to sex differences in certain brain structures (e.g., the posterior corpus callosum). Skrandies et al., (1999) found a consistently larger global field power in females suggesting that during visual information processing different neural assemblies are activated in males and females. Empirical evidence favoring sex differences in physiological parameters of cortical activation comes also from PET, fMRI, and brain nerve conduction velocity (NCV) studies. It was found that for figural tasks males show significantly stronger parietal activation, while females show significantly greater frontal activation (Weiss et al., 2003). A similar greater left frontal brain activation in females was also observed in relation to verbal intelligence scores (Pfleiderer et al., (2004). Nyberg et al.,

(2000) observed sex differences in brain activation during memory retrieval, while Haier and Benbow (1995) reported a positive relationship in glucose metabolic rate in temporal lobe regions and mathematical reasoning ability only in men. A similar finding was also reported by Mansour et al., (1996). In a recent study by Reed, et al., (2004) NCV, the speed at which impulses travel along nerves, was compared in the visual nerve pathway of males and females. It was found that the mean NCV of males was about 4% faster than in females.

Summarizing these findings suggests that gender related differences in intelligence can be observed in relation to the type of task (verbal/figural), and activated brain regions (frontal versus temporal-occipital and parieto-occipital areas). A tentative conceptual framework for the differences observed could be provided by age changes in white matter in the brain. It is now established that during childhood and adolescence the volume of white matter (WM: nerve axons, myelin around the axons, and glial cells) in the brain steadily increases. In males this volume probably increases faster than in females (De Bellis et al., 2001). This would also explain the finding, that among adults, males have an advantage of approximately 4 IQ points (Colom and Lynn, 2004). The increase in WM could be due to increased myelination, increased axon size, glial proliferation, or a combination of these (De Bellis et al., 2001). Miller (1994) proposed that myelination could also be an explanation of the neural efficiency theory of intelligence – the more focused use of specific task-relevant brain areas in high intelligent individuals could be the result of less leakage and cross-talk between neurons.

Does this mean that girls and boys should be taught separately, even in mixed schools? The conclusion of several researchers is that at present our knowledge base is too weak to use for any policy making on such issues (O'Boyle and Gill, 1998; Hansen and Monk, 2002).

4.4. Brain development

The vast majority of brain development is completed very early, perhaps by the age of 6 (Goldman-Rakic, 1996). The concept of plasticity — both neural and cognitive — lies at the heart of the brain-behavior relationship across the lifespan. Plasticity of the nervous system allows learning and environmental adaptation. Plasticity – developmental changes in synaptic density and synaptic pruning, the key role of cell loss, and the growth and myelination of white matter – are greatest in childhood (Craik, 2006). One of many interesting points is the fact that synaptic density peaks in the frontal cortex at the age of 4 years; it is worth noting that Tulving (2005) has suggested that true episodic memory and self-awareness does not develop until the same age. However there is also evidence that there is some plasticity and fine-tuning that continues across the lifespan. Maguire et al. (2000) found that in London taxi-drivers the posterior region of the hippocampus is much larger than in the rest of population, whereas the front region is much smaller. There is also preliminary evidence that extensive practice of intellectual skills is associated with higher performance on some cognitive tasks. For example, Bialystok et al. (2004) have shown that lifelong bilinguals display an advantage over monolinguals on simple tasks requiring inhibitory control. Such differences could point to anatomical change in a healthy adult brain due to learning. The growing evidence for cortical plasticity in middle-aged and elderly adults would suggest that we need more time to help our adolescents develop their thinking skills than traditional sharp stage theory may indicate.

5. WHAT CAN COGNITIVE NEUROSCIENCE OFFER TO E-LEARNING?

Physiological studies of e-learning and computer supported multimedia teaching can be classified into two broad categories: 1) physiological studies using virtual reality or computers as a means of placing subjects into a predefined and highly controlled environment, and 2) studies that make use of physiological measurements to assess any bodily reaction to e-learning (Pugnetti et al., 2001). The second approach is of special interest to educators and can help in the design of computer supported instructional material. As stressed by Mikropoulos (2001) there are only a few studies reporting results on brain activity in e-learning. Bayliss and Ballard (1998a, 1998b) have reported findings on the cognitive activity of subjects who were told to stop their virtual cars at the red traffic light. Strickland and Chartier (1997) have reported on EEG measurements in a virtual reality headset, concluding that differences do exist between real and virtual image processing. In a PET study Maguire et al. (1998) showed that a parahippocampal involvement in encoding object locations in virtual large scale space could be observed that was not activated during explorations of empty virtual environments. A study by Mikropoulos (2000) showed that the human brain operates in a different way when it receives signals coming from synthetic environments such as the computer-generated environments. These studies are more general and have only limited educational relevance.

In a recent study, Gerlič and Jaušovec (1999) investigated the cognitive processes involved in learning information presented in multimedia and text format using EEG. Students learned material presented with a text; text, sound, and picture; and text, sound and video. Alpha power which is inversely related to mental effort was analyzed. For the text presentation, the alpha power measures showed higher amplitudes (less mental activity) over the occipital and temporal lobes, and less alpha power (higher mental activity) over the frontal lobes. The results support the assumption that the video and picture presentations induced visualization strategies, whereas the text presentation mainly generated processes related to verbal processing. The results further showed that gifted students displayed less mental activity during all three formats of presentation. These differences were especially pronounced for the video format. No gender-related differences in EEG patterns related to the format of presentation were observed. In a second study, Gerlič and Jaušovec (2001) investigated the cognitive processes of students while learning physics. Experts and novices in the domain of physics learned material presented by text, and in a computer supported multimedia format, while their EEG was recorded. Alpha power measures as well as coherence measures were analyzed. The results taken altogether suggest that learning with multimedia was rather demanding, yet provoked less transfer of information between brain areas, and had no beneficial influence on the amount of learned material. Another finding was that experts in the domain of physics learned more than did novices, regardless of the type of presentation. The EEG patterns differed mainly in the lower alpha band, thus pointing to the superior control of attentional processes in experts. Similar findings were also reported by Mikropoulos (2001) for a virtual environment form of presentation. Eye-movement measurements showed that the subjects were more attentive when navigating in the virtual world. Lower theta activity in the virtual task demonstrated that the subjects invested less mental effort in the virtual task. McCluskey (1997) tried to relate cerebral hemisphericity to the performance of different computer tasks. He could show that right-brain dominant individuals significantly out performed their left-brain and mixed-brain dominant counterparts in several areas.

This overview showed that neuropsychological research into e-learning and computer supported multimedia presentations is just slowly emerging. At present there is a lack of a systematical research approach which would focus on the differences between e-learning and classical classroom presentations. In our opinion the goals of neuropsychological research on e-learning should stress the following points:

- study brain activity of different types of multimedia presentation (e.g., animation in combination with text or narrative audio presentation)
- study brain activity of different cognitive styles and ability levels in computer assisted learning environments
- How do brain activation patterns change in relation to training/learning?
- What are the specific changes in individuals brain activity involved in E-learning sessions?

REFERENCES

Anderson, O.R. (1997). A neurocognitive perspective on current learning theory and science instructional strategies. *Science Education*, 81, 67-89.

Anokhin, A.P., Lutzenberger, W., and Birbaumer, N. (1999). Spatiotemporal organization of brain dynamics and intelligence: an EEG study in adolescents. *International Journal of Psychophysiology*, 33, 259-273.

Ansari, D., and Coch, D. (2006). Bridges over troubled waters: education and cognitive neuroscience. *Trends in Cognitive Sciences*, 4, 146-151

Baddeley, A. (1986). *Working memory*. New York, USA: Oxford University Press.

Bayliss, J.D., and Ballard, D.H. (1998). *Single trial P300 recognition in virtual environment* . The University of Rochester, Computer Science Department, Technical Report 98.1 . Available at www.cs.rochester.edu/trs/robotics_trs.htm

Bayliss, J.D., and Ballard, D.H. (1998). *The effect of eye tracking in a VR helmet on EEG recordings*. The University of Rochester, Computer Science Department, Technical Report 685. Available at www.cs.rochester.edu/trs/robotics_trs.htm

Beringer, V.W., and Abbott, R.D. (1992). The unit of analysis and the constructive processes of the learner: Key concepts for educational neuropsychology. *Educational Psychologist*, 27, 223-242.

Bialystok, E., Craik, F.I.M., Klein, R., Viswanathan, M. (2004). Bilingualism, aging, and cognitive control: evidence from the Simon task. *Psychology and Aging,* 19, 290–303.

Binder, R.J., and Rao, S.M. (1994). *Human brain mapping with functional magnetic resonance imaging*. In A., Kertesz (Ed.). Localization and Neuroimaging in neuropsychology (pp.185-212). San Diego: Academic Press.

Blakemore, S. J., and Frith, U. (2005). *The Learning Brain: Lessons for Education*. Blackwell, Oxford, UK.

Bouras, C., and T. Tsiatsos,T. (2006) Educational virtual environments: design rationale and architecture. *Multimed Tools Appl.* 29, 153–173

Bruer, J.T. (1997). Education and the brain: A bridge to far. *Educational Researcher*, 26, 4-16.

Butler, S.R., and Glass, A. (1976). *EEG correlates of cerebral dominance*. In A. H Reisen, and R.F. Thompson (Eds.) Advances in psychology Vol. 3 (pp. 219-384). NY, USA: John Wiley

Byrnes, J.P., and Fox, N., A. (1998). The educational relevance of research in cognitive neuroscience. *Educational Psychology Review*, 10, 297-341.

Cabeza, R. and Nyberg, L. (2000). Imaging cognition II: An empirical review of 275 PET and fMRI studies. *Journal of Cognitive Neuroscience*, 12, 1-47.

Cohen, M.S. (1996). *Rapid MRI and functional applications*. In Toga, A.W., and Mazziotta, J.C. (Eds.), Brain Mapping: The Methods. Academic Press, Orlando FL, pp. 191-219.

Colom, R., and Lynn, R. (2004). Testing the developmental theory of sex differences in intelligence on 12–18 year olds. *Personality and Individual Differences*, 36, 75-82.

Condliffe Lagemann, E. (2000) *An Elusive Science: The Troubling History of Education Research*. University of Chicago Press.

Corsi-Cabrera, M., Arce, C., Ramos, J., and Guevara, M. A. (1997). Effect of spatial abilityand sex on inter- and intrahemispheric correlation of EEG activity. Electroencephalography and Clinical. *Neurophysiology*, 102, 5–11.

Craik, F.I.M. (2006) Brain–behavior relations across the lifespan: A commentary. *Neuroscience and Biobehavioral Reviews* , 30, 885–892

De Bellis, M. D., Keshavan, M. S., Beers, S. R., Hall, J., Frustaci, K., and Masalehdan, A. et al. (2001). Sex differences in brain maturation during childhood and adolescence. *Cerebral Cortex*, 11, 552–557.

Detterman, D.K. (1994). *Intelligence and the brain*. In P. A. Vernon (Ed.) The neuropsychology of individual differences. (pp. 35-57). London, UK: Academic Press INC.

Donchin, E., Kutas, M., and McCarthy, G. (1977). *Electrocortical indices of hemispheric specialization*. In S. Harnad, R.W. Doty, L. Goldstein, J. Jaynes and G. Krauthamer (Eds.) Lateralization in the nervous system (pp. 339-384). New York, USA: Academic Press.

Dunn, B., Dunn, D., Andrews, D., and Languis, M.L. (1992). Metacontrol: A cognitive model of brain functioning for psychophysiological study of complex learning. *Educational Psychologist*, 27 455-471.

Etevenon, P. (1986). *Applications and perspectives of EEG cartography*. In F.H. Duffy (Ed.) Topographic mapping of brain electrical activity. Stoneham MA: Butterworth Publishers.

Gerlič, I., and Jaušovec, N. (1999). Multimedia: Differences in cognitive processes observed with EEG. *Educational Technology Research and Development*,47, 5-14.

Gerlič, I., and Jaušovec, N. (2001). Differences in EEG power and coherence measures related to the type of presentation: Text versus multimedia. *Journal of Educational Computing Research*, 25, 177-195.

Gevins, A., and Smith, M.E. (2000). Neurophysiological measures of working memory and individual differences in cognitive ability and cognitive style. *Cerebral Cortex*, 10, 830-839.

Gill, H.S., and O'Boyle, M.W. (1997). Sex differences in matching circles and arcs: A preliminary EEG investigation. *Laterality*, 2, 33-48.

Glass, A. (1964). Mental arithmetic and blocking of the occipital alpha rhythm. *Electroencephalography and Clinical Neurophysiology*, 16, 595-603.

Goldman-Rakic, P.S. (1986). Setting the stage:Neural development before birth. In Pterson, S.L., Klivington, K.A., and Peterson, R.W. (Eds.). *The Brain, Cognition and Education*, Academic, New York, USA, pp. 233-258.

Goldman-Rakic, P.S. (1996). *What can neuroscience contribute to education?* In Briding the gap between neuroscience and education, Education Comission of the States, Denver, CO, pp. 11-12.

Gonzales, P. et al. (2004). *Highlights from the Trends in International Mathematics and Science Study*: TIMSS 2003, National Center for Education Statistics

Goswami, U. (2004). Neuroscience and education: from research to practice. *Nature Reviews Neuroscience*. Available at http://www.nature.com/reviews/neuro

Gutierrez, S., and Corsi-Cabrera, M. (1988). EEG activity during performance of cognitive atsks demanding verbal and/or spatial processing. *International Journal of Neuroscience*, 62 , 149-155.

Haier, R.J., Neuchterlein, K.H., Hazlett, E., Wu, J.C. Paek, J., Browning, H.,L., and Buchsbaum, M.S. (1988). Cortical glucose metabolic rate correlates of abstract reasoning and attention studied with positron emission tomography. *Intelligence*, 12, 199-217

Haier, R.J., Siegel, B., Tang, C., Abel, L., and Buchsbaum, M.S. (1992). Intelligence and changes in regional cerebral glucose mezabolic rate following learning. *Intelligence*, 16, 415-426

Haier, R.J., Benbow, C.P. (1995). Sex differences and lateralization in temporal lobe glucose metabolism during mathematical reasoning. *Developmental Neuropsychology*, 4, 405-414

Haier, R.J., White, N.S., and Alkire, M.T. (2003). Individual differences in general intelligence correlate with brain function during nonreasoning tasks. *Intelligence*, 31, 429-441.

Hansen, L., and Monk, M. (2002). Brain development, structuring of learning and science education: Where are we now? A review of some recent research. International Journal of Science Education, 24, 343-356.

Haxby, J.V., Horwitz, B., Ungerleider, L.G., Maisog, J.M., Pietrini, P., Grady C.L., (1994). The functional organization of human extrastriate cortex: A PET-rCBF study of selective attention to faces and locations. *Journal of Neuroscience*, 14, 6336-6353.

Hinshaw, S.P. (1994). *Attention deficits and Hyperactivity in children*. Sage Publications, Thousand Oaks, CA.

Hunt, N.P. (1998). *Designing instruction for the Web: Incorporating new conceptions of the learning process.* In ED-MEDIA/ED-TELECOM 98 World Conference on Educational Multimedia and Hypermedia and World Conference on Educational Telecommunication. Proceedings (10th, Freiburg, Germany, June 20-25, pp 334-342.

Jaušovec, N., Jaušovec, K., and Gerlič, I. (2006). The influence of Mozart's music on brain activity in the process of learning. *Clinical Neurophysiology*, 117, 2703-2714.

Jaušovec, N. (1996). Differences in EEG alpha activity related to giftedness. *Intelligence*, 23, 159-173.

Jaušovec, N. (1998). Are gifted individuals less chaotic thinkers? *Personality and Individual Differences,* 25, 253-267.

Jaušovec, N. (2000). Differences in cognitive processes between gifted, intelligent, creative and average individuals while solving complex problems: An EEG study. *Intelligence*, 28, 213-237

Jaušovec, N., and Jaušovec, K. (2000)a. Differences in resting EEG related to ability. *Brain Topography*, 12, 229-240.

Jaušovec, N., and Jaušovec, K. (2000) b. Correlations between ERP parameters and intelligence: a reconsideration. *Biological Psychology*, 50, 137-154.

Jaušovec, N., and Jaušovec, K. (2001). Differences in EEG current density related to intelligence. *Cognitive Brain Research*, 12, 55-60.

Jaušovec, N., and Jaušovec, K. (2003). Spatiotemporal brain activity related to intelligence: a low resolution brain electromagnetic tomography study. *Cognitive Brain Research*, 16, 267-272.

Jaušovec, N., and Jaušovec, K. (2004) a. Intelligence related differences in induced brain activity during the performance of memory tasks. *Personality and Individual Differences*, 36, 597-612.

Jaušovec, N., and Jaušovec, K. (2004) b. Differences in induced brain activity during the performance of learning and working-memory tasks related to intelligence. *Brain and Cognition*, 54, 65-74.

Jaušovec, N., and Jaušovec, K, (2005). Differences in induced gamma and upper alpha oscillations in the human brain related to verbal/performance and emotional intelligence. *International Journal of Psychophysiology*, 56, 223-235.

Jensen, A.R. (1992). Understanding g in terms of information processing. *Educational Psychology Review*, 4, 271-308

Kaput, J.J. (1992). *Technology and mathematics education*. In D.A. Grouws (Ed.), Handbook of research on mathematics teaching and learning. (pp. 693-719). NY, USA: Simon and Schuster.

Klimesch, W., Schimke, H., and Pfurtscheller, G. (1993). Alpha frequency, cognitive load and memory performance. *Brain Topography*, 5, 1-11.

Klimesch, W., Doppelmayr, M., Schimke, H., and Ripper, B. (1997a). Theta synchronization and alpha desynchronization in a memory task. *Psychgophysiology*, 34, 169-176.

Klimesch, W., Doppelmayr, M., Pachinger, Th., and Ripper, B. (1997b). Brain oscillations and human memory: EEG correlates in the upper alpha and theta band. *Neuroscience Letters*, 238, 9-12.

Klimesch, W. (1999). EEG alpha and theta oscillations reflect cognitive and memory performance: a review and analysis. *Brain Research Reviews*, 29, 169-195.

Kosslyn, S.M., and Koenig, O. (1992). *Wet mind: The new cognitive neuroscience*. The Free Press, New York, USA.

Lutzenberger, W., Elbert, T., Birbaumer, N., and Ray, W.J. (1992). The scalp distribution of the fractal dimension of the EEG and its variation with mental tasks. *Brain Topography*, 5, 27-34

Maguire, E.A., Firth, C.D., Burgess, N., Donnett, J.G., and O'Keefe, J. (1998). Knowing where things are: Parahippocampal involvement in encoding object locations in virtual large-scale space. *Journal of Cognitive Neuroscience*, 10, 61-76.

Maguire, E.A., Gadian, D.G., Johnsrude, I.S., Good, C.D., Ashburner, J., Frackowiak, R.S.J., and Frith, C.D. (2000). *Navigation-related structural change in the hippocampi of taxi drivers*. Proceedings of the National Academy of Sciences, USA, 97, 4398-4403.

Mangun, G.R., and Hillyard, S.A. (1995). *Mechanisms and models of selective attention*. In M.D. Rugg, and M.G.H. Coles (Eds.), Electrophysiology of mind: Event-related brain potentials and cognition. Oxford University Press, Oxford, pp. 40-85.

Mansour, C.S., Haier, R.J., and Buchsbaum, M.S. (1996). Gender comparison of cerebral glucose metabolic rate in healthy adults during a cognitive task. *Personality and Individual Differences*, 20, 183-191.

Martinez, J. and Kesner, R. (1998). Neurobiology of learning and memory. Academic Press, San Diego.

Mayer, J.D., Caruso, D.R., and Salovey, P. (2000). Emotional intelligence meets traditional standards for an intelligence. *Intelligence*, 27, 267-298.

Mayer, R.E., Moreno, R. (2002). Animation as an aid to multimedia learning. *Educational Psychology Review*, 14, 87-99.

McCluskey, J.J. (1997). An exploratory study of the possible impact of cerebral hemisphericity on the performance of selected linear, non-linear, and spatial computer tasks. *Journal of Educational Computing Research*, 16, 269-279.

Metter, E.J., and Hanson, W.R. (1994). Use of positron emition tomography to study aphasia. In Kertesz (Ed.). *Localization and Neuroimaging in neuropsychology* (pp.123-149). San Diego: Academic Press.

Mikropoulos, T.A. (2000). *Design, development and evaluation of advanced learning environments*. An overall approach. Presented at the HERMES Advanced systems for teaching and learning over the world wide web, B42-B52, September 1-3 (Samos, Greece).

Mikropoulos, T.A. (2001). Brain activity on navigation in virtual environments. *Journal of Educational Computing Research*, 24, 1-12.

Miller, E.M. (1994). Intelligence and brain myelination: A hypothesis. *Personality and individual differences*, 17, 803-833.

Mölle, M., Marshall, L., Wolf, B., Fehm, H., and Born, J. (1999). EEG complexity and performance measures of creative thinking. *Psychophysiology*, 36, 95-104.

Najjar, L.J. (1996). Multimedia information and learning. *Journal of Educational Multimedia and Hypermedia*, 2, 129-150.

Nunez, P.L. (1995). *Mind, brain, and electroencephalography*. In P. L. Nunez (Ed.) Neocortical dynamics and human EEG rhythms. (pp. 133-194) NY, USA: Oxford University Press.

Neubauer, V., Freudenthaler, H.H., and Pfurtscheller, G. (1995). Intelligence and spatiotemporal patterns of event-related desynchronization. *Intelligence*, 3, 249-266.

Neubauer, A.C., Sange, G., and Pfurtscheller, G. (1999). *Psychometric intelligence and event-related desynchronization during performance of a letter matching task*. In G. Pfurtscheller and F.H. Lopes da Silva (Ed.) Handbook of electroencephalography and clinical neuropsychology, Vol. 6: Event-related desynchronization. Amsterdam: Elsevier, pp. 219-232.

Neubauer A.C., Fink, A., and Schrausser, D.G. (2002). Intelligence and neural efficiency: The influence of task content and sex on the brain – IQ relationship. *Intelligence*, 30, 515-536.

Neubauer, A.C., and Fink, A. (2003). Fluid intelligence and neural efficiency: effects of task complexity and sex. *Personality and Individual Differences*, 35, 811-827.

Nyberg, L., Habib, R., and Herlitz, A. (2000). Brain activation during episodic memory retrieval: sex differences. *Acta Psychologica*, 105, 181-194.

O'Boyle, M.W., and Gill, H.S. (1998). On the relevance of research findings in cognitive neuroscience to educational practice. *Educational Psychology Review*, 10, 397-409.

O'Boyle, M.W., Benbow, C.P., and Alexander, J.E. (1995). Sex differences, hemispheric laterality, and associated brain activity in the intellectually gifted. *Developmental Neuropsychology*, 4, 415-443.

Petsche, H. (1996). Approaches to verbal, visual and musical creativity by EEG coherence analysis. *International Journal of Psychophysiology*, 24, 145-159.

Petsche, H. (1997). *EEG coherence and mental Activity.* In F. Angeleri, S. Butler, S. Giaquinto, and J. Majakowski (Ed.). Analysis of the electrical activity of the brain. (pp. 141-168). Chichester: John Wiley and Sons Ltd.

Pfleiderer,B., Ohrmann,A, P., Suslow, B.T., Wolgast, B.M., Gerlach, B.A.L., Heindela, C.W., and Michael, N. (2004). N-acetylaspartate levels of left frontal cortex are associated with verbal intelligence in women but not in men: a proton magnetic resonance spectroscopy study. *Neuroscience,* 123, 1053-1058.

Pfurtscheller, G. (1999). *Quantification of ERD and ERS in the time domain.* In G. Pfurtscheller and F.H. Lopes da Silva (Ed.) Handbook of electroencephalography and clinical neuropsychology, Vol. 6: Event-related desynchronization. Amsterdam: Elsevier, pp. 89-105.

Posner, M.I., Peterson, S.E., Fox, P.T., and Raichle, M.E. (1988). Localization of cognitive operations in the human brain. *Science*, 240, 1627-1631.

Posner, M.I., Rothbart, M.K. (2005), Influencing brain networks: implications for education. *Trends in Cognitive Sciences*, 9, 99-103

Pugnetti, L., Mendozzi, L., and Meehan, M. (2001). Psychophysiological correlates of virtual reality. *Teleoperators and Virtual environments*, 10, 384-401.

Reed, T.E., Vernon, P.A., and Johnson, A.M. (2004). Sex difference in brain nerve conduction velocity in normal humans. *Neuropsychologia*, 42, 1709–1714.

Rees, G., Frith, C.D., and Lavie, N. (1997). Modulating irrelevant motion perception by varying attentional load in an unrelated task. *Science*, 278, 1616-1619.

Reimann, P. (1999). The role of external represenations in distributed problem solving. *Learning and Instruction*, 9, 411-418.

Rescher, B., and Rappelsberger, P. (1999). Gender dependent EEG-changes during a menatl rotation task. *International Journal of Psychophysiology*, 33, 209-222.

Ring, G., and Mathieux, G. (2002, February). *The key components of quality learning.* Paper presented at the ASTD Techknowledge 2002 Conference, Las Vegas.

Rossett, A. (2002). *Waking in the night and thinking about e-learning.* In A. Rossett (Ed.), The ASTD e-learning handbook (pp. 3-18). New York, USA: McGraw-Hill.

Rueda, M. R., Rothbart, M. K., McCandliss, B. D., Saccomanno, L., and Posner, M. L. (2005) *Training, maturation and genetic influences on the development of executive attention.* Proc. Natl Acad. Sci. USA 102, 14931–14936.

Rugg, M.D., and Coles, M.H.G. (1995). *Electrophysiology of mind.* New York, USA: Oxford University Press.

Salomon, G. (1998). Novel constructivist learning environments and novel technologies: Some issues to be concerend with. *Research Dialogue in Learning and Instruction*, 1, 3-11.

Salomon, G., Perkins, D.N., and Globerson, T. (1991). Partners in cognition: extending human intelligence with intelligent technologies. *Educational Researcher*, 20, 2-9.

Schaverien, L., and Cosgrove, M. (1999). A biological basis for generative learning in technology-and-science part I: A theory of learning. *International Journal of Science Education*, 21, 1223-1235.

Schaverien, L., and Cosgrove, M. (2000). A biological basis for generative learning in technology-and-science part II: Implications for technology-and-science education. *International Journal of Science Education*, 22, 13-35.

Sejnovski, T.J., and Churchland, P.S. (1989). *Brain and cognition*. In Posner, M.I. (Eds.), Foundations of cognitive science, pp.301-358.

Shaywitz, B.A., Shaywitz, S.E., Pugh, K.R., Constable, R.T., Skudlarski, P., Fulbright, R.K., Brronen, R.A., Fletcher, J.M., Shankweiler, D.P., Katz, L., and Gore, J.C. (1995). Sex differences in the functional organization of the brain for language. *Nature,* 373, 607-609.

Skrandies, W., Reik, P., and Kunze, Ch. (1999). Topography of evoked brain activity during mental arithmetic and language tasks: sex differences. *Neuropsychologia,* 37, 421-430.

Stein A, and Petsche, H. (1995) EEG synchronization seems to reflect functional properties of the underlying cortical networks in the human brain. *European Journal of Neuroscience*, 8, 32-37.

Strickland, D., and Chartier, D. (1997). *EEG measurements in a virtual reality headset.* Presence: Teleoperators and Virtual Environments, 6, 581-588.

Thorndike, E.L. (1920). Intelligence and its use. *Harper's Magazine*, 140, 227-235.

Traub, R.D., Whittington, M.A., Buhl, E.H., Jefferys, J.G.R., and Faulkner, H.J. (1999).On the mechanisms of the $\gamma \to \beta$ frequency shift in neuronal oscillations induced in rat hippocampal slices by tetanic stimulation. *The Journal of Neuroscience*, 19, 1088-1105.

Tulving, E. (1983). *Elements of episodic memory*. Oxford, UK: Clarendon Press.

Tulving, E. (2005). *Episodic memory and autonoesis: uniquely human?* In: Terrace, H.S., Metcalfe, J. (Eds.), The Missing Link in Cognition: Origins of Self-re.ective Consciousness. Oxford University Press, New York, USA, pp. 3–56.

Van Someren, M., Boshuizen, E., de Jong, T., and Reimann, P. (1998). *Multiple represenations for problem solving and learning*. London, UK: Elsevier.

Vernon, P.A., and Mori, M. (1992). Intelligence, reaction times, and peripheral nerve conduction velocity. *Intelligence*, 16, 273-288.

Vigotsky, L.S. (1978). *Mind and Society*. Harvard University Press, Cambridge, MA.

Weiss, E., Siedentopf, C.M., Hofer, A., Deisenhammer, E.A., Hoptman, M.J., Kremser, C., Golaszewski, S., Felber, S., and Fleischhacker, W.W. (2003). Sex differences in brain activation pattern during a visuospatial cognitive task: a functional magnetic resonance imaging study in healthy volunteers. *Neuroscience Letters*, 344, 169-172.

In: E-Learning: 21st Century Issues and Challenges
Editor: A.R. Lipshitz and S. P. Parsons, pp. 225-234

ISBN : 978-1-60456-156-2
©2008 Nova Science Publishers, Inc.

Chapter 12

TAILORING AND WEBCASTING FOR PATIENT AND STUDENT HEALTH EDUCATION

Ray Jones and Inocencio Maramba
University of Plymouth, UK

ABSTRACT

This chapter is about the 'connectedness' of different ways of presenting health information. Information for individual patients can be tailored via 'user-models' which may include the patient's own medical record. There is evidence that tailoring information in this way can make it more relevant and useable for patients and their families. For example, in rigorous randoamised trials we have shown that tailored information is more likely to be shown by cancer patients to their confidants. There may be impact on psychological wellbeing, but this has been more difficult to show.

Traditional e-learning for students has well known advantages such as convenience of time and being able to work at the student's own pace and review material in different ways. However, the reduced 'connection' with the lecturer and other students may mean that students are less motivated to engage with the material. We have been developing simple ways of delivering live webcasting with a simultaneous chat room. User reaction from students has been favourable but there are many practical aspects to improve. Although there is evidence that computers can be used successfully for psychological therapy and patient education approaches to this could be improved by inclusion of live webcasting. For example, computerised cognitive behavioural therapy has proved successful for anxiety and depression but there is also some evidence that this approach is less successful if there is no human contact. A combination of live webcasting to provide human contact and motivation together with tailored information education may be the best way forward.

However, there are many unanswered questions about the use of these technologies particularly amongst new user groups. For example, how does the use of asynchronous methods such as email differ from synchronous methods such as chat rooms. Chat rooms may provide more 'connection' but perhaps users need time to think. We will be exploring such issues with groups of older people.

INTRODUCTION

Information for patients comes in many formats. Most patients get the majority of their information face-to-face from health professionals. However, information from TV, the press, books, leaflets, and of course the Internet plays an increasing role. Information may be 'pushed' by professionals – in the form of (for example) an anti-smoking or safe sex campaign, or may be 'pulled' by patients seeking more information about their condition. Information may be sought to help in making a joint decision with the health care provider, or may be sought simply for 'peace of mind'. Information can be targeted at particular groups by the language and imagery used and by the medium and timing of the output. Health promoters use the services of marketing experts to help develop images and phraseology suitable for their target audiences. Charities and other providers of condition specific information develop and test their booklets, leaflets, and web pages with focus groups and interviews amongst the target populations. However, information cannot only be targeted at particular groups but also tailored to the individual patient. This chapter is about studies that have sought to take that further step from targeting a particular group of patients to tailoring the information for individuals.

Tailoring is just one way of trying to 'connect' better with the user. Another way is through the use of synchronous methods such as webcasting and in this chapter we describe our experience of live webcasting with simultaneous chat room both for students and for patients.

TAILORED INFORMATION FOR PATIENTS

Information for individual patients can be made more relevant, enabling them to 'connect' with the information by tailoring it via 'user-models' and information about the patient, from onscreen questionnaire or some other source such as the patient's own medical record [1]. There is evidence that tailoring information in this way can make it more useable by patients and their families. For example, we have carried out two randomised trials comparing tailored information with general information for patients with cancer receiving radiotherapy in a hospital in Glasgow, Scotland [2,3]. The first study [2] included 525 patients with breast, prostate, cervical, or laryngeal cancer just starting a course of radiotherapy. One group were offered general cancer information on a touch screen computer located in the outpatient area of the hospital, together with a paper copy of what they viewed on screen. Another group of patients used the same computer but instead of seeing just general information started with information from their own medical record, and then as they navigated away from that moved into more general information. We found that patients offered this tailored information were more likely to show the paper copy of the information to someone else, were more likely to rate the information highly and showed a greater reduction in anxiety (as measured by the Hospital Anxiety and Depression Scale [4]) over 3 months than those with general information only. A subsequent study [3] of 400 patients and their confidants confirmed that patients were more likely to show booklets including, and tailored by, personal information, to their confidants.

This approach of giving patients access to their own medical record and using the information to tailor further explanation about their condition can be extended to virtually all groups. In another study we successfully took this approach with patients with schizophrenia in a day centre in the Gorbals in Glasgow [5]. We had no major problems in sharing the medical record and tailoring information for this more difficult-to-engage group.

Information for patients can be tailored in a number of ways. For example, Grasso [6] attempted to develop a conversational method to put counter arguments to users about their dietary choices. In her approach the arguments presented to users were tailored according to their previous responses.

Others, such as Marsden [7], have used online questionnaires. She recruited female university students and asked them to complete online questionnaires about their dietary, exercise, and other lifestyle choices. She compared the impact of tailored versus general emails sent to the students encouraging behaviour that might help prevent subsequent development of osteoporosis. She used Prochaska and Di Clemente's [8] stages of change model to choose which type of message to send.

Kroez, Werkman, and Brug [9] recently reviewed the use of tailored information in dietary advice. Most of the studies used online questionnaires about food, exercise, other lifestyle issues such as whether the user smoked to generate advice or a health plan as a letter or a leaflet. Most studies found that those with personalized advice increased their daily servings of fruits and vegetables.

Another way of tailoring is to make better use of the information already seen onscreen or given via leaflet. Many websites now record the pathway that users have followed. This information could be used to tailor information. This approach was pioneered by Mellish and others in Edinburgh in a novel experiment in museums in which a handset was to give audio information about the exhibits being viewed. The aim was that the handset would send the users position to a computer which could then generate an explanation such as 'This exhibit that you are looking at is similar to the one that you have just seen in that. In comparison to the XXX exhibit that you saw before on the second floor this piece. In the end, the main system was delivered through a standard web interface, but the idea could be revisited [10].

The information needs of patients change over time. A person newly diagnosed with cancer requires different information to someone who has been living with cancer for some time and had multiple treatments. Information for patients needs to be built up over time. In face to face dialogue with a health professional, they professional will partly remember what has already been discussed but also confirm this to gradually help the patient to build an understanding of the situation. If this is to be done in some form of automated dialogue the computer program needs to adapt to current questions or information requests and build upon what has been said before. Dialogue systems are well described by Bickmore and Giorgino [11] with illustrations from their work with Fitrack exercise advisor [12] and other systems.

Lastly, these approaches to tailoring information normally assume some 'user model' by which to select and modify the information presented. One of the most well known consumer websites which constructs a dynamic user model is Amazon (www.amazon.com). Most readers will know how this site, based on the user's current choice, suggests books that other readers who have made the same choice, have gone on to buy. The same approach can of course be made with health information and can be particularly useful where there is a very large amount of information for which a 'dynamic' index could be constructed, tailored to the particular user.

In general, tailoring helps people connect with the information. A systematic review of tailored information in a range of settings and conditions has explored the effects of using computers to tailor printed information to the individual patient, with positive effects on patient satisfaction, knowledge, and anxiety [13].

WEBCASTING FOR HEALTH EDUCATION

Other ways of improving the connectedness of computerised approaches to health education include better connection with the author or therapist, for example, through synchronous direct connection such as some form of video connection or chat room. The same technologies can be used to improve connectedness in e-learning for health students. We describe here how we tried, then abandoned, the use of interactive satellite TV and have since taken two main approaches to the development of live webcasting. These methods are being developed for use with students and patients separately, as well as for joint learning between students and patients.

In the 1990s the University of Plymouth acquired a link from their TV studio to the TDS4b satellite uplink, on loan from the European Space Agency (ESA). The ESA satellite had a 'footprint' of the whole of Europe and provided high quality delivery giving access to learners at sites where terrestrial networks was restricted, for example, due to the non-availability of high bandwidth links. Between 2002 and 2005 this facility was used for interactive TV panel discussions with audience interaction via telephone or email to the panel chair. Although the format of the programmes worked well, expansion to new sites was difficult because of the cost of installing a satellite receiver. Broadcast costs, including TV studio time and satellite connect time, were also prohibitive with a total cost typically of £600 per one hour programme. Finally, at existing sites access to rooms where the satellite receivers were connected was a problem [14]. Our experience with satellite TV emphasised the need to be able to deliver education via the Internet. A webcasting facility was developed in 2005.

We have developed webcasting mini-studios comprising a camera, computer, and mixer with connection to video streamer. Initially we simply streamed video and interacted with the audience via email. Since then we have used two software environments enabling a simultaneous chat room.

GoodMood WIP is a webcasting application (www.goodmood.net/GoodMood/Products) that includes a number of features in addition to video, such as presentation media, whiteboard, audience feedback, audience polling, speaker biography and document attachment. In some initial trials of GoodMood we had two 'windows' for users the direct video feed of talking head and the Powerpoint converted as a 'flash'. However, this approach seemed to remove a certain amount of the control from the lecturer, particularly in the need to prepare the 'flash' from Powerpoint some time before the time of webcast. Using the ministudio, from where the presenter, in real time, mixed the Powerpoint and 'talking head' output and just used the GoodMood chatroom overcame this problem.

The other approach has been to develop a chatroom within which we embed the videostream. The web chat software used was ajaxchat (http://www.ajaxchat.org), which is free software, licensed under the Gnu Public Licence (GPL). Ajaxchat is written in PHP, a web scripting language, and uses the MySQL relational database to store messages and data. Among the features of ajaxchat are fast response time, use of avatars, personal messaging, emoticons, and inline URLs. We modified the ajaxchat programme code to embed the webcast stream. The ajaxchat method has a limitation in the length of the message that can be posted to the chat room compared to GoodMood WIP. We also have had some concerns about the bandwidth required on the server. However, it currently has many other advantages. GoodMood requires Active X and some of our non-University users do not have administrative rights on their computers to install this. We have also had problems with firewalls for GoodMood that we have not had with ajaxchat. We have so far not reproduced the useful ajaxchat features of avatars, list of signed-on members, and parallel chatrooms, within GoodMood WIP. The main advantage of the ajaxchat approach is that it is free of charge and open source. We continue to pursue the use of both methods so as to identify and use the most useful features of each.

We have used live webcasting with chatroom for a number of events for our own University students and others. For example, in early May 2007 we ran a one day online e-health workshop. We had 15 participants from Malaysia, Pakistan, Iran, Germany, Scotland and England and three presenters. Comments from participants included: *'all in all an enjoyable learning experience for me, with lots of potential'*, *'the potential for web casting is enormous'*, *'I much liked the discussion and its momentum. I also liked that you did not use voice as a medium for communication, but used text based chat for this purpose'*, *'I've never done a chatroom ever, so being able to chat with many people in real time online was really interesting and beneficial'*.

Various practical issues about delivery arose and these are being addressed. They include the need for practice and guidance for the facilitators in this new medium, getting the right balance between presentation and discussion, and deciding which elements need to be live and which can be pre-recorded and made available beforehand.

LIVE WEBCASTING IN PATIENT EDUCATION AND ONLINE THERAPY

We are currently exploring the use of live webcasting for patients with anxiety or depression. Depression and anxiety are common problems and impose large economic and social burdens. These costs can be substantially reduced by effective treatment and patients generally prefer psychological therapies to medication. Computerised cognitive behavioural therapy has been shown effective. In the UK, the National Institute of Clinical Excellence reviewed computerised cognitive behavioural therapy (CCBT) for anxiety and depression [15] and have recommended use of CCBT. However, the effectiveness of CCBT may suffer through lack of human contact. In our own work we developed a multimedia CCBT package to help patients in the management of stress. The pilot study [16], in which a research assistant introduced the computer system to patients and asked how they 'got on' with the package after use the package seemed very successful in reducing anxiety. However, in a subsequent randomised trial [17] in which patients had to access the system without any support in a public library the package was less successful. We concluded that human contact was an important feature of use of CCBT. Others have found the same [18].

We are currently working with Williams, Martinez, Prestwich and others (University of Glasgow), authors of www.livinglifetothefull.org.uk, a self help cognitive behaviour website for people with anxiety or depression. We are exploring different ways in which we can improve the connection between patients, website and therapist. For example, live webcasting, in which a therapist appears live on the patient's computer and leads a chat room discussion with patients typing their anonymous questions and comments, should provide more 'connection' than a simple email. However, it requires that patients log on to their computer at a certain time and that they have both the technical ability and the requisite hardware to participate. Furthermore, live webcasting will be more costly than a simple email. Methods need to be easy to use so as to remain accessible to the widest population possible (accepting that the target population is already limited to Internet users) and the trade-off between extra cost and possible additional effectiveness needs to be examined. In our current research we aim to compare different types of motivational support and their acceptability to users, the feasibility of long term implementation and maintenance of these interventions, and how they impact on 'connectedness'.

Unlike our webcasting for students (above) in which we used webcasting ministudios, in this new work, therapists will be working from their office or home and the videostream will be 'captured' on a webcam. We have so far encountered a number of problems in pursuing this approach including interruptions in the video stream. This occurred during multicasting (sending video to more than one viewer) and was due to network bandwith limitations. Some have these have been overcome by using a streaming media server, such as Microsoft Media Server, which receives video being "pushed" from the therapist's computer and rebroadcasts it to the viewers. This results in a more stable video output because the streaming server has a larger dedicated network bandwidth as well as greater computing power. But as of yet, we have not found a totally robust solution suitable for use with novice Internet users, particularly those with anxiety or depression.

FINDING APPROPRIATE MEASURES OF CONNECTEDNESS

We are exploring different ways of measuring 'connectedness'. 'Connectedness' between therapist and patients is part of the concept of therapeutic alliance and the Working Alliance Inventory developed by Horvath and Greenberg [19] a frequently used measure. They developed therapist and client versions both designed to yield three alliance scales, corresponding to the supposed (according to Bordin [18]) three components of the therapeutic alliance: Goal, Task, and Bond. Shortened versions of these scales were produced by Tracey and Kokotovic [21] and used in a recent study of Internet-based cognitive behavioural therapy [22-23]. Knaevelsrud and Maercker studied 96 patients with posttraumatic stress reactions allocated to 10 sessions of German language CCBT and concluded that a stable and positive online therapeutic relationship can be established through the Internet which improved during the treatment process. Studies of Internet –based patient information where the 'therapist' (or site author) is less clearly identified, have used various measures of usability. For example, in our cancer studies [2,3] we used a series of Likert style questions asking about the relevance, ease of use comprehensiveness, understandability, etc of the information. Finding or developing appropriate measures of connectedness, for therapists with virtual patients, or for lecturers with e-learning students will be necessary to have consistent ways of comparing different technologies.

CONNECTION VERSUS 'TIME TO THINK'

Although methods such as webcasting may make participants feel more 'connected' there may also be a disadvantage in that with synchronous methods people do not have time to reflect and construct appropriate communications. Even healthy young adults often prefer asynchronous modes of social contact—such as mobile phone text messaging—over real time voice calls for managing challenging interpersonal exchanges [24]. We are currently exploring whether older people come to value the opportunity for thoughtful and unhurried reflection on message content afforded by email and bulletin board messaging, and differentiate this from the more immediate but cognitively challenging demands of Internet chat and instant messaging.

SHARED LEARNING BETWEEN STUDENTS, PATIENTS AND THE PUBLIC

Although there is no strong evidence as yet, there may be benefits in 'efficiency', and for patients and students, from shared e-learning. We have explored the possibility of live webcasts shared by students and patients. Patients may be experts in their own conditions and have a role to play in educating health professionals and other patients, about the impact and effects of the condition [25]. Their expertise has been under-utilised, but there is insufficient evidence about the costs and effectiveness of service user involvement in e-learning and whether it is beneficial to try to inform and educate patients and staff in the same learning environment. It is not clear whether students of the health professions and patients will be comfortable learning with each other, nor whether the information needs of patients and professionals are too disparate to make shared learning possible. There is certainly evidence that nursing students may use information aimed at patients to help with coursework [26] while many patients access 'professional' literature [27], indicating that it may be possible to share some materials or 'events' even though each group might require other sources of information more specific to their needs. We broadcast a number of programmes aimed at patients, students and staff. These included prostate cancer, epilepsy, hypertension, access to health information, diabetic foot ulcers, head injury, and multiple sclerosis. We aim to develop this idea with webcasts aimed at combined audiences but with follow up information tailored to groups or even individuals.

CONCLUSION

In conclusion, tailoring information and live webcasting are both ways in which we can help patients and students connect more both with the information and the therapist or lecturer. Ways of combining these approaches should be a productive line of research but there are both practical and theoretical issues to be addressed.

ACKNOWLEDGMENTS

We would like to thank Dave Hurrell, Zoe Portman, Adrian Vranch, Matt Newcombe, Gail Wilson, Faye Doris, Fraser Reid and others who have helped with this work.

REFERENCES

[1]   Bental, D.S., Cawsey, A.J., Jones, R. (1999). Patient Information Systems that Tailor to the Individual. *Patient Education and Counseling*, 36, 171-180.

[2]   Jones, R.B., Pearson, J., McGregor, S., Cawsey, A., Barrett, A., Atkinson, J.M., Craig, N., Gilmour, W.H., McEwen, J. (1999). Randomised trial of personalised computer based information for cancer patients. *BMJ,* 319, 1241-1247.

[3]   Jones, R.B., Pearson, J., Cawsey, A.J., Bental, D., Barrett, A., White, J., White, C.A., Gilmour, W.H. (2006). Effect of different forms of information produced for cancer patients on their use of the information, social support, and anxiety: randomised trial. *BMJ*, 332, 942 – 948

[4]   Zigmond, A.S., Snaith, R.P. (1983). The Hospital Anxiety and Depression Scale. *Acta Psychiatrica Scan*, 67, 361-370.

[5]   Jones, R., Atkinson, J.M., Coia, D.A., Paterson, L., Morton, A.R., McKenna, K., Craig, N., Morrison, J., Gilmour, W.H. (2001). Randomised trial of computer-based education for patients with schizophrenia, *BMJ*, 322, 835-840.

[6]   Grasso, F., Cawsey, A., Jones, R.B. (2000). Dialectical argumentation to solve conflicts in advice giving: a case study in the promotion of healthy nutrition in *International Journal of Human Computer Studies*, 53 (6), 1077-1115.

[7]   Marsden, J. (2003). Primary prevention of osetoporosis in young British women: a comparison of electronic stage-based tailored messages versus non-tailored intervention. University of Glasgow. PhD Thesis.

[8]   Prochaska, J.O., DiClemente, C.C., Norcross, J.C. (1992 Sep). In search of how people change. Applications to addictive behaviors. *Am Psychol.*47(9), 1102-14.

[9]   Kroeze, W., Werkman, A., Brug, J. A. (2006). Systematic Review of Randomized Trials on the Effectiveness of Computer-Tailored Education on Physical Activity and Dietary Behaviors. *Annals of Behavioral Medicine,* 31 (3), 205-223.

[10]   O'Donnell, M., Knott, A., Mellish, C., Oberlander, J. (2001). ILEX:The architecture of a dynamic hypertext generation system. *Natural Language Engineering*, 7, 225-250.(More information at http://www.hcrc.ed.ac.uk/ilex/)

[11]   Bickmore., and Giorgino. Some novel aspects of health communication from a dialogue systems perspective. In *Proceedings of the AAAI fall symposium on dialogue systems for health communication*. Washington, DC. (Downloaded from http://www.misu.bmc.org/~bickmore/dshc/bickmore.pdf August 2007)

[12]   Bickmore, T., Gruber, A., Picard, R. (2005). Establishing the computer-patient working alliance in automated health behavior change interventions. *Patient Education and Counseling*, 59 (1), 21-30.

[13]   Treweek, S.P., Glenton, C., Oxman, A.D. (2002). Computer-generated patient education materials: Do they affect professional practice? A systematic review. *Journal American Medical Information Association*, 9 (4), 346-358

[14]   Jones, R., Skirton, H., McMullan, M. (2006). Feasibility of combining e-health for patients with e-learning for students using synchronous technologies. *Journal of Advanced Nursing*, 56 (1), 99-110.

[15]   Kaltenthaler, E., Shackley, P., Stevens, K., et al. (2002). *Computerised Cognitive Behavioural Therapy for Depression and Anxiety*. Report commissioned by NHS R&D HTA Programme on behalf of NICE.

[16]   White, J., Jones, R,, McGarry, E. (2000). Cognitive behavioural computer therapy for the anxiety disorders: A pilot study. *J Mental Hlth*, 9, 505-516.

[17]   Jones, R. B., Kamarzaman, Z., Naven, L. M., Morton, W. R., Marriott, C., Craig, N., and Gilmour, W. H. (2001). Cognitive behavioural computer therapy for anxiety: difficulties in carrying out a randomised trial and lessons learned. University of Glasgow. Submission to NICE.

[18]   Gellatly, J., Bower, P., Hennessy, S., Richards, D., Gilbody, S., Lovell, K. (2007). What makes self-help interventions effective in the management of depressive symptoms? Meta-analysis and meta-regression. *Psychol Med*, 11, 1-24. (published on-line early).

[19]   Horvath, A.O., Greenberg, L.S. (1989). Development and validation of the Working Alliance Inventory. *Journal of Counselling Psychology*, 36, 223–233.

[20]   Bordin, E.S. (1979). The generalizability of the psychoanalytic concept of the working alliance. *Psychotherapy: Theory, Research and Practice*, 16, 252–260.

[21]   Tracey, T.J., Kokotovic, A.M. (1989). Factor structure of the Working Alliance Inventory. *Psychological Assessment: A Journal of Consulting and Clinical Psychology*, 1, 207–210.

[22]   Knaevelsrud, C., Maercker, A. (2007). Internet-based treatment for PTSD reduces distress and facilitates the development of a strong therapeutic alliance: a randomized controlled trial. *BMC Psychiatry*, 7:13 doi:10.1186/1471-244X-7-13.

[23]   Knaevelsrud, C., Maercker, A. (2006). Does the Quality of the Working Alliance Predict Treatment Outcome in Online Psychotherapy for Traumatized Patients? *J Med Internet Res*, 8(4), e31 <URL: http://www.jmir.org/2006/4/e31/>

[24]   Reid, F.J.M., Reid, D.J. (in press).The expressive and conversational affordances of mobile messaging. *Behaviour & Information Technology*.

[25]   Jones, R., Tweddle, S., Hampshire, M., Hill, A., Moult, B., and McGregor, S. (2000). *Patient-led learning for the clinical professions in fulfilling the information needs of patients*. Published by NHS Information Authority, June 2000. Ref 2000-IA-280. Available   from

http://www.nhsia.nhs.uk/informatics/pages/resource_informatics/patient_led_learning
.pdf

[26] Wilson, E.J. (1995). Use of a public access health information system by student nurses. *Master of Public Health Thesis*, University of Glasgow.

[27] Budtz, S., and Witt, K. (2002). Consulting the Internet before visit to general practice. Patients'use of the Internet and other sources of health information. *Scand J Prim Health Care,* 20(3), 174-176.

INDEX

D

F

G

H

I

M

N

Q

R

S